Sensors and Data Analysis for Biomechanics and Physical Activity

Sensors and Data Analysis for Biomechanics and Physical Activity

Guest Editor

Francisco Pinho

MDPI

Basel • Beijing • Wuhan • Barcelona • Belgrade • Novi Sad • Cluj • Manchester

Guest Editor
Francisco Pinho
H^{2}M—Health and Human Movement Unit
Polytechnic University of Health, CESPU
Vila Nova de Famalicão
Portugal

Editorial Office
MDPI AG
Grosspeteranlage 5
4052 Basel, Switzerland

This is a reprint of the Special Issue, published open access by the journal *Sensors* (ISSN 1424-8220), freely accessible at: https://www.mdpi.com/journal/sensors/special_issues/208JS10163.

For citation purposes, cite each article independently as indicated on the article page online and as indicated below:

Lastname, A.A.; Lastname, B.B. Article Title. *Journal Name* **Year**, *Volume Number*, Page Range.

ISBN 978-3-7258-8181-9 (Hbk)
ISBN 978-3-7258-8182-6 (PDF)
https://doi.org/10.3390/books978-3-7258-8182-6

Contents

About the Editor

Francisco Pinho

Francisco Pinho is a physiotherapist and electronics and informatics engineer, and he holds a PhD in Biomedical Engineering. He is a higher education professor and director of a research unit in human movement, with around 25 years of academic, scientific, and professional experience. His work focuses on human movement analysis, biomechanics, physiotherapy, biomedical instrumentation, physiological signal acquisition and processing, electromyography, motion capture, force platforms, and technologies applied to health, rehabilitation, sport, education, and research. His profile combines clinical expertise with engineering and technological development, particularly in the design and implementation of biomedical devices, embedded systems, wireless sensors, and quantitative tools for functional assessment and applied research.

sensors

MDPI

Article

Estimation of Forces and Powers in Ergometer and Scull Rowing Based on Long Short-Term Memory Neural Networks

Lorenzo Pitto [1,2], Frédéric R. Simon [1,2], Geoffrey N. Ertel [1,2], Gérome C. Gauchard [1,2,3] and Guillaume Mornieux [1,2,3,*]

1 Development Adaptation Handicap (DevAH) Research Unit, Université de Lorraine, 54000 Nancy, France; lorenzo.pitto@univ-lorraine.fr (L.P.); frederic.simon@univ-lorraine.fr (F.R.S.); geoffrey.ertel@univ-lorraine.fr (G.N.E.); gerome.gauchard@univ-lorraine.fr (G.C.G.)
2 CARE Grand Est, Université de Lorraine, 54000 Nancy, France
3 Faculty of Sport Sciences, Université de Lorraine, 54000 Nancy, France
* Correspondence: guillaume.mornieux@univ-lorraine.fr

Abstract

Analyzing performance in rowing, e.g., analyzing force and power output profiles produced either on ergometer or on boat, is a priority for trainers and athletes. The current state-of-the-art methodologies for rowing performance analysis involve the installation of dedicated instrumented equipment, with the most commonly employed systems being PowerLine and BioRow. This procedure can be both expensive and time-consuming, thus limiting trainers' ability to monitor athletes. In this study, we developed an easier-to-install and cheaper method for estimating rowers' forces and powers based only on cable position sensors for ergometer rowing and inertial measurement units (IMUs) and GPS for scull rowing. We used data from 12 and 11 rowers on ergometer and on boat, respectively, to train a long short-term memory (LSTM) network. The LSTM was able to reconstruct the forces and power at the gate with an overall mean absolute error of less than 5%. The reconstructed forces and power were able to reveal inter-subject differences in technique, with an accuracy of 93%. Performing leave-one-out validation showed a significant increase in error, confirming that more subjects are needed in order to develop a tool that could be generalizable to external athletes.

Keywords: machine learning; rowing; IMU; kinetics; LSTM

1. Introduction

Rowing is a sport that requires the precise coordination of all the body segments, making technique a determinant factor for performance, with the result of a race possibly being decided by differences as small as a fraction of a second [1,2]. Rowing involves cyclic movements, and each cycle is usually decomposed into two phases, namely, the drive and recovery phases. The 'drive' phase begins when the oars are inserted into the water; this event is called the 'catch.' During the drive, the oars remain immersed in the water and propel the boat forward [1]. During this phase, the sequential movement of the legs, trunk, and arms generates power that is ultimately transferred to the water through the oars [1]. At the end of this movement, the oars are extracted from the water, marking the event called 'finish' and the beginning of the 'recovery' phase. During this phase, the oars remain out of the water, and the rowers pull the boats with their feet in order to prepare for the following cycle.

When weather conditions are unsuitable for rowing on water, rowers often train indoors using rowing ergometers [3]. Some ergometers have been designed to reproduce as closely as possible the forces and movements of boat rowing by including a free-floating mechanism that allows the frame of the ergometer to slide in the horizontal direction [3].

In recent years, significant efforts have been made to precisely measure and quantify the rowing technique (commonly referred to as the "athlete signature" [4]) and performance through the integration of motion and force sensors on boats and ergometers [4–12]. Force and power profiles are of particular interest because they correlate with performance [1,13] and the spinal loads associated with low back pain, which has a high prevalence among rowers [14,15]. The analysis of force–time profiles is also used as a criterion for selecting crew members in double and four boats [1,16]. Additionally, the decomposition of the total power generated by the rowers into the contributions of the different body segments (i.e., arms, trunk, and legs) is a powerful tool that can be used to characterize a rower's technique and, thus, identify and correct technical errors [1,17,18]. To quantitatively describe these force and power profiles, technical determinants, such as the time to peak (T2P), mean to peak ratio (M2P), and work ratio (WR), are typically used. More uniform force profiles, characterized by a higher M2P [12,13], as well as an earlier peak in the force transferred to the oars (i.e., a lower T2P) [9,12], have been associated with higher performance. Furthermore, an earlier peak of maximum trunk power has been associated with higher performance [17], a factor that can be directly targeted by using real-time biofeedback to improve a rower's technique [18].

While measuring the forces generated by rowers provides important information to trainers, it requires the replacement of certain components of a boat or ergometer with specialized, instrumented versions. Two of the most commonly used systems for analyzing rowing performance are BioRow (BioRow Tech, London, UK) and PowerLine (Peach Innovation, Cambridge, UK). The proposed solutions (Figure 1) involve replacing the foot stretcher (the component that connects to the rowers' feet, allowing the transfer of pushing and pulling forces) in both boat and ergometer rowing, replacing the oarlocks at the boat gates (components of the boat that hold the oars in place, allowing them to pivot during the rowing stroke), and adding a strain gauge at the handle in ergometer rowing (on an ergometer, the oars are replaced by a single rigid handle attached to a chain) [4,5,8,12,19]. This type of equipment can be expensive, and significant effort is required to keep the same rigging when parts are replaced, especially in scull rowing, where boats are finely adjusted according to the anthropometry and preferences of each rower [1]. These factors inevitably limit the number of boats or ergometers that can be equipped simultaneously and the frequency at which the instrumented parts can be installed on different boats, which, in turn, limits the amount of attention paid by trainers to each rower. A method allowing the estimation of the forces and powers generated by rowers without necessitating the replacement of boat or ergometer parts would be extremely helpful, allowing multiple rowers within a club to be quickly equipped and monitored.

Machine learning methods have been widely applied to the detection of human behavior, particularly within the field of biomechanics. These applications range from the classification and detection of specific features of motion, like gait abnormalities [20,21] and swimming styles [22], to the estimation of joints [23], bones [24], and ground reaction forces [25]. Recently, companies have started developing machine learning methods based on physics-informed biomechanical simulations for estimating body internal and contact forces from videos [26,27]. When applied to rowing practice, machine learning methods have been used to cluster rowers based on kinematics [28], separate novice from expert rowers based on posture measured with inertial measurement units (IMUs) [29], and assign rowers to specific events based on kinematics and demographics [30].

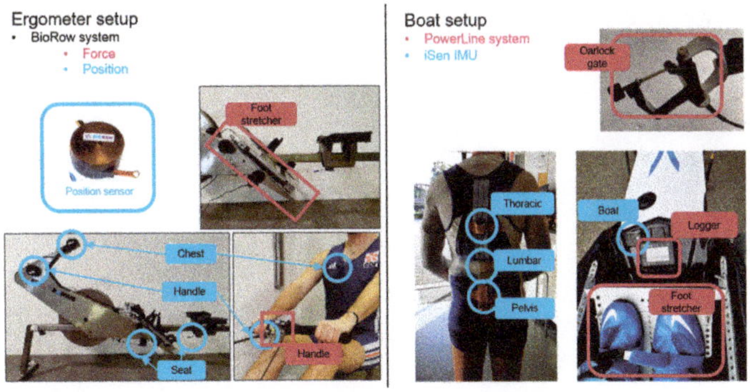

Figure 1. Sensor setup for ergometer and boat rowing.

An alternative to machine learning is the use of traditional biomechanical simulations. In particular, predictive and tracking simulations have been successfully employed to study human motion [31–33] and are well suited for estimating forces and power output in rowing applications. Tracking simulations execute forward dynamics while forcing the motion to closely match the recorded kinematics, enabling the generation of dynamically consistent kinematics and kinetics even in the absence of measured forces [31]. However, this approach suffers from the drawback of being more computationally demanding and requiring expert users to handle the different aspects of the simulation, such as defining models that describe muscle architecture and force generation, as well as interactions with the environment.

To the best of our knowledge, there are currently no machine learning methods for estimating the force and power generated by rowers, and the gold standard for rowing performance analysis remains the post-session analysis of PowerLine or BioRow data. This paper contributes to the state of the art by providing a tool for estimating rowing forces and powers based on measured kinematics.

Our main goal was to estimate the time profiles of force and power throughout the rowing cycle rather than clustering rowers based on technique [28] or using classifiers to define their performance [29]. Given the sequential nature of the rowing movement, characterized by time-dependent variations in forces and a sequential involvement of the body segments, we chose to base this work on a recurrent neural network. Long short-term memory (LSTM) networks are particularly well suited for processing time series information and have been extensively employed for sequence-to-sequence tasks in various applications for several years [34], including in biomechanics tasks, to recognize motor activities [34], predict falls [35], gait kinematics [36,37], and gait phases [36]. The functioning of LSTM networks has been described exhaustively in many publications [37–40] and is beyond the scope of this paper. In short, the architecture of LSTM networks allows them to capture long-term relationships within sequences, with the ability to selectively retain or forget information [40].

The input data for the proposed model should come from sensors that are cost-effective and easy to install. When rowing on an ergometer, cable-based sensors can be used to measure the displacement of different body parts [17,18]. These sensors consist of a spring-loaded cable that can be easily attached and detached to a rower's clothes or ergometer seat. On a boat, the most versatile method for measuring rowers' movements involves the use of IMUs. IMUs are compact and lightweight sensors that can be comfortably worn by rowers without restricting their movement and installed on the boat without any alteration of the rigging. Thanks to their versatility, IMUs have been extensively used to measure human motion [32,41–43].

The purpose of this study was to train an LSTM network to determine the forces and powers generated by rowers during boat and ergometer rowing without the use of force sensors. In particular, we aimed at computing the forces at the feet and gates or handle, the power transferred to the gates or handle, and the powers generated by the arms, trunk, and legs. We hypothesized that the accuracy of force and power estimation would be enough to describe the rowers' techniques, characterized by features such as peak timing and the development ratio.

2. Materials and Methods

2.1. Participants

Data for this study were collected as part of previously published studies [12,18]. This included data from 12 male rowers on a scull boat (20.0 ± 2 years old, 185 ± 5 cm, 79.0 ± 6.7 kg) and from 11 male rowers on the ergometer (22.3 ± 2.2 years, 185.5 ± 7.1 cm, 77.4 ± 7.0 kg). Participants did not suffer any recent injury.

2.2. Test Procedure

Concerning the dataset collected from rowing on water, rowers were asked to row at their personal competition rate, which was, on average, 32.5 strokes per min (spm), and used their personal scull boat. The dataset on the ergometer included rowing sessions with two different stroke rates, i.e., 20 spm and their personal competition rate, which was, on average, 35.8 spm.

2.3. Setup and Data Acquisition

The ergometer (RP3®, Care RowPerfect BV, Hardenberg, The Netherlands) was equipped with BioRow sensors. These included force sensors at the feet and handle and displacement sensors at the handle, seat, and chest (Figure 1). The position sensors consisted of spring-loaded cables. These sensors were connected to an acquisition card (National Instruments, "NI USB-6000 Multifunction I/O Device," National Instruments, Austin, TX, USA) connected to Matlab (MATLAB, version R2022b, The MathWorks, Inc., Natick, MA, USA) and sampled at 150 Hz. The ergometer was utilized in its dynamic configuration, and all measurements were performed at the same wheel resistance (i.e., 5 on the RP3 wheel).

The personal scull boats of the rowers were equipped with a PowerLine system (version 4.12.0.0). This system included force sensors at the foot stretcher and oarlock gates and oar angle sensors at the oarlock gates (Figure 1). The sensors were connected to a logger unit positioned in front of the rowers, which also collected data from an integrated GPS and IMU and provided real-time feedback, such as stroke rate and power output. PowerLine data were collected at 50 Hz on the logger and downloaded after the rowers finished their training session. Additionally, four IMUs (version 2022.0, iSen, STT Systems, San Sebastian, Spain), collecting data at 100 Hz, were included: three on the back of the rower (pelvis, lumbar, and thoracic spine) [42] and one on the boat to facilitate synchronization with the PowerLine data. These IMUs are compact and lightweight (46 g, 56 mm × 38 mm × 18 mm), minimizing interference with the rowing motion. They incorporate built-in sensor fusion algorithms that enable direct export of the unit 3D pose and free acceleration data. Data from IMUs were wirelessly transmitted to a receiver placed on a boat closely following the athletes. Given this limitation, iSen data sequences were limited to a series of around 15 consecutive strokes and were, therefore, much shorter than the ones stored on the PowerLine logger.

2.4. Data Analysis

Data from the iSen and PowerLine systems were synchronized based on the boat velocity measured from the PowerLine GPS and the boat velocity computed from the acceleration of the iSen IMU installed on the boat. Specifically, the IMU acceleration measured along the direction of movement was time-integrated and high-pass filtered (0.1 Hz) to remove drift; the velocity measured by the GPS was similarly filtered. The points of minimum velocity were automatically identified and used to determine rowing cycles and the instantaneous stroke rate. This allowed the identification of the cycles recorded during the short iSen sequences within the much longer PowerLine sequences. After synchronization, all data from the boat rowing sessions were interpolated at 100 Hz.

Rowing cycles were segmented based on the starboard position of the oar for scull rowing and on the handle position for ergometer rowing. In both cases, the lowest value defined the catch event, and the highest value the finish event. After discarding the cycles with missing data and artifacts, the datasets consisted of 396 cycles for boat rowing and 2005 cycles for ergometer rowing.

In both rowing conditions, we considered only the force along the axis of motion (defined by the boat axis and the ergometer rail). This translates to the horizontal component of the foot stretcher force. Similarly, for the force measured at the oarlock gates, only the propulsive component, along the direction of motion, was considered. For the force at the ergometer handle, the installed strain gauge only measured a unidirectional force, specifically the tension of the chain.

The cable sensors installed on the ergometer measured the position of the handle, chest, and seat with respect to the ergometer (X^h_{ergo}, X^c_{ergo}, and X^s_{ergo}, respectively). The length of the arms (X^a_{ergo}) and the trunk opening (X^t_{ergo}) were computed as:

$$X^a_{ergo} = X^h_{ergo} - X^c_{ergo}, \tag{1}$$

$$X^t_{ergo} = X^c_{ergo} - X^s_{ergo}, \tag{2}$$

The leg extension was assumed to be the same as X^s_{ergo}. The velocities of the handle and the three body segments V^h_{ergo}, V^a_{ergo}, V^t_{ergo}, and V^l_{ergo} were obtained by taking the time derivatives of X^h_{ergo}, X^a_{ergo}, X^t_{ergo}, and X^s_{ergo}, respectively (Figure 2).

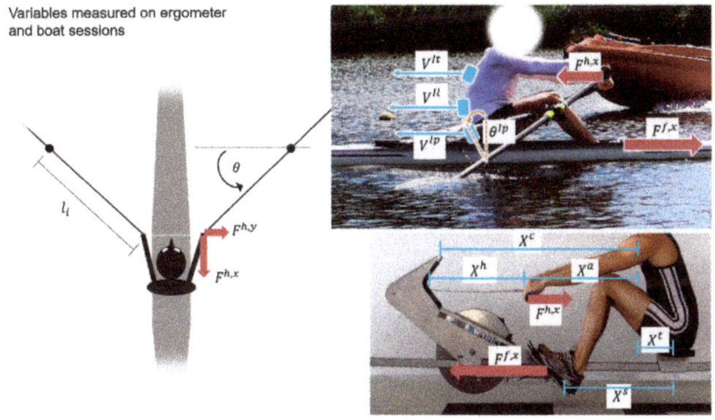

Figure 2. Graphical representation of the base variables included in the study.

For the ergometer, power at the handle and segments was computed following Kleshnev [44]. Specifically:

$$P^{h,x}_{ergo} = V^{h}_{ergo} F^{h,x}_{ergo}, \tag{3}$$

$$P^{a}_{ergo} = V^{a}_{ergo} F^{h,x}_{ergo}, \tag{4}$$

$$P^{t}_{ergo} = V^{t}_{ergo} F^{h,x}_{ergo}, \tag{5}$$

$$P^{l}_{ergo} = V^{l}_{ergo} F^{f,x}_{ergo}, \tag{6}$$

where $P^{h,x}_{ergo}$, P^{a}_{ergo}, P^{t}_{ergo}, and P^{l}_{ergo} are the powers for the handle, arms, trunk, and legs, respectively; $F^{h,x}_{ergo}$ is the force measured at the handle, and $F^{f,x}_{ergo}$ is the force measured at the feet along the horizontal direction.

For the boat, we computed the corresponding powers. However, given the differences in the systems and sensors, we used a different approach. In particular, the total power transferred to the oars (P^{h}_{boat}) was computed as:

$$P^{h}_{boat} = (F^{h,x}_{boat} l_i \cos(\theta) + F^{h,y}_{boat} l_i \sin(\theta))\dot{\theta} = P^{h,x}_{boat} + P^{h,y}_{boat}, \tag{7}$$

where l_i is the internal lever arm of the oar; $F^{h,x}_{boat}$ and $F^{h,y}_{boat}$ are the x and y components of the force at the handle; θ and $\dot{\theta}$ are the oar angle and angular velocity, respectively. Forces and powers at the handle are the sum of the board and starboard components.

The powers of the trunk and leg segments were computed as:

$$P^{l}_{boat} = F^{f,x}_{boat} V^{l}_{boat}, \tag{8}$$

$$P^{t}_{boat} = F^{h,x}_{boat} V^{t}_{boat}, \tag{9}$$

where V^{t}_{boat} and V^{l}_{boat} are the velocities of the trunk and leg segments:

$$V^{t}_{boat} = V^{It}_{boat} V^{Ip}_{boat}, \tag{10}$$

$$V^{l}_{boat} = V^{Ip}_{boat} - l^{Ip} \dot{\theta}^{Ip} \cos\left(\theta^{Ip}\right), \tag{11}$$

where V^{It}_{boat} and V^{Ip}_{boat} are the velocities of the IMUs placed on the thoracic spine and pelvis, obtained by time-integration of the IMUs acceleration; l^{Ip} is the distance from the pelvis IMU to the seat (we used a value of 15 cm for all subjects); θ^{Ip} and $\dot{\theta}^{Ip}$ are the angle of the pelvis IMU from the vertical axis and its time-derivative.

The calculation of the power arms was based on Hofmijster et al. [45], proposing that the total power generated by the rower should be determined by the power transferred to the oar plus the power used to accelerate the center of mass. Modeling the rower's body with only three segments capable of generating power, we obtain the power generated by the arms as:

$$P^{a}_{boat} = P^{h}_{boat} + \left(F^{f,x}_{boat} - F^{h,x}_{boat}\right) V_{boat} - P^{t}_{boat} - P^{l}_{boat}, \tag{12}$$

where V_{boat} is the boat velocity obtained from the GPS embedded in the PowerLine box.

In summary, the sequences used as targets for the LSTM network, hereafter referred to as 'measured sequences,' were: $F^{f,x}$, $F^{h,x}$, $P^{h,x}$, P^{a}, P^{t}, P^{l}, for both ergometer and boat rowing.

2.5. LSTM Architecture

For this study, a vanilla LSTM [40] was chosen and implemented using the built-in functions of the Deep Learning Toolbox in MATLAB. Preliminary analyses indicated that adding extra LSTM layers did not significantly improve performance while increasing training time. Consequently, the random search was conducted using a single LSTM layer. The base architecture was defined as:

- Sequence input layer (nI)
- Fully connected layer (nI)
- LSTM layer
- Dropout layer (DOp)
- Fully connected layer (nO)
- Regression layer

Where nI is the number of input features (18 for the boat and 16 for the ergometer, Table 1); DOp is the dropout percentage; and nO is the number of output sequences (six for both ergometer and boat sessions). We performed a random search to find the best values of the following hyperparameters: number of units within the LSTM layers (log-uniform sampling between 10 and 500) and dropout percentage (0%, 5%, and 10%). To select the best architecture after the random search, we based the decision on the mean absolute error (*MAE*) computed over the effective drive phase (refer to the session LSTM performance evaluation).

Table 1. List of features included in the LSTM network for boat and ergometer cases.

Input Features	Ergometer	Boat
Oar angular velocity	−	+
Boat horizontal velocity	−	+
Boat acceleration	−	+
IMU thoracic horizontal velocity WRT boat	−	+
IMU lumbar horizontal velocity WRT boat	−	+
IMU pelvis horizontal velocity WRT boat	−	+
IMU thoracic 1PCA [1] acceleration	−	+
IMU lumbar 1PCA [1] acceleration	−	+
IMU pelvis 1PCA [1] acceleration	−	+
IMU thoracic 1PCA [1] angular velocity	−	+
IMU lumbar 1PCA [1] angular velocity	−	+
IMU pelvis 1PCA [1] angular velocity	−	+
Average boat speed in the previous cycle	−	+
Max boat speed previous cycle	−	+
Height of rower	+	+
Weight of rower	+	+
Duration of the previous drive	+	+
Duration of current drive	+	+
Position of handle	+	−
Position of chest	+	−
Position of seat	+	−
Velocity of handle	+	−
Velocity of arms	+	−
Velocity of trunk	+	−
Velocity of seat	+	−
Acceleration of handle	+	−
Acceleration of trunk	+	−
Acceleration of legs	+	−
Maximum handle speed in the previous cycle	+	−
Time elapsed: maximum handle speed to beginning the current cycle	+	−

[1] First principal component.

2.6. LSTM Training

We performed the first training during the random search and then used the so-defined architecture for a leave-one-out validation (similar to the method used by Su et al. [36]). For the random search training, we split the data into 80% training and 20% validation. For the leave-one-out validation, we used N-1 subjects as training and the remaining subject as validation, repeating the process N times. We set a stopping criterion to the training if 20 epochs [46] elapsed without improvement in the validation data reconstruction, measured as the root mean squared error (RMSE) over the rowing cycle [36]. The parameters used for the training included the following: max epochs: 10,000; learning rate: 0.001; minibatch size: 32; Adam optimization algorithm. Boat and ergometer sessions LSTM were trained separately.

2.7. LSTM Data

For both the ergometer and boat, the target series were six sequences describing: $F^{f,x}$, $F^{h,x}$, $P^{h,x}$, P^a, P^t, P^l. For both the ergometer and boat, the sequences defined were segmented into rowing cycles starting at the finish event and ending at the following finish event. Rowing cycles were considered in absolute time rather than being time-normalized. Before training, data were normalized to the mean and standard deviation. The selection of input features was different for the ergometer and boat, as data were obtained with different kinds of sensors and described two systems that differ in terms of body movement and interactions with the environment. Specifically, for the ergometer sessions LSTM, we included 16 features: position of handle, chest, and seat (X^h, X^c, and X^s); velocities of the handle, arms, trunk opening, and leg extension (V^h, V^a, V^t, and V^l); acceleration of the trunk and legs, computed by the time derivative of the respective velocities. Additional features were added to include information about the subjects and the rowing session: height and weight of the rower, duration of previous and current drive phases, maximum handle speed of the previous stroke, and time elapsed between the maximum speed and the catch event of the current stroke. The reason behind the last two is that the resistance felt at the handle depends on the spinning velocity of the wheel, which decreases during the recovery phase when no force is applied to it. Thus, the time elapsed from the maximum should provide information about the wheel spinning velocity at the start of the drive phase. For the boat sessions LSTM, we included 18 features: gate angular velocity ($\dot{\theta}$); boat horizontal velocity (from the GPS integrated into the PowerLine box) and acceleration (from the accelerometer integrated into the PowerLine box); horizontal velocity with respect to the boat reference system of IMU thoracic, lumbar, and pelvis (V^{It}_{boat}, V^{Il}_{boat}, and V^{Ip}_{boat}); first principal component of acceleration and angular velocity of the three IMUs. Similarly to the ergometer, additional features were added to include information about the subjects and the rowing session: height and weight of the rower; average and maximum boat velocity in the previous cycle (providing information about the change in speed of the boat and thus to the power transferred to the oars); duration of the previous and current drive phases (providing information about the stroke rate, which is known to correlate with power output).

2.8. LSTM Performance Evaluation

To compare the performances of the networks, we used metrics computed over the effective drive phase duration, as there are little to no forces and powers during the recovery phase, making it of little value for performance evaluation. The effective drive phase, for both ergometer and boat rowing, was automatically detected within each cycle based on the handle force, as it is usually computed with the Peach software. Specifically, the phase began when the gait force exceeded 20 kg and ended when the force decreased below 10 kg. Although sessions at different stroke rates on the ergometer were included in the LSTM training to improve the generalizability of the reconstruction, only the sessions at 20 spm were considered for the subsequent performance analysis, as this condition included the highest numbers of consistent cycles. As a measure of performance, we considered the mean absolute error (*MAE*) between the target and reconstructed sequences (i.e., $F^{f,x}$, $F^{h,x}$, $P^{h,x}$, P^{a}, P^{t}, P^{l}) for all cycles and the *MAE* over the average curve over multiple cycles (*cMAE*). As each cycle input sequence was of a different duration, we interpolated the reconstructed sequences over 50 timeframes describing the effective drive phase.

$$MAE = \frac{1}{CT}\sum_{c=1}^{C}\sum_{t=1}^{T}|y_t^c - \hat{y}_t^c|, \quad (13)$$

$$cMAE = \frac{1}{CT}\sum_{t=1}^{T}\left|\sum_{c=1}^{C}(y_t^c - \hat{y}_t^c)\right|, \quad (14)$$

where T = 50 timeframes; C is the number of cycles included in the validation set. During leave-one-out validation, C refers to all of the cycles associated with a single subject. *MAE* and *cMAE* were also expressed as a percentage of the associated curve:

$$(c)MAE_{norm} = \frac{(c)MAE}{mean(|V|)}, \quad (15)$$

where V is any of the time-normalized target variables.

We evaluated how technical determinants used to describe and evaluate a rower's technique were affected by the process of estimation. Specifically, we calculated time to peak (T2P), defined as the instant at which the curves reach the peak, expressed in percent of the entire drive phase (i.e., catch to finish); mean to peak (M2P), defined as the ratio between the mean and maximum value of a curve times 100, over the entire drive phase; and work ratio (WR), defined as the ratio of the area under the curve before the peak to the total area under the curve times 100, also over the entire drive phase [17]. To determine whether the rowers' technique could be accurately described from the estimated sequences, we performed two-sample *t*-tests (ttest2 function in MATLAB, with significance level 0.05) comparing the means of the technical determinants calculated from the measured sequences with those derived from the estimated sequences. We also assessed whether the technical determinants derived from the estimated sequences could distinguish between the techniques of different subjects, specifically in cases where the technical determinants derived from the measured sequences of two subjects showed significant differences. This was conducted by performing two-sample *t*-tests to compare the mean values of the technical determinants of each pair of rowers. Inter- and intrasubject *t*-tests were performed only on data from ergometer sessions since the number of cycles for each subject in the boat sessions was too small in some cases.

For the intrasubject differences, we computed the accuracy:

$$As = \frac{HA}{HA + HR} * 100, \quad (16)$$

where *HA* denotes the subjects for which the null hypothesis of equal mean could not be rejected (p-value > 0.05) and *HR* the subjects where the null hypothesis was rejected.

For the inter-subject differences, we computed the accuracy:

$$Ap = \frac{CH}{CH + DH} * 100, \quad (17)$$

where *CH* denotes subject pairs where the null hypothesis of the two subjects having equal mean for the analyzed technical determinant was similarly rejected or accepted when conducting the test on the measured and LSTM curves; *DH* denotes the subject pairs where there was no agreement on the null hypothesis rejection.

3. Results

The optimized architectures were found to be 1 layer, 500 neurons, and 0% dropout for the ergometer condition and 1 layer, 53 neurons, and 10% dropout for the boat condition. The average measured and estimated curves for the forces and powers of four representative subjects for the ergometer and boat sessions are depicted in Figure 3. The performance for all subjects combined, expressed in terms of absolute and normalized *MAE* and *cMAE* for all force and power variables, is presented in Table 2. The average values of MAE_{norm} were 3.20% and 4.90% for ergometer and boat sessions, respectively; the average values of $cMAE_{norm}$ were 0.53% and 0.90% for ergometer and boat sessions, respectively. The MAE_{norm} observed in the leave-one-out validation was on average 19.94% and 14.02% for the sessions on ergometer and on boat, respectively (Table 2); the $cMAE_{norm}$ was on average 7.95% and 12.38% for the ergometer and boat sessions, respectively. Figure 4 shows the performance metrics detailed subject by subject. The variable with the highest *MAE* and *cMAE* was $P^{h,x}$, and the variable with the highest MAE_{norm} and $cMAE_{norm}$ was instead P^{a}.

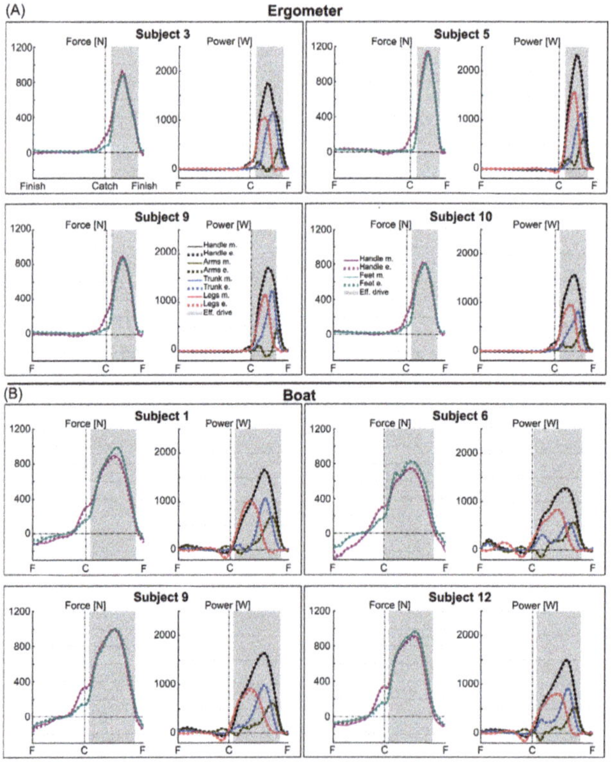

Figure 3. Measured (continuous lines) and estimated (dashed lines) force and power profiles for four representative subjects during ergometer (**A**) and boat (**B**) rowing. The curves represent the average over the cycles used for validation, time normalized over the finish-to-finish period. The vertical line defines the catch event; the shaded area defines the effective drive phase.

Table 2. LSTM performance. *MAE* and *cMAE*, absolute and normalized, are computed for the cycles in the validation set. Results reported for the leave-one-out validation (LOOV) consist of the mean errors over all subjects.

		MAE	*cMAE*	*MAE* Norm	*cMAE* Norm	LOOV *MAE*	LOOV *MAE* Norm	LOOV *cMAE*	LOOV *cMAE* Norm
Ergometer	$F^{f,x}$	19.15 N	2.67 N	3.06%	0.43%	66.20 N	10.40%	58.74 N	9.22%
	$F^{h,x}$	17.69 N	2.40 N	2.87%	0.39%	47.73 N	7.63%	39.53 N	6.32%
	$P^{h,x}$	37.04 W	5.44 W	2.96%	0.43%	95.81 W	7.69%	78.55 W	6.30%
	P^{a}	8.87 W	1.77 W	4.40%	0.88%	26.26 W	13.24%	22.37 W	11.23%
	P^{t}	14.50 W	1.68 W	2.88%	0.33%	35.64 W	7.05%	28.43 W	5.55%
	P^{l}	18.07 W	4.20 W	3.05%	0.71%	59.43 W	10.20%	57.79 W	9.07%
Boat	$F^{f,x}$	22.89 N	3.66 N	3.58%	0.57%	72.80 N	11.54%	65.94 N	10.49%
	$F^{h,x}$	23.15 N	4.13 N	3.33%	0.59%	61.40 N	8.91%	52.71 N	7.67%
	$P^{h,x}$	34.76 W	5.14 W	3.55%	0.52%	110.17 W	11.29%	97.48 W	10.03%
	P^{a}	20.52 W	3.13 W	8.25%	1.26%	60.89 W	25.15%	53.43 W	22.39%
	P^{t}	19.01 W	5.38 W	5.06%	1.43%	46.89 W	13.19%	39.48 W	11.25%
	P^{l}	27.26 W	4.91 W	5.64%	1.02%	67.81 W	14.05%	60.8 W	12.43%

P^{l} 27.26 W 4.91 W 5.64% 1.02% 67.81 W 14.05% 60.8 W 12.43%

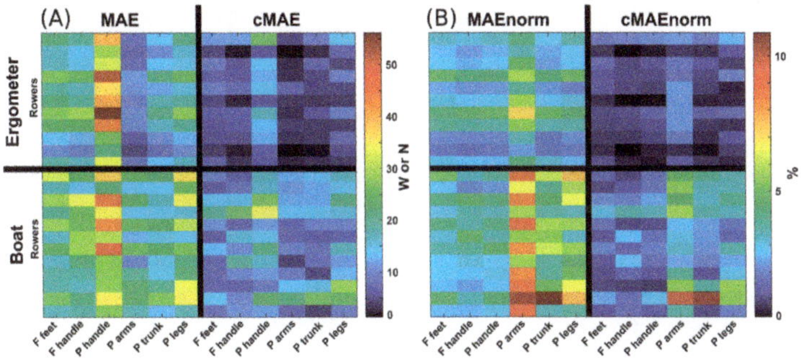

Figure 4. *MAE* and *cMAE* are reported in absolute values (**A**) and normalized to the average value of the target curve (**B**). Units are N for the forces (F) and W for the powers (P). Rows correspond to individual rowers.

The technical determinants describing the rowers' technique (i.e., T2P, M2P, and WR) are shown in Figure 5 for four representative subjects. In both boat and ergometer rowing, a clear sequencing of legs, trunk, and arms was observed, with T2P occurring at approximately 40%, 60%, and 70% of the cycle, respectively. Subjects rowing on ergometers showed a variety of strategies regarding the involvement of the arms, as seen by the inter-subject variations in M2P and WR. Subjects on the boat showed more inter-subject variability in the involvement of the trunk and legs. The overall *MAE* of the T2P was 0.78% and 1.55%; the overall *MAE* for M2P was 0.66% and 0.96%; the overall *MAE* for WR was 2.05% and 3.32% for the boat and ergometer sessions, respectively (Table 3). When focusing on the ergometer sessions, no significant differences between T2P, M2P, and WR, based on the LSTM curves and on the measured curves, were found (Figure 6). When comparing pairs of subjects, technique differentiation for T2P for the power of the arms, trunk, and legs showed an accuracy of 90.9%, 94.5%, and 90.9%, respectively. These accuracies were 94.5%, 96.4%, and 98.2%, respectively, for the M2P; 98.2%, 85.4%, and 90.9% when based on the WR of the different segments.

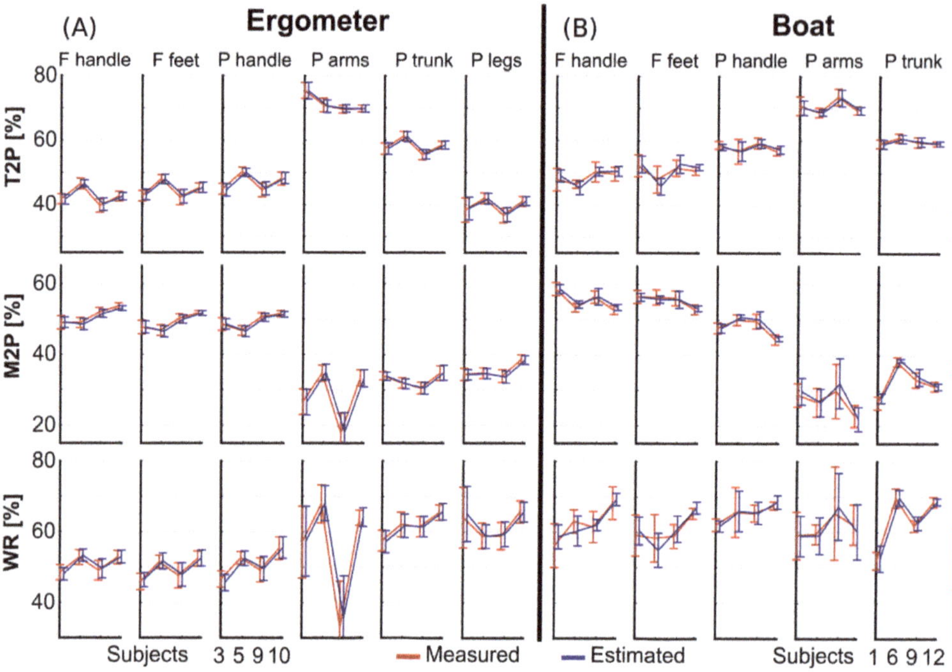

Figure 5. Technical determinants T2P, M2P, and WR were computed on the measured (red) and reconstructed (blue) forces and power sequences for four representative subjects in ergometer (**A**) and boat (**B**) rowing sessions. Mean and standard deviation were calculated across all cycles in the validation dataset.

Table 3. Mean ± standard deviation and mean absolute error (*MAE*) over all the cycles in the validation dataset for the technical determinants time to peak (T2P), mean to peak (M2P), and work ratio (WR).

		T2P (% Drive Phase)	**T2P *MAE***	**M2P (%)**	**M2P *MAE***	**WR (%)**	**WR *MAE***
Ergometer	$F^{f,x}$	0.05 ± 1.59	0.97	−0.25 ± 1.09	0.86	0.11 ± 2.93	2.07
	$F^{h,x}$	0.02 ± 1.69	1.06	−0.16 ± 1.03	0.75	−0.08 ± 3.01	2.18
	$P^{h,x}$	0.00 ± 1.61	0.96	−0.13 ± 1.06	0.80	−0.15 ± 2.92	2.04
	P^{a}	−0.07 ± 1.07	0.48	0.04 ± 0.78	0.59	0.33 ± 3.55	2.25
	P^{t}	−0.02 ± 1.44	0.42	−0.05 ± 0.63	0.47	−0.12 ± 3.45	1.51
	P^{l}	0.23 ± 1.92	0.80	−0.12 ± 0.65	0.48	0.15 ± 4.30	2.25
Boat	$F^{f,x}$	0.31 ± 3.45	2.67	0.17 ± 1.39	1.15	0.59 ± 6.15	4.88
	$F^{h,x}$	0.20 ± 3.49	2.39	−0.16 ± 1.11	0.89	0.49 ± 5.99	4.13
	$P^{h,x}$	0.11 ± 1.72	1.22	0.25 ± 0.92	0.74	0.48 ± 3.12	2.35
	P^{a}	−0.34 ± 1.17	0.88	0.44 ± 1.64	1.26	−0.28 ± 4.17	3.15
	P^{t}	−0.06 ± 0.83	0.57	0.55 ± 0.92	0.80	0.29 ± 2.37	1.89
	P^{l}	0.26 ± 2.27	1.54	−0.19 ± 1.28	0.96	0.84 ± 4.92	3.55

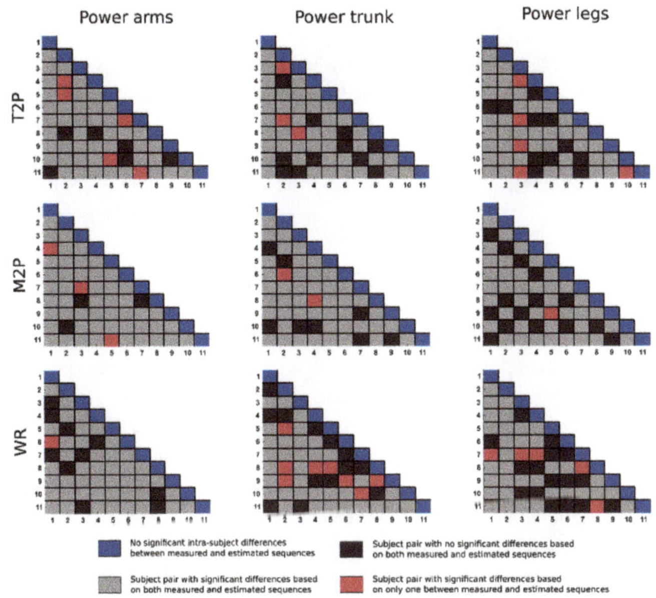

Figure 6. Two-sample *t*-test results between the measured and LSTM-estimated sequences for the T2P, M2P, and WR derived from the power arms, trunk, and legs. Values along the diagonal represent the intra-subject differences between measured and reconstructed sequences. Values outside the diagonal are comparisons between pairs of subjects performed on both the measured and estimated sequences. The colors indicate whether the inter-subject differences detected from the estimated sequences are consistent with those detected from the measured sequences.

4. Discussion

In this article, we propose a method for estimating the forces and powers generated during rowing with minimal setup and without requiring the installation of force sensors. The goal was to create a simple method that could be used by trainers during everyday practice and possibly serve as the basis for real-time feedback for rowers. In contrast, the use of traditional biomechanical approaches [31,33] would require more complex simulations, requiring expert users and more time-consuming analysis. Since rowing is a sequential movement with a straightforward relationship between velocity and power, we opted for an LSTM network, as such networks have been proven to yield successful results for sequential motions like gait [36].

The LSTM network was able to reconstruct the forces and powers generated by the rowers with an overall mean absolute error smaller than 5% in ergometer and on-water rowing. Averaging over multiple cycles, justified by the repetitive and highly repeatable movements of rowing [47], brought the average error down to below 1%. Moreover, the individual rowers' techniques, characterized by peak timing, mean to peak, and work ratio, were identified by the LSTM network with an error smaller than 4%. Finally, inter-individual differences in rowing technique were identified with an accuracy above 90%, except for the trunk power work ratio during ergometer rowing. The proposed method was thus able to quantify, with good accuracy, variables that are important for the evaluation of rowers' performance [1,13] and techniques [9,12,17].

The estimation of the curve was accurate enough to identify fine details in the rowers' techniques that could be addressed in training. For instance, in Figure 3A, the rowers on the ergometer show different strategies in terms of their arm power development, with subject 9 showing an early peak, followed by a session at negative power. This kind of curve is seen as a technical fault [1,48] since it means that some of the power generated by the rowers is absorbed by the arms instead of being transferred to the handle or oars. For this particular rower, the proposed method would facilitate the delivery of targeted feedback to correct the identified technical fault (i.e., a reduction in negative power, as highlighted on a monitor in front of the rower) while also providing objective metrics that the trainer can track over time (e.g., watts of negative power, ideally tending to zero). Real-time feedback has been proven to be helpful in boat and ergometer rowing [11,48,49], and the possibility of having targeted feedback with minimal equipment for both ergometers and boats would greatly benefit trainers and athletes.

The accuracy of body segment power estimation was lower than that of force estimation, particularly in the case of arm power, which was the segment with the lowest power production and presented the largest relative error. This result was expected since the forces are quantities that can be measured directly, while body segment power calculation is based on several assumptions combining multiple measurements. For instance, differences in sensor placement between subjects might lead to over- or underestimation of arm length and velocity, creating noise in power computation but not in the force measurements. We also identified additional sources of noise that limit the performance of our LSTM network. In the first place, the forces that we measured were unidirectional, but in reality, rowers can also exert forces in the vertical and lateral directions, which would affect the behavior of the boat and ergometer but not be captured by the sensors. Other sources of noise, while limiting the performance of the LSTM network on a cycle-by-cycle basis, could be mitigated when averaging the curves over multiple cycles. In particular, these sources include environmental interactions with water and wind, which might change within a single session [50], or oscillations of the ergometer along the rail. For instance, the average speed of the ergometer is obviously zero, but there might be cycle-by-cycle differences where the center of mass of the system (i.e., the rower plus the ergometer) moves a few centimeters backward or forward. These cycle-by-cycle variations make the model, in its current state, unsuitable for precisely identifying instantaneous changes in someone's technique. However, given the repeatability of the rowing gesture [47], data averaged over a few cycles will provide important information regarding technique and performance progress over time. Some quantities could be more sensitive than others to these errors, such as the T2P of a curve with a large plateau, where small changes can have a larger effect on the peak position (e.g., for ergometer subject 3, leg power T2P exhibited less accuracy in discriminating between rowers). While the current method may not be accurate enough to discriminate between subjects with very similar techniques, the errors in identifying technical determinants were smaller than the variability observed among subjects employing different techniques. Indeed, the technical parameters used for describing rowers' techniques showed good agreement between the measured and estimated sequences. When comparing the techniques between pairs of rowers, the determinants based on the estimated sequences had an accuracy of 93%, meaning legs–trunk–arms sequencing could be accurately estimated and used to inform crew selection based on the similarity of force and power profiles [16].

The accuracy of force and power estimation was much lower in the leave-one-out validation, with great variability between subjects. Considering the small number of subjects, this result was expected. Indeed, the rowers included in the study exhibited great variability in height, weight, and technique and might lie outside of the distribution of the small training set. In future research, more data should be collected to improve generalizability to larger populations of rowers [1]. In particular, the current sample was composed of only male rowers with similar ages and comparable skill levels and techniques [1]. Extending the analysis to women and younger or older rowers is a necessary step to include a variety of body types in the training set. Furthermore, the inclusion of data obtained from unskilled rowers (e.g., beginners or rowers on gym ergometers) could help the model learn specific mechanics behind the rowing movement that would be underrepresented in data collected from skilled rowers. The inclusion of these data might lead to the development of a computational tool capable of predicting the forces, powers, and technical profiles of any rower, whatever the rowing condition. Nonetheless, even in the current state, with a network trained on a small data sample corresponding to an average rowing club, this method shows promising results, allowing rowers' techniques to be predicted in different settings, provided they had been previously evaluated once while using the complete biomechanical setup. Building on these promising results, future research should explore the feasibility of estimating force and power exclusively through video data. Such methods have already been successfully implemented for more complex movement types [25], and their application to rowing, particularly in the controlled environment of ergometer rowing, appears highly plausible.

Overall, the proposed method should significantly reduce the costs of performance analysis. Equipping an ergometer with only cable sensors could reduce costs by more than half, with video-based systems offering the potential for even greater savings. Similarly, while the cost of equipping a rowing boat currently exceeds EUR 2000, a set of IMUs and GPS devices can be acquired for less than half this cost, offering the advantage of being easily transferrable between rowers and boats.

To conclude, equipping rowing boats and ergometers with force and displacement sensors can be costly and time-consuming. The proposed method only requires the application of IMUs or cable sensors (ideally, for indoor rowing, these could also be replaced by video motion captures) and can quantify rowers' performance and techniques with good accuracy.

Author Contributions: Conceptualization, L.P. and G.M.; methodology, L.P., G.N.E. and F.R.S.; software, L.P.; validation, L.P.; formal analysis, L.P.; investigation, L.P.; resources, G.M.; data curation, L.P.; writing—original draft preparation, L.P.; writing—review and editing, L.P., F.R.S., G.N.E., G.C.G. and G.M.; visualization, L.P.; supervision, G.M.; project administration, G.M.; funding acquisition, G.C.G. and G.M. All authors have read and agreed to the published version of the manuscript.

Funding: This research was funded by a grant from the PIA (Programme d'Investissements d'Avenir) via the ANR (Agence Nationale de la Recherche) with the reference ANR-20-STHP-0006.

Institutional Review Board Statement: This study was approved by the Sud-Ouest et Outre-Mer III ethics committee (approval reference 20.07.21.43000-ID_9115) and conformed to the requirements stipulated in the Declaration of Helsinki.

Informed Consent Statement: Written informed consent was obtained from all subjects involved in the study.

Data Availability Statement: Data will be made available upon request. Code available at: https://github.com/loPitto/LSTM-scull-ergo (accessed on 4 January 2025).

Acknowledgments: The authors would like to thank the trainers and athletes of the Pôle Aviron Nancy for their availability and valuable support.

Conflicts of Interest: The authors declare no conflicts of interest.

References

1. Kleshnev, V. *The Biomechanics of Rowing*, 2nd ed.; Crowood Press: Marlborough, UK, 2016.
2. Dawson, R.G.; Lockwood, R.J.; Wilson, J.D.; Freeman, G. The Rowing Cycle: Sources of Variance and Invariance in Ergometer and on-the-Water Performance. *J. Mot. Behav.* **1998**, *30*, 33–43. [CrossRef] [PubMed]

3. Colloud, F.; Bahuaud, P.; Doriot, N.; Champely, S.; Chèze, L. Fixed versus Free-Floating Stretcher Mechanism in Rowing Ergometers: Mechanical Aspects. *J. Sports Sci.* **2006**, *24*, 479–493. [CrossRef] [PubMed]
4. Mpimis, T.; Gikas, V.; Gourgoulis, V. A Rigorous and Integrated On-Water Monitoring System for Performance and Technique Improvement in Rowing. *Sensors* **2023**, *23*, 6150. [CrossRef]
5. Warmenhoven, J.; Cobley, S.; Draper, C.; Harrison, A.J.; Bargary, N.; Smith, R. Assessment of Propulsive Pin Force and Oar Angle Time-series Using Functional Data Analysis in On-water Rowing. *Scand. J. Med. Sci. Sports* **2017**, *27*, 1688–1696. [CrossRef] [PubMed]
6. Warmenhoven, J.; Cobley, S.; Draper, C.; Harrison, A.; Bargary, N.; Smith, R. How Gender and Boat-Side Affect Shape Characteristics of Force–Angle Profiles in Single Sculling: Insights from Functional Data Analysis. *J. Sci. Med. Sport* **2018**, *21*, 533–537. [CrossRef] [PubMed]
7. Warmenhoven, J.; Cobley, S.; Draper, C.; Smith, R. Over 50 Years of Researching Force Profiles in Rowing: What Do We Know? *Sports Med.* **2018**, *48*, 2703–2714. [CrossRef]
8. Holt, A.C.; Ball, K.; Siegel, R.; Hopkins, W.G.; Aughey, R.J. Relationships between Measures of Boat Acceleration and Performance in Rowing, with and without Controlling for Stroke Rate and Power Output. *PLoS ONE* **2021**, *16*, e0249122. [CrossRef]
9. Holt, A.C.; Aughey, R.J.; Ball, K.; Hopkins, W.G.; Siegel, R. Technical Determinants of On-Water Rowing Performance. *Front. Sports Act. Living* **2020**, *2*, 589013. [CrossRef] [PubMed]
10. Lintmeijer, L.L.; Hofmijster, M.J.; Schulte Fischedick, G.A.; Zijlstra, P.J.; Van Soest, A.J. "Knoek" Improved Determination of Mechanical Power Output in Rowing: Experimental Results. *J. Sports Sci.* **2018**, *36*, 2138–2146. [CrossRef] [PubMed]
11. Lintmeijer, L.L.; Knoek Van Soest, A.J.; Robbers, F.S.; Hofmijster, M.J.; Beek, P.J. Real-Time Feedback on Mechanical Power Output: Facilitating Crew Rowers' Compliance with Prescribed Training Intensity. *Int. J. Sports Physiol. Perform.* **2019**, *14*, 303–309. [CrossRef] [PubMed]
12. Pitto, L.; Ertel, G.N.; Simon, F.R.; Gauchard, G.C.; Mornieux, G. Influence of Neuromuscular Activity and Technical Determinants on Scull Rowing Performance. *Appl. Sci.* **2024**, *14*, 9055. [CrossRef]
13. Smith, R.; Draper, C. Skill Variables Discriminate between the Elite and Sub-Elite in Coxless Pair-Oared Rowing. *Int. Soc. Biomech. Sport.* **2006**, *24*, 1–4.
14. Trompeter, K.; Fett, D.; Platen, P. Back Pain in Rowers: A Cross-Sectional Study on Prevalence, Pain Characteristics and Risk Factors. *Sportverletz. Sportschaden* **2019**, *33*, 51–59. [CrossRef] [PubMed]
15. Wilson, F.; Thornton, J.S.; Wilkie, K.; Hartvigsen, J.; Vinther, A.; Ackerman, K.E.; Caneiro, J.P.; Trease, L.; Nugent, F.; Gissane, C.; et al. 2021 Consensus Statement for Preventing and Managing Low Back Pain in Elite and Subelite Adult Rowers. *Br. J. Sports Med.* **2021**, *55*, 893–899. [CrossRef]
16. Baudouin, A. A Biomechanical Review of Factors Affecting Rowing Performance. *Br. J. Sports Med.* **2002**, *36*, 396–402. [CrossRef]
17. Simon, F.R.; Ertel, G.N.; Duchene, Y.; Maciejewski, H.; Gauchard, G.C.; Mornieux, G. Prediction of Rowing Ergometer Performance by Technical and Core Stability Parameters. *J. Sports Sci.* **2023**, *41*, 399–407. [CrossRef]
18. Pitto, L.; Simon, F.; Banet, L.; Ertel, G.; Mornieux, G. Real-Time Biofeedback to Control Trunk Power Production in Ergometer Rowing. *ISBS Proc. Arch.* **2024**, *42*, 760.
19. Warmenhoven, J.; Smith, R.; Draper, C.; Harrison, A.J.; Bargary, N.; Cobley, S. Force Coordination Strategies in On-water Single Sculling: Are Asymmetries Related to Better Rowing Performance? *Scand. J. Med. Sci. Sports* **2018**, *28*, 1379–1388. [CrossRef]
20. Ejaz, N.; Khan, S.J.; Azim, F.; Asif, M.; Teuțan, E.; Pleșa, A.; Păcurar, R.; Stan, S.-D. Automatic Gait Classification Model Empowered by Machine Learning for People with and without Osteoporosis Using Smart Walker. *Appl. Sci.* **2024**, *14*, 3874. [CrossRef]
21. Yang, Z. An Efficient Automatic Gait Anomaly Detection Method Based on Semisupervised Clustering. *Comput. Intell. Neurosci.* **2021**, *2021*, 8840156. [CrossRef]
22. Worsey, M.T.O.; Pahl, R.; Espinosa, H.G.; Shepherd, J.B.; Thiel, D.V. Is Machine Learning and Automatic Classification of Swimming Data What Unlocks the Power of Inertial Measurement Units in Swimming? *J. Sports Sci.* **2021**, *39*, 2095–2114. [CrossRef]
23. Stetter, B.J.; Ringhof, S.; Krafft, F.C.; Sell, S.; Stein, T. Estimation of Knee Joint Forces in Sport Movements Using Wearable Sensors and Machine Learning. *Sensors* **2019**, *19*, 3690. [CrossRef]
24. Matijevich, E.S.; Scott, L.R.; Volgyesi, P.; Derry, K.H.; Zelik, K.E. Combining Wearable Sensor Signals, Machine Learning and Biomechanics to Estimate Tibial Bone Force and Damage during Running. *Hum. Mov. Sci.* **2020**, *74*, 102690. [CrossRef] [PubMed]
25. Johnson, W.R.; Mian, A.; Donnelly, C.J.; Lloyd, D.; Alderson, J. Predicting Athlete Ground Reaction Forces and Moments from Motion Capture. *Med. Biol. Eng. Comput.* **2018**, *56*, 1781–1792. [CrossRef] [PubMed]
26. ForceTeck. Available online: https://www.forceteck.com/ (accessed on 24 December 2024).
27. Model Health. Available online: https://www.modelhealth.io (accessed on 24 December 2024).

28. Wilaikaew, P.; Noisriphan, W.; Chen, C.C.; Charoensuk, J.; Ruengitinun, S.; Chootong, C. Apply Machine-Learning Model for Clustering Rowing Players. In Proceedings of the ACM International Conference Proceeding Series, Osaka Japan, 15 December 2023; Association for Computing Machinery: New York, NY, USA, 2023; pp. 218–224.
29. Bosch, S.; Shoaib, M.; Geerlings, S.; Buit, L.; Meratnia, N.; Havinga, P. Analysis of Indoor Rowing Motion Using Wearable Inertial Sensors. In Proceedings of the BodyNets International Conference on Body Area Networks, Sydney, Australia, 28–30 September 2015.
30. Li, Y.; Koldenhoven, R.; Jiwan, N.; Zhan, J.; Liu, T. Automated Rower Assignment to Rowing Events: A Machine Learning Approach. *ISBS Proc. Arch.* **2024**, *42*, 592.
31. Nitschke, M.; Marzilger, R.; Leyendecker, S.; Eskofier, B.M.; Koelewijn, A.D. Change the Direction: 3D Optimal Control Simulation by Directly Tracking Marker and Ground Reaction Force Data. *PeerJ* **2023**, *11*, e14852. [CrossRef]
32. Dorschky, E.; Nitschke, M.; Seifer, A.K.; van den Bogert, A.J.; Eskofier, B.M. Estimation of Gait Kinematics and Kinetics from Inertial Sensor Data Using Optimal Control of Musculoskeletal Models. *J. Biomech.* **2019**, *95*, 109278. [CrossRef] [PubMed]
33. Falisse, A.; Pitto, L.; Kainz, H.; Hoang, H.; Wesseling, M.; Van Rossom, S.; Papageorgiou, E.; Bar-On, L.; Hallemans, A.; Desloovere, K.; et al. Physics-Based Predictive Simulations to Explore the Differential Effects of Motor Control and Musculoskeletal Deficits on Gait Dysfunction in Cerebral Palsy: A Retrospective Case Study. *Front. Hum. Neurosci.* **2020**, *14*, 497821. [CrossRef]
34. Ordóñez, F.; Roggen, D. Deep Convolutional and LSTM Recurrent Neural Networks for Multimodal Wearable Activity Recognition. *Sensors* **2016**, *16*, 115. [CrossRef]
35. Nait Aicha, A.; Englebienne, G.; Van Schooten, K.S.; Pijnappels, M.; Kröse, B. Deep Learning to Predict Falls in Older Adults Based on Daily-Life Trunk Accelerometry. *Sensors* **2018**, *18*, 1654. [CrossRef] [PubMed]
36. Su, B.; Gutierrez-Farewik, E.M. Gait Trajectory and Gait Phase Prediction Based on an LSTM Network. *Sensors* **2020**, *20*, 7127. [CrossRef] [PubMed]
37. Zaroug, A.; Lai, D.T.H.; Mudie, K.; Begg, R. Lower Limb Kinematics Trajectory Prediction Using Long Short-Term Memory Neural Networks. *Front. Bioeng. Biotechnol.* **2020**, *8*, 527709. [CrossRef]
38. Greff, K.; Srivastava, R.K.; Koutník, J.; Steunebrink, B.R.; Schmidhuber, J. LSTM: A Search Space Odyssey. *IEEE Trans. Neural Netw. Learn. Syst.* **2016**, *28*, 2222–2232. [CrossRef]
39. Graves, A. Generating Sequences with Recurrent Neural Networks. *arXiv* **2013**, arXiv:1308.0850.
40. Zaroug, A.; Garofolini, A.; Lai, D.T.H.; Mudie, K.; Begg, R. Prediction of Gait Trajectories Based on the Long Short Term Memory Neural Networks. *PLoS ONE* **2021**, *16*, e0255597. [CrossRef]
41. Brice, S.M.; Millett, E.L.; Philippa, B. The Validity of Using Inertial Measurement Units to Monitor the Torso and Pelvis Sagittal Plane Motion of Elite Rowers. *J. Sports Sci.* **2022**, *40*, 950–958. [CrossRef]
42. Li, Y.; Koldenhoven, R.M.; Jiwan, N.C.; Zhan, J.; Liu, T. Trunk and Shoulder Kinematics of Rowing Displayed by Olympic Athletes. *Sports Biomech.* **2020**, *22*, 1095–1107. [CrossRef] [PubMed]
43. Chia, L.; Andersen, J.T.; McKay, M.J.; Sullivan, J.; Megalaa, T.; Pappas, E. Evaluating the Validity and Reliability of Inertial Measurement Units for Determining Knee and Trunk Kinematics during Athletic Landing and Cutting Movements. *J. Electromyogr. Kinesiol.* **2021**, *60*, 102589. [CrossRef]
44. Kleshnev, V. Power in Rowing. In Proceedings of the 18 International Symposium on Biomechanics in Sports, Hong Kong, China, 25–30 June 2000; pp. 2–5.
45. Hofmijster, M.J.; Lintmeijer, L.L.; Beek, P.J.; van Soest, A.J.K. Mechanical Power Output in Rowing Should Not Be Determined from Oar Forces and Oar Motion Alone. *J. Sports Sci.* **2018**, *36*, 2147–2153. [CrossRef] [PubMed]
46. Karakish, M.; Fouz, M.A.; ELsawaf, A. Gait Trajectory Prediction on an Embedded Microcontroller Using Deep Learning. *Sensors* **2022**, *22*, 8441. [CrossRef]
47. Fohanno, V.; Nordez, A.; Smith, R.; Colloud, F. Asymmetry in Elite Rowers: Effect of Ergometer Design and Stroke Rate. *Sports Biomech.* **2015**, *14*, 310–322. [CrossRef] [PubMed]
48. Gorman, A.J.; Willmott, A.P.; Mullineaux, D.R. The Effects of Concurrent Biomechanical Biofeedback on Novel Skill Acquisition. *Sports Biomech.* **2022**, *21*, 297–311. [CrossRef] [PubMed]
49. Gorman, A.J.; Willmott, A.P.; Mullineaux, D.R. The Effects of Concurrent Biomechanical Biofeedback on Rowing Performance at Different Stroke Rates. *J. Sports Sci.* **2021**, *39*, 2716–2726. [CrossRef]
50. Binnie, M.J.; Astridge, D.; Watts, S.P.; Goods, P.S.R.; Rice, A.J.; Peeling, P. Quantifying On-Water Performance in Rowing: A Perspective on Current Challenges and Future Directions. *Front. Sports Act. Living* **2023**, *5*, 1101654. [CrossRef] [PubMed]

sensors

MDPI

Article

The Reliability of 20 m Sprint Time Using a Novel Assessment Technique

Patrick M. Holmberg, Mico H. Olivier and Vincent G. Kelly *

School of Exercise and Nutrition Sciences, Queensland University of Technology, Brisbane, QLD 4000, Australia; patrick.holmberg@hdr.qut.edu.au (P.M.H.); micohannes.olivier@hdr.qut.edu.au (M.H.O.)
* Correspondence: v6.kelly@qut.edu.au

Abstract

Sprint acceleration is critical for success in team sports. This study aimed to (a) establish the test–retest reliability of a novel method for assessing 20 m sprint performance and (b) determine the magnitude of meaningful change in 20 m sprint times. Thirty highly trained male team sport athletes completed sprint testing (2 × 20 m [separated by 5 min]) on two separate occasions, separated by 7 days. Sprint times (0–20, 0–10, 10–20 m) were recorded using infrared timing gates (Brower Timing Systems, West Valley City, UT, USA) connected to a motion start sensor positioned at the participant's rear leg while in a 2-point starting stance. 0–20, 0–10, and 10–20 m sprint times demonstrated acceptable reliability (CV = 0.52–1.36%, ICC = 0.89–0.95). Additionally, the smallest worthwhile change (SWC) was greater than the typical error (TE [95% CI]) for 0–20 (0.025 s) and 0–10 m (0.016 s) sprint times, indicating that meaningful changes can be reliably detected between testing sessions. However, the SWC was less than the TE for 10–20 m sprint times. This suggests the method may not reliably detect meaningful changes in sprint performance over this distance. As such, the minimal detectable change (95% CI) should be considered the threshold for meaningful change (0.033 s). The consistent and low TE across sprint distances highlights the test–retest reliability of the method for assessing 0–20 m sprint times in this population of highly trained male team sport athletes.

Keywords: motion start sensor; reliability; sprint testing; team sports; timing gates

1. Introduction

Sprinting is critical for success in team sports [1]. However, sprint efforts during competitions are often brief, lasting only 2–3 s [2]. Alternatively, maximal velocity is rarely achieved in team sports [3], suggesting that speed testing in team sports should concentrate on acceleration over the initial 20 m compared with longer sprint distances [1]. This raises the important question of how best to assess sprint times over 20 m to guide and evaluate training prescriptions.

Considering their simplicity and relatively low cost, timing gates are a popular method for speed assessment in applied settings [4,5]. A limitation of timing gate systems is the standardisation of the self-regulated start [6]. Momentum from extraneous body movements, such as a rocking motion caused by stepping or leaning backward from a 2-point starting stance, can reduce the reliability of recorded sprint times, particularly when using a single-beam timing system [4,7,8]. Although Darrall-Jones et al. [9] observed acceptable test–retest reliability (CV = 1.8–3.1%) for 0–20 and 0–10 m sprint times in junior rugby players, the typical error (TE) was greater than the smallest worthwhile change (SWC). This suggests that the method may not be able to reliably detect meaningful changes in sprint times over these distances [10].

Previous studies replaced the initial timing gate with a motion start sensor, activated by the participant's thumb or foot whilst they are in a 3-point starting stance [6,11]. This method was suggested to reduce the extraneous movement that often occurs before the activation of the electronic timing in a 2-point start [6]. Whereas the different starting techniques (foot and thumb starts) produced minimal differences in TE (~0.02 s or <1%), Duthie et al. [6] reported large differences in 10 m sprint time in junior rugby players. Additionally, 10 m sprint times for the foot start condition varied significantly between trials (0.02 ± 0.02 s, $p < 0.05$) [6]. The TE was lower than previous research, which reported typical errors of ~0.04 s for 10 m sprint time using a single-beam timing system [5]. However, the TE was greater than the SWC, suggesting that the method may not be able to reliably detect meaningful changes in 10 m sprint times [6].

The variation in 10 m sprint times was partly attributed to the participants' lack of experience with the 3-point starting stance [6]. This may have caused their centre of mass to shift, increasing momentum before timing was initiated [4,7,8]. Although the 3-point start was suggested to reduce momentum, it may require additional familiarisation, particularly for team sport athletes who have not been exposed to this technique [6]. Considering that reliability was similar for the 2- and 3-point starts, the latter may not be advisable for this population [6].

No studies have examined the reliability of using a motion start sensor positioned at participants' rear leg whilst they are in a 2-point starting stance to assess 0–20 m sprint times (Figure 1). If team sport athletes are familiarised with the method, it may reduce the error typically observed in 0–20 m sprint tests involving a timing gate system [5,6,9]. This could produce more precise measurements, allowing for the detection of meaningful changes in sprint times over this distance. Therefore, this study aimed to establish the test–retest reliability of a novel method for assessing 20 m sprint performance in highly trained team sport athletes. A secondary aim was to determine the magnitude of meaningful change in 20 m sprint times. It was hypothesised that the method would be a reliable tool for assessing meaningful changes (i.e., SWC > TE) in 0–20 m sprint performance.

Figure 1. Set-up for 20 m sprint assessment using the motion start sensor.

2. Methods

2.1. Experimental Approach to the Problem

To establish the test–retest reliability of 20 m (0–20, 0–10, 10–20 m) sprint times and determine the magnitude of meaningful change in these variables, a group of highly trained male team sport athletes [12] were familiarised with experimental procedures on two separate occasions. Participants then completed two testing sessions involving 2 × 20 m sprints (separated by 5 min), with the sessions separated by 7 days. Sprint testing was conducted at the same time of day (±1 h) to account for diurnal variation [13]. Ethical approval was granted by an Institutional Research Ethics Committee, approval number 6399.

2.2. Subjects

Thirty highly trained male athletes (age: 19.56 [±2.40] years, height: 178.16 [±8.51] cm, body mass [BM]: 74.73 [±9.12] kg) provided written consent before participation. This sample size is considered sufficient to establish reliability and detect meaningful performance changes [14]. Inclusion criteria were individuals aged 18–24 years, highly trained athletes [12], currently performing $\geq$ 2 lower-body training sessions involving resistance exercise and sprint-specific activities per week, and injury-free.

Participants were instructed not to perform any lower-body exercise in the 72 h before testing sessions. Any non-lower-body exercise completed 72 h before testing sessions was recorded in an activity diary and standardised across testing sessions. Participants also completed a 3-day nutritional intake diary before the initial testing session and were instructed to replicate their nutritional intake and timing for the subsequent testing session. Compliance with these instructions was verified before testing sessions through physical activity diaries, nutritional logs, brief interviews, and a signed form confirming adherence to the outlined protocols.

2.3. Procedures

Sprint performance was assessed using a 20 m sprint with a split time recorded at 10 m. Participants performed two maximal 20 m sprints separated by a 5 min rest period. Before sprint testing, participants completed a standardised warm-up involving dynamic stretching and progressively faster runs (2 × 70%, 2 × 80%, 2 × 90%, and 1 × 100% of maximal effort [separated by 2–4 min]). Sprint times were recorded using infrared timing gates (Brower Timing Systems, Utah, USA) with 0.01 s accuracy. The timing gates were positioned at approximately hip height (90 cm above the ground) at 10 and 20 m. The timing system was connected to a motion start sensor, which had a sensitivity range of 2–10 cm and sampled at 500 Hz. Participants assumed a split-stance crouch position (i.e., 2-point stance) [15] 50 cm behind tape affixed to the ground, denoting the "starting line" [9]. Upon taking their preferred starting stance (dominant leg and stance length were recorded during the familiarisation sessions), the motion start sensor was placed on a stable surface ~5 cm above ground and manually positioned 10 cm from the lateral malleolus of the participant's rear leg. After confirmation that the motion start sensor was in position, participants were instructed to begin each maximal trial at their readiness. Timing of maximal sprints was initiated upon the movement of the rear foot and concluded upon completion of the specified distance. The accuracy of the motion start sensor was confirmed using 2-dimensional motion capture filmed 1 m to the left or right of participants (depending on their starting leg) at a height of 40 cm (Hudl Technique; Ubersense Inc., Chicago, IL, USA). Participants were instructed to sprint maximally over the 20 m, with cones positioned at 22 m to encourage maximal speed through the "finish line". Verbal encouragement was provided throughout each maximal sprint. The best trial (based on sprint time) was used to assess sprint performance [5]. All sprinting activities were completed outdoors on field turf, with participants wearing cleats.

2.4. Statistical Analysis

The normality of the data was assessed using the Shapiro–Wilk test. Test–retest reliability was assessed with the intraclass correlation coefficient (ICC), and 95% confidence intervals (CI) were reported. When normality assumptions were violated, skewness was assessed to determine the appropriate bootstrapping method for constructing 95% CI. If $|\text{skewness}| < 1$, bootstrap t-intervals (5000 samples, 95% CI) were used; if $|\text{skewness}| \geq 1$, bias-corrected and accelerated bootstrapping (5000 samples, 95% CI) was applied to correct for non-normality [16]. Paired t-tests were used to compare 0–20, 0–10, and 10–20 m sprint times between sessions [17]. Statistical significance was set at $p < 0.05$ a priori. The ICC was calculated using a two-way mixed effects model with single measures for absolute agreement and interpreted as follows: >0.90 = excellent, 0.75–0.90 = good, 0.50–0.74 = moderate, and <0.50 = poor [18]. The CV was calculated as the percentage of each participant's mean score [19] based on the mean difference and standard deviation (SD) across trials [20]. The CV was interpreted as follows: <5% = good, 5–10% = moderate, and >10% = poor [21]. The TE was calculated and presented with a 95% CI to quantify within-subject variation [22,23]. The standard error of measurement (SEM) was calculated to assess the precision of 20 m sprint times, and SWC was calculated using 0.2 x between-subject SD [22]. An increase or decrease in 0–20 m sprint times greater than the SWC was used as the threshold for a meaningful change in sprint performance [20]. Additionally, the minimal detectable change with 95% CI (MDC_{95}) was calculated to determine practically meaningful changes in sprint times [24,25]. Descriptive statistics for 20 m sprint times are presented as mean (±SD) with 95% CI. All statistical analyses were performed using R Studio (version 4.3.1) with the following packages: '*BlandAltmanLeh*', '*psych*', and '*irr*'.

3. Results

Reliability measurements for 20 m sprint times are presented in Table 1. Sprint times were considered reliable based on the following criteria: CV ≤ 10% and ICC ≥ 0.80 [26]. 0–20 m sprint time showed excellent test–retest reliability (CV = 0.52%, ICC = 0.95 [0.89, 0.97]) and was able to detect the SWC (i.e., SWC > TE). 0–10 m sprint time also demonstrated excellent test–retest reliability (CV = 0.67%, ICC = 0.93 [0.86, 0.97]) and was able to detect the SWC. Additionally, 10–20 m sprint time showed acceptable test–retest reliability (CV = 1.36%, ICC = 0.89 [0.78, 0.95]). However, the SWC was less than the TE, indicating that meaningful changes in sprint performance over this distance may not be reliably detected.

Table 1. Descriptive and test–retest reliability statistics for 20 m sprint times.

Sprint Times	Mean ± SD	CV (%)	ICC (95% CI)	TE (90% CI)	SEM	SWC (0.2)	SWC ≥ TE	MDC_{95}
0–20 m (s)	3.09 ± 0.13	0.52	0.95 (0.90, 0.98)	0.016 (0.012, 0.021)	0.029	0.025	Yes	0.057
0–10 m (s)	1.82 ± 0.08	0.67	0.93 (0.86, 0.97)	0.012 (0.009, 0.016)	0.022	0.016	Yes	0.044
10–20 m (s)	1.26 ± 0.05	1.36	0.89 (0.78, 0.95)	0.017 (0.013, 0.023)	0.017	0.010	No	0.033

CV: coefficient of variation; *CI:* confidence interval; *ICC:* intraclass correlation; MDC_{95}: minimal detectable change calculated with 95% probability; *SWC:* smallest worthwhile change; *SD:* standard deviation; *SEM:* standard error of measurement; *TE:* typical error.

Normality was violated for 0–20 m sprint times. Bootstrapping with 5000 samples (95% CI) produced a mean difference of 0.005 s (95% CI: −0.009, 0.020), indicating no significant difference between testing sessions. The Bland–Altman plot showed a mean difference of 0.005 s, suggesting no systematic bias (Figure 2). The Limits of Agreement (LOA) indicated that 95% of 0–20 m sprint times were between −0.077 s (lower LOA) and 0.087 s (upper LOA), with no evidence of proportional bias.

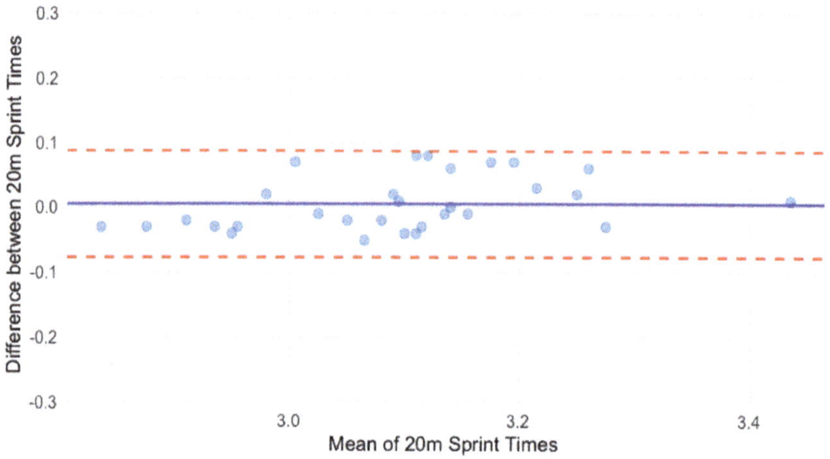

Figure 2. Bland–Altman plot for 0–20 m sprint time.

A paired *t*-test revealed no significant difference in 0–10 m sprint times between testing sessions ($p = 0.77$, 95% CI: [−0.010, 0.013]). The Bland–Altman plot showed a mean difference of 0.001 s, indicating no systematic bias (Figure 3). The LOA ranged from −0.060 s (lower LOA) to 0.064 s (upper LOA), with 95% of 0–10 m sprint times within this range. No evidence of proportional bias was observed.

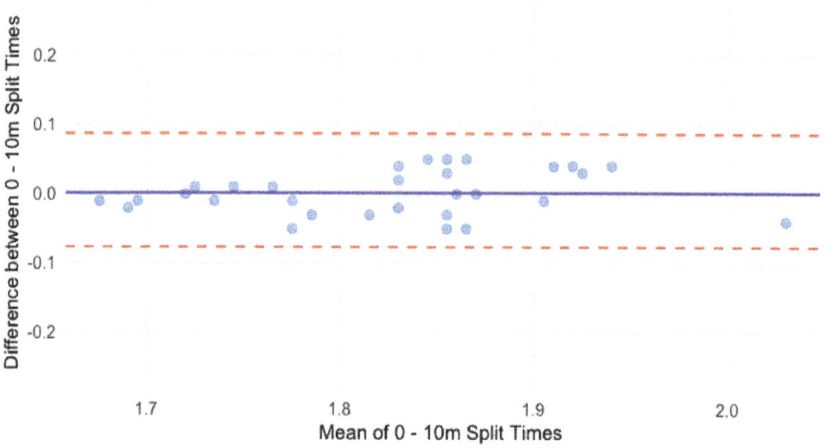

Figure 3. Bland–Altman plot for 0–10 m sprint time.

A paired *t*-test showed no significant difference in 10–20 m sprint times between testing sessions ($p = 0.71$, 95% CI: [−0.010, 0.007]). The Bland–Altman plot indicated a mean difference of 0.001 s, indicating no systematic bias (Figure 4). The upper and lower LOA were 0.046 s and −0.049 s. This suggests that 95% of 10–20 m sprint times were within this range. No evidence of proportional bias was observed.

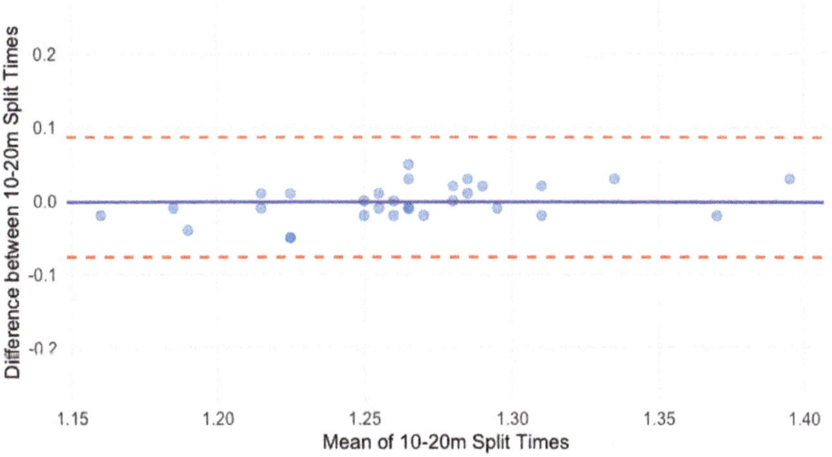

Figure 4. Bland–Altman plot for 10–20 m sprint time.

4. Discussion

This study aimed to establish the test–retest reliability of a novel method for assessing 20 m sprint performance. A secondary aim was to determine the magnitude of meaningful change in 0–20 m sprint times. The main finding was that 0–20, 0–10, and 10–20 m sprint times demonstrated acceptable test-retest reliability (CV = 0.52–1.36%, ICC = 0.89–0.95). Additionally, the SWC was greater than the TE for 0–20 and 0–10 m sprint times, indicating that meaningful changes can be reliably detected between testing sessions. However, the SWC was less than the TE for 10–20 m sprint times. This suggests that the method may not reliably detect meaningful changes in sprint performance over this distance.

The TE for 0–20, 0–10, and 10–20 m sprint times was 0.016 (0.012, 0.021), 0.012 (0.009, 0.016), and 0.017 (0.013, 0.023) seconds, respectively. These TE values were lower than those reported for 0–20 and 0–10 m sprint times in junior rugby players [6,9]. Darrall-Jones et al. [9] used a single-beam timing system, which may have increased the likelihood of false signals (e.g., the infrared beam being broken by limbs rather than the torso), possibly affecting the recorded times [4,7,8]. Duthie et al. [6] reported a similarly low TE for 10 m sprint times (0.015 [0.011–0.029] seconds) using a method that replaced the initial timing gate with a motion start sensor activated by the thumb or foot. Whilst the different starting techniques resulted in minimal differences in the TE (~0.02 s or <1%), differences in 10 m sprint time were found between testing sessions [6]. Despite the foot start having the lowest TE, a substantial decrease in 10 m sprint time was observed between these sessions [6]. The decrease was attributed to rugby players' limited exposure to the 3-point start [6]. In contrast, no differences in 0–20, 0–10, and 10–20 m sprint times were observed in the present study, likely due to participants' experience with the 2-point starting technique and the additional familiarisation sessions. The consistent and low typical error across sprint distances highlights the reliability of the method for assessing 0–20 m sprint times in this population of highly trained team sport athletes.

The SWC was greater than the TE for 0–20 (0.025 s) and 0–10 m (0.016 s) sprint times, indicating that meaningful changes can be reliably detected between testing sessions. However, the SWC was less than the TE for 10–20 m sprint times. This suggests the method may not reliably detect meaningful changes in sprint performance over this distance. Applying SWC allows practitioners to make informed decisions based on testing data and report individual changes in response to training interventions [9,10]. Due to time constraints in most practical environments, using TE and SWC from a similar population is considered an acceptable approach for assessing changes in physical performance measures [9,27,28]. As such, practitioners working with highly trained male team sport athletes can apply these findings when assessing changes in 0–20 m sprint times. The findings highlight the importance of selecting reliable testing methods and demonstrate the value of using SWC relative to TE to accurately assess changes in 0–20 m sprint speed and inform training decisions.

The MDC_{95} for 0–20, 0–10, and 10–20 m sprint times were 0.057, 0.044, and 0.033 s, respectively. Whereas the TE (95% CI) provides an estimate of reliability, it does not specify the magnitude of change required to identify a practically meaningful change in performance. In contrast, the MDC_{95} establishes a clear threshold for the smallest change that exceeds measurement error and can confidently be considered practically meaningful [19]. As such, it can be particularly useful in applied settings to understand whether a change in sprint performance occurred due to the training intervention or random variation. Practitioners working with highly trained male team sport athletes can use this information to develop accurate sprint performance standards and determine practically meaningful changes in 0–20 m sprint times.

This study has several limitations. The absence of independent validation for the motion start sensor raises uncertainty about its accuracy and reliability relative to established methods, warranting direct comparisons with laser timing systems to assess its precision and potential advantages. The findings are specific to highly trained male team sport athletes. Thus, further research is required to determine whether the method demonstrates similar reliability and sensitivity to meaningful changes in other sporting populations, such as female athletes or individuals with different training backgrounds. Standardising the shin angle and stance width may have improved the consistency of the sprint measures. Additionally, testing sessions occurred outdoors. As such, air temperature and wind speed may have affected the recorded sprint times [29]. Finally, increasing the sample size and number of trials could have increased the precision of the TE, improving the test's ability to reliably detect meaningful changes in 0–20 m sprint times [10].

The findings showed acceptable test–retest reliability for 0–20, 0–10, and 10–20 m sprint times. Additionally, the SWC was greater than the TE for 0–20 and 0–10 m sprint times, indicating that meaningful changes can be reliably detected between testing sessions. In contrast, the SWC was less than the TE for 10–20 m sprint times. Thus, the method may not reliably detect meaningful changes in sprint performance over this distance. As such, the MDC_{95} should be considered the threshold for meaningful change. If participants are sufficiently familiarised, the results suggest that this novel method is a useful tool to assess 20 m sprint times in highly trained male team sport athletes.

Author Contributions: Conceptualisation, P.M.H.; methodology, P.M.H.; statistical analysis and visualisation, M.H.O. and P.M.H.; writing—original draft preparation, P.M.H.; writing—review and editing, P.M.H., V.G.K. and M.H.O. All authors have read and agreed to the published version of the manuscript.

Funding: This research received no external funding.

Institutional Review Board Statement: The study was conducted in accordance with the Declaration of Helsinki and approved by the Institutional Review Board of Queensland University of Technology (6399, 22 March 2023).

Informed Consent Statement: Informed consent was obtained from all subjects involved in the study.

Data Availability Statement: The raw data supporting the conclusions of this article will be made available by the authors on request.

Acknowledgments: We would like to acknowledge the invaluable contribution of Madison Griess, Lucas Quinn, and Sinjin Todd in this study.

Conflicts of Interest: The authors declare no conflicts of interest.

References

1. Simperingham, K.D.; Cronin, J.B.; Ross, A. Advances in sprint acceleration profiling for field-based team-sport athletes: Utility, reliability, validity and limitations. *Sports Med.* **2016**, *46*, 1619–1645. [PubMed]
2. Vigne, G.; Gaudino, C.; Rogowski, I.; Alloatti, G.; Hautier, C. Activity profile in elite Italian soccer team. *Int. J. Sports Med.* **2010**, *31*, 304–310. [PubMed]
3. Lindsay, A.; Draper, N.; Lewis, J.; Gieseg, S.P.; Gill, N. Positional demands of professional rugby. *Eur. J. Sport Sci.* **2015**, *15*, 480–487. [PubMed]
4. Ellis, L. Protocols for the physiological assessment of the team sport players. *Physiol. Tests Elite Athl.* **2000**, 128–144.
5. Moir, G.; Button, C.; Glaister, M.; Stone, M.H. Influence of familiarization on the reliability of vertical jump and acceleration sprinting performance in physically active men. *J. Strength Cond. Res.* **2004**, *18*, 276–280.
6. Duthie, G.M.; Pyne, D.B.; Ross, A.A.; Livingstone, S.G.; Hooper, S.L. The reliability of ten-meter sprint time using different starting techniques. *J. Strength Cond. Res.* **2006**, *20*, 251.
7. Earp, J.E.; Newton, R.U. Advances in electronic timing systems: Considerations for selecting an appropriate timing system. *J. Strength Cond. Res.* **2012**, *26*, 1245–1248.
8. Kraan, G.A.; Van Veen, J.; Snijders, C.J.; Storm, J. (2001). Starting from standing; why step backwards? *J. Biomech.* **2001**, *34*, 211–215.
9. Darrall-Jones, J.D.; Jones, B.; Roe, G.; Till, K. Reliability and usefulness of linear sprint testing in adolescent rugby union and league players. *J. Strength Cond. Res.* **2016**, *30*, 1359–1364.
10. Hopkins, W.G. Measures of reliability in sports medicine and science. *Sports Med.* **2000**, *30*, 1–15.
11. Brooks, B.T. Relative Effects of Running Surface, Equipment, and Competitive Test Conditions upon Sprinting Speed of Football Players. Master's Thesis, The Pennsylvania State University, University Park, PA, USA, 1976.
12. McKay, A.K.A.; Stellingwerff, T.; Smith, E.S.; Martin, D.T.; Mujika, I.; Goosey-Tolfrey, V.L.; Sheppard, J.; Burke, L.M. Defining training and performance calibre: A participant classification framework. *Int. J. Sports Physiol. Perform.* **2022**, *17*, 317–331. [PubMed]
13. Drust, B.; Waterhouse, J.; Atkinson, G.; Edwards, B.; Reilly, T. Circadian rhythms in sports performance—An update. *Chronobiol. Int.* **2005**, *22*, 21–44. [PubMed]
14. Borg, D.N.; Bach, A.J.; O'Brien, J.L.; Sainani, K.L. Calculating sample size for reliability studies. *PM&R* **2022**, *14*, 1018–10255.
15. Cronin, J.B.; Green, J.P.; Levin, G.T.; Brughelli, M.E.; Frost, D.M. Effect of starting stance on initial sprint performance. *J. Strength Cond. Res.* **2007**, *21*, 990–992.
16. Wilcox, R.R. *Understanding and Applying Basic Statistical Methods Using R*, 1st ed.; Wiley: Hoboken, NJ, USA, 2016; pp. 139–173.
17. Smithies, T.D.; Toth, A.J.; Campbell, M.J. Test–retest reliability and practice effects on a shortened version of the Category Switch Task—A pilot study. *J. Cogn. Psychol.* **2024**, *36*, 742–753.
18. Koo, T.K.; Li, M.Y. A guideline of selecting and reporting intraclass correlation coefficients for reliability research. *J. Chiropr. Med.* **2016**, *15*, 155–163.
19. Hopkins, W.G. Reliability from Consecutive Pairs of Trials (Excel Spreadsheet). 2000. Available online: http://sportsci.org/resource/stats/xrely.xls (accessed on 1 December 2024).
20. Turner, A.; Brazier, J.; Bishop, C.; Chavda, S.; Cree, J.; Read, P. Data analysis for strength and conditioning coaches: Using Excel to analyze reliability, differences, and relationships. *Strength Cond. J.* **2015**, *37*, 76–83.
21. Duthie, G.; Pyne, D.; Hooper, S. The reliability of video-based time motion analysis. *J. Hum. Mov. Stud.* **2003**, *44*, 259–272.
22. Hopkins, W.G.; Batterham, A.M.; Marshall, S.W.; Hanin, J. Progressive statistics. *Sportscience* **2009**, *13*.

23. Lexell, J.E.; Downham, D.Y. How to assess the reliability of measurements in rehabilitation. *Am. J. Phys. Med. Rehabilit.* **2005**, *84*, 719–723.
24. Bucher, E.; Millet, G.; Wehrlin, J.; Steiner, T. Test–retest reliability of ski-specific aerobic, sprint, and neuromuscular performance tests in highly trained cross-country skiers. *Scand J. Med. Sci. Sports* **2023**, *33*, 2482–2498. [PubMed]
25. Ettema, M.; Brurok, B.; Baumgart, J.K. Test–retest reliability of physiological variables during submaximal seated upper-body poling in able-bodied participants. *Front. Physiol.* **2021**, *12*, 749356.
26. Lindberg, K.; Solberg, P.; Bjørnsen, T.; Helland, C.; Rønnestad, B.; Frank, M.T.; Haugen, T.; Østerås, S.; Kristoffersen, M.; Midttun, M.; et al. Strength and power testing of athletes: A multicenter study of test–retest reliability. *Int. J. Sports Physiol. Perform.* **2022**, *17*, 1103–1110. [PubMed]
27. Buchheit, M.; Rabbani, A.; Beigi, H.T. Predicting changes in high-intensity intermittent running performance with acute responses to short jump rope workouts in children. *J. Sports Sci. Med.* **2014**, *13*, 476–482.
28. Pyne, D.B. Interpreting the Results of Fitness Testing. In Proceedings of the International Science and Football Symposium, Melbourne, VIC, Australia, 16–20 January 2007.
29. Arsac, L.M.; Locatelli, E. Modeling the energetics of 100-m running by using speed curves of world champions. *J. Appl. Physiol.* **2002**, *92*, 1781–1788.

sensors

MDPI

Article

Enhancing Multi-User Activity Recognition in an Indoor Environment with Augmented Wi-Fi Channel State Information and Transformer Architectures

MD Irteeja Kobir, Pedro Machado, Ahmad Lotfi, Daniyal Haider * and Isibor Kennedy Ihianle *

Department of Computer Science, Nottingham Trent University, 50 Shakespeare St., Nottingham NG1 4FQ, UK; md.kobir2023@my.ntu.ac.uk@ntu.ac.uk (M.I.K.); pedro.machado@ntu.ac.uk (P.M.); ahmad.lotfi@ntu.ac.uk (A.L.)
* Correspondence: daniyal.haider@ntu.ac.uk (D.H.); isibor.ihianle@ntu.ac.uk (I.K.I.)

Abstract: Human Activity Recognition (HAR) is crucial for understanding human behaviour through sensor data, with applications in healthcare, smart environments, and surveillance. While traditional HAR often relies on ambient sensors, wearable devices or vision-based systems, these approaches can face limitations in dynamic settings and raise privacy concerns. Device-free HAR systems, utilising Wi-Fi Channel State Information (CSI) to human movements, have emerged as a promising privacy-preserving alternative for next-generation health activity monitoring and smart environments, particularly for multi-user scenarios. However, current research faces challenges such as the need for substantial annotated training data, class imbalance, and poor generalisability in complex, multi-user environments where labelled data is often scarce. This paper addresses these gaps by proposing a hybrid deep learning approach which integrates signal preprocessing, targeted data augmentation, and a customised integration of CNN and Transformer models, designed to address the challenges of multi-user recognition and data scarcity. A random transformation technique to augment real CSI data, followed by hybrid feature extraction involving statistical, spectral, and entropy-based measures to derive suitable representations from temporal sensory input, is employed. Experimental results show that the proposed model outperforms several baselines in single-user and multi-user contexts. Our findings demonstrate that combining real and augmented data significantly improves model generalisation in scenarios with limited labelled data.

Keywords: Human Activity Recognition (HAR); Channel State Information (CSI); data augmentation; deep learning; CNN; transformer; signal processing; time-series analysis; multi-user recognition; privacy-preserving sensing

1. Introduction

Human Activity Recognition (HAR) is a foundational task in ubiquitous computing, offering critical insights into human behaviour with broad applications in healthcare monitoring, smart environments, ambient assisted living, and elder care [1]. Traditional HAR systems typically rely on ambient sensors, wearable sensors or vision-based systems. Although effective, these modalities pose considerable limitations; ambient sensors such as motion detectors do not provide accurate information about a specific activity, wearable devices demand user compliance, regular charging, and maintenance, while vision-based systems suffer from occlusion, varying illumination, and severe privacy concerns [2–4]. To preserve the privacy of users, some research with thermal vision employing thermal sensor arrays has shown promising results [5].

To address these limitations, recent advances have led to device-free HAR using wireless sensing, particularly Wi-Fi Channel State Information (CSI). CSI captures fine-grained changes in radio signal propagation due to human motion, enabling passive, contactless, and privacy-preserving activity detection [6]. The advantage of this approach lies in the sensing through obstacles and across rooms without requiring user-worn devices. However, CSI-based HAR systems face challenges including sensitivity to ambient noise, temporal drift, and multipath interference. Performance often degrades in dynamic or densely populated multi-user environments due to overlapping activities and spatial interference [7]. The limited availability of labelled datasets, especially for diverse user configurations and rare activities, hinders the training of generalisable models [8]. Multi-user HAR is further complicated by simultaneous movements, unpredictable patterns, and spatial entanglement, requiring models capable of extracting discriminative features from noisy, entangled signals and generalising across varying spatial configurations [9–11]. Traditional machine learning techniques, relying on handcrafted features and rigid assumptions, are often inadequate in these contexts [12]. Deep learning, particularly convolutional and attention-based models, offers an alternative. However, many current studies treat preprocessing, feature extraction, and classification as discrete stages, potentially missing the benefits of an integrated pipeline.

Another inherent challenge associated with CSI-based HAR is data scarcity, which significantly limits the training of deep learning models, especially in complex multi-user and real-world scenarios where manual annotation is inefficient. Data augmentation provides a viable strategy to address this and improve model robustness [12,13]. Unlike image augmentation, time-series augmentation for CSI data must preserve signal continuity, statistical integrity, and temporal dynamics. Techniques like jittering (Gaussian noise), scaling (amplitude modulation), magnitude warping (non-linear time scaling), and slice shuffling (temporal segment permutation) generate realistic signal variations mimicking unseen behaviours or environments [14]. The application of these augmentations increases data diversity and enhances the generalisation of models trained with limited data.

Recent advances in deep learning highlight the potential of hybrid architectures combining convolutional layers for local pattern recognition with Transformers for capturing long-range dependencies [11,15–17]. However, their multi-user application, device-free HAR, remains largely unexplored. Transformers, particularly when augmented with relative positional encoding, are well-suited for modelling the complex temporal relationships inherent in overlapping or concurrent human activities [18]. To address these limitations, a unified, augmentation-aware framework for CSI-based HAR is proposed, specifically designed to handle the challenges of multi-user recognition and limited training data. Our approach integrates signal denoising, advanced data augmentation, domain-informed feature engineering, and deep multimodal learning. As part of this, a custom CNN + Transformer model is introduced to learn both local and global patterns in the CSI signal space. It is trained using an augmented dataset mimicking real-world activity variability.

The scientific contributions resulting from the research presented in this paper are as follows:

- An integrated CSI preprocessing and augmentation pipeline is introduced, combining Butterworth filtering, Discrete Wavelet Transform (DWT), and random transformation strategies to augment and enrich training diversity while preserving statistical properties.
- A custom integration of CNN and Transformer components for effective local and global temporal feature extraction, specifically adapted for multi-user activity recognition using augmented CSI data.

- The proposed architecture is benchmarked against three state-of-the-art hybrid models, demonstrating better performance and generalisability across varying augmentation levels and user concurrency.
- Extensive experiments to evaluate different multi-user scenarios are conducted, demonstrating the effectiveness of the proposed model in mitigating signal overlap and spatial interference.

The remainder of the paper is organised as follows: Section 2 presents a review of related work, while Section 3 details the proposed model and augmentation methods. Section 4 describes the experimental setup and results, followed by discussion in Section 5. The paper concludes in Section 6, offering final reflections and directions for future research.

2. Related Work

Advances in HAR using CSI have seen a notable shift from conventional machine learning methods to advanced deep learning models, with Transformer-based architectures emerging as a powerful alternative in recent years. This is driven by the increasing need for scalable, device-free, and privacy-conscious activity recognition systems, especially in smart homes and IoT-enabled environments [1,4,6,7]. Classical machine learning algorithms like Support Vector Machines (SVM) and Random Forests (RF) have inherent limitations in feature generalisation and sensitivity to noise, prompting a transition toward deep learning models [7,17]. CNN architectures learn spatial representations directly from spectrograms of CSI signals, outperforming hand-engineered features [4,6,7,17]. To enhance temporal modelling for capturing sequential dependencies in activities, hybrid architectures have been utilised by combining CNN architectures with recurrent models such as LSTM and GRU. Recent approaches have also explored contrastive learning frameworks and diffusion-based methods for HAR, which learn robust representations by maximising inter-class separability and modelling temporal dynamics in latent space [19,20]. Diffusion-based techniques have also been proposed for data augmentation and sensing enhancement in Wi-Fi-based HAR, offering generative mechanisms for more realistic and diverse training samples [21,22]. Although these methods show promise, our work focuses on supervised learning with architectural emphasis on CNN and Transformer integration to support interpretability and scalability in multi-user environments.

Advances in Transformer-based architectures are emerging in CSI-HAR by incorporating self-attention to capture long-range temporal dependencies, offering a robust alternative to recurrence [11,15,16]. For example, a multichannel attention-based Transformer achieved high accuracy in HAR [23], and a lightweight Transformer optimised for edge computing maintained a good performance—92.4% accuracy with reduced complexity [24]. However, attention-only models can struggle with fine-grained local features to discriminate similar activities. To overcome this, hybrid CNN–Transformer architectures have emerged, combining CNNs for spatial pattern extraction with Transformers for global contextual modelling. Incorporating relative positional embeddings in these frameworks enhances temporal precision and activity segmentation [23,25]. These hybrid designs improve recognition accuracy and balance local and global sequence modelling, often a trade-off in Transformer-only systems.

Table 1 presents a summary of recent advances in CSI-HAR, showcasing a range of datasets, modelling techniques, signal processing approaches, and evaluation protocols. The field has evolved significantly from classical machine learning models like SVM and Random Forest to more adaptive and accurate deep learning architectures such as CNNs [26], attention-based BiLSTM models [27], and compact Transformer-based models. More recent efforts also focus on hybrid frameworks that address domain variability through domain adaptation and generalisation [28,29].

Table 1. Literature summary table.

Authors (Year)	Dataset/Source	Model(s) Used	Signal Processing/Augmentation	Evaluation Method	Key Findings
Muaaz et al. (2021) [26]	WiFi NICs CSI	CNN	CSI ratio, PCA, spectrogram	Experimental evaluation	97.78% accuracy; robust to environmental variations
Shi et al. (2022) [28]	WiFi CSI	CNN + Domain Adaptation	CSI enhancement	Cross-domain evaluation	One-fits-all model with improved generalisation to new environments
Wang et al. (2022) [29]	WiFi CSI data	Domain Generalisation (AFFAR)	Adaptive feature fusion	Cross-domain testing	Combined domain-specific and domain-invariant features for robustness
Abuhoureyah et al. (2024) [30]	Custom multi-user CSI data	Deep learning + ICA + CWT	ICA, CWT	Experimental evaluation	Separated overlapping signals; enabled robust multi-user location-independent HAR
Wang et al. (2021) [31]	CSI-based HAR dataset	Few-shot Learning	Data augmentation	Experimental evaluation	Few-shot learning enabled improved accuracy in limited-data settings
Zhang et al. (2022) [32]	Custom WiFi CSI	Graph Few-shot Learning	Augmented graph features	Few-shot evaluation	Generalised well across tasks using limited labelled samples effectively
Xiao et al. (2024) [33]	Synthetic WiFi CSI	Diffusion + Contrastive Learning	Diffusion-based augmentation	Contrastive accuracy eval	Outperformed baseline models in generalisation under limited data
Zhang et al. (2022) [34]	CSI-based HAR dataset	Zero-effort cross-domain (Widar3.0)	None specified	Cross-domain evaluation	Achieved high accuracy without requiring user calibration
Shi et al. (2020) [35]	WiFi CSI	One-shot Learning + CSI enhancement	CSI signal denoising	Experimental testing	Enabled recognition with few samples and improved signal quality
Xiao et al. (2023) [33]	WiFi CSI synthetic data	Diffusion Model + MLP	GAN/Diffusion-based augmentation	Comparative experiments	Improved training effectiveness using synthetic CSI data
Elkelany et al. (2023) [27]	CSI dataset (12 activities, 3 environments)	ABiLSTM	Spectrogram conversion	10-fold CV	Achieved up to 94.03% accuracy across environments

A recurring challenge across many studies is the limited generalisability of models in unseen or changing environments. To address this, several works have proposed strategies like few-shot learning [31,32], one-shot recognition [35], and zero-effort cross-domain adaptation [34]. These methods aim to reduce the reliance on large, curated training datasets, enabling models to adapt more flexibly to novel contexts or user behaviours.

Another major focus is data augmentation. Diffusion-based methods [33] have emerged as a powerful way to create more realistic synthetic CSI samples, often in combination with contrastive learning to improve performance under limited supervision. These approaches have shown promise in boosting accuracy and resilience, especially when training data is scarce or noisy.

Despite these improvements, recognising activities in multi-user environments remains a complex problem. Overlapping signals often reduce model accuracy, even when advanced techniques are used to separate them. Abuhoureyah et al. [30] tackled this by applying independent component analysis (ICA) and continuous wavelet transform (CWT), demonstrating improved performance for location-independent, multi-user HAR. However, such solutions are still sensitive to dynamic spatial configurations and signal interference.

Finally, evaluation inconsistency remains a barrier to progress. Studies vary significantly in their methodologies, with some using 10-fold cross-validation [27], or contrastive frameworks [33]. This lack of standardisation makes it difficult to compare models directly or replicate published results reliably.

In light of these ongoing challenges, our proposed work introduces a hybrid CNN + Transformer framework that is designed with generalisability and scalability in mind. By combining spatial–temporal feature extraction with efficient preprocessing and augmentation strategies, the model aims to deliver robust performance in both single- and multi-user scenarios, with real-world applicability at its core.

3. Proposed Methods

A four-stage approach for HAR using CSI is proposed. The schematic diagram of the proposed framework is illustrated in Figure 1, designed to enhance recognition performance, particularly in complex multi-user home environments. The pipeline of the proposed approach comprises data acquisition, preprocessing, augmentation, and model training/classification. The data acquisition involves transmitting Wi-Fi signals through an indoor space where human activities occur. Motion-induced perturbations of these signals are captured as CSI measurements at the receiver, inherently encoding characteristics of static postures and dynamic movements, forming the raw dataset.

A multi-stage preprocessing pipeline extracts meaningful information from raw CSI. Subcarrier averaging reduces redundancy and smooths signal fluctuations. Butterworth filtering eliminates high-frequency noise, and Discrete Wavelet Transform (DWT) decomposes the signal, preserving essential features across scales, improving signal quality and retaining informative temporal dynamics. To improve generalisability and reduce overfitting given limited CSI data, a random transformation-based augmentation module generates diverse and realistic variations while preserving activity class semantics. This module incorporates jittering, scaling, slice shuffling, and magnitude warping. The augmented dataset is then partitioned for model development.

The classification stage trains baseline (CNN, LSTM) and advanced hybrid deep learning models CNN with Transformer - the proposed model, BiLSTM, GRU and LSTM to better capture spatial and temporal dependencies inherent in CSI data, enhancing recognition of complex, multi-user activities due to their increased representational capacity.

Finally, the trained models are evaluated using accuracy and F1-score metrics to assess their effectiveness and robustness.

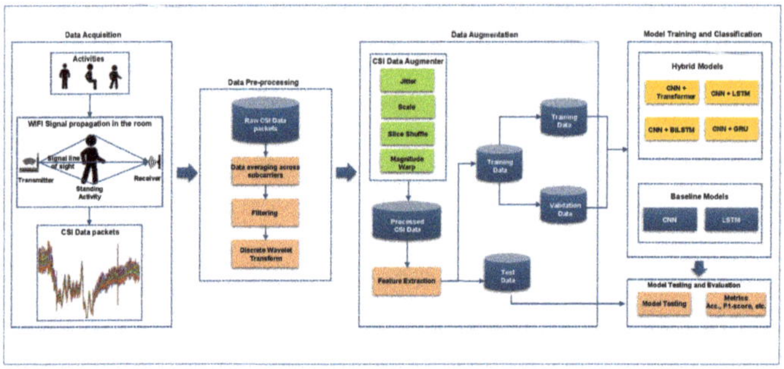

Figure 1. Overview of the proposed Human Activity Recognition framework using CSI data. The pipeline consists of four main stages: data acquisition through Wi-Fi signal propagation, signal preprocessing using filtering and wavelet transformation, data augmentation via random transformation techniques (jittering, scaling, slice shuffling, and magnitude warping), and classification using both baseline and hybrid deep learning models.

3.1. Data Acquisition

A publicly available CSI-based HAR dataset [36], specifically designed to investigate the feasibility of indoor activity recognition using fine-grained CSI from wireless signals, is utilised. The dataset was collected in a controlled laboratory environment, simulating a typical indoor room measuring 3 m by 2.8 m.

As illustrated in Figure 2, the experimental setup involved two Universal Software Radio Peripheral (USRP) devices: a USRP X300 as the transmitter and a USRP X310 as the receiver. Both were equipped with VERT2450 omnidirectional antennas and operated at a frequency of 3.75 GHz within the 5G sub-6 GHz band, chosen for its ability to capture subtle human motion with low interference and high signal resolution. The transmitter and receiver were positioned diagonally opposite each other in the room to establish a reliable communication link and maximise spatial signal coverage. Within the defined activity zone, consisting of four chairs arranged in a 1 m grid, participants performed various daily activities. During these activities, the USRP devices continuously collected CSI data using the GNU Radio software environment. The communication protocol used Orthogonal Frequency-Division Multiplexing (OFDM), providing robust frequency-domain information. The raw CSI data was initially logged in plain text format and subsequently converted to CSV files for preprocessing and machine learning analysis [36].

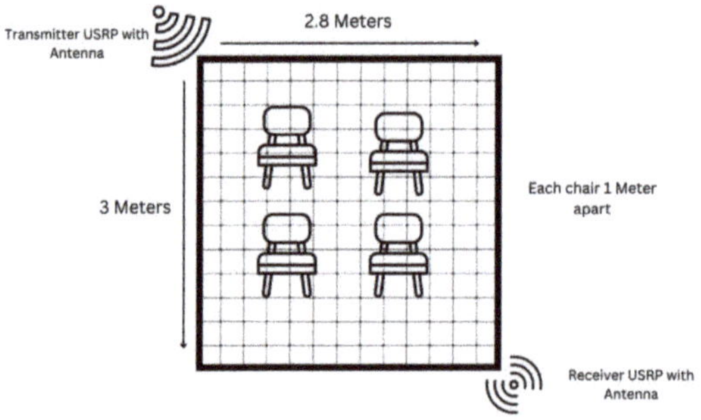

Figure 2. Experimental setup for capturing human activities using the 5G frequency band. The indoor environment measures 3 m by 2.8 m. A USRP X300 (transmitter) and a USRP X310 (receiver) are positioned at opposite corners. Four chairs are arranged 1 m apart to define the human activity space.

3.2. Data Processing

To ensure accurate HAR, a data processing pipeline is designed to denoise raw CSI streams and extract meaningful time–frequency features. A Butterworth low-pass filter was applied first to eliminate high-frequency noise. Subsequently, a DWT was used to extract hierarchical temporal–frequency components, capturing subtle variations induced by human activity. This dual-stage approach effectively handles both single-user and multi-user scenarios, where overlapping motion patterns often introduce complex signal artifacts [24,37]. The initial step involved averaging the raw CSI data across all 51 subcarriers to standardise the input and reduce variability, resulting in a single representative time series $\bar{x}(t)$, as defined by Equation (1):

$$\bar{x}(t) = \frac{1}{N}\sum_{i=1}^{N} x_i(t), \quad \text{where } N = 51 \tag{1}$$

To mitigate high-frequency noise originating from hardware, environmental factors, and multipath effects, which can distort activity-related dynamics, a fourth-order Butterworth low-pass filter was applied. The maximally flat passband response enables effective noise suppression while preserving critical signal patterns, with the denoised signal $\tilde{x}(t)$ obtained through zero phase filtering:

$$\tilde{x}(t) = \mathcal{F}_{\text{LP}}[\bar{x}(t)], \tag{2}$$

where $\mathcal{F}_{\text{LP}}$ denotes the zero-phase Butterworth filtering operation, which avoids phase shifts that might distort time-domain features. Figure 3 illustrates the filtering effect on CSI signals for single- and multi-user activities.

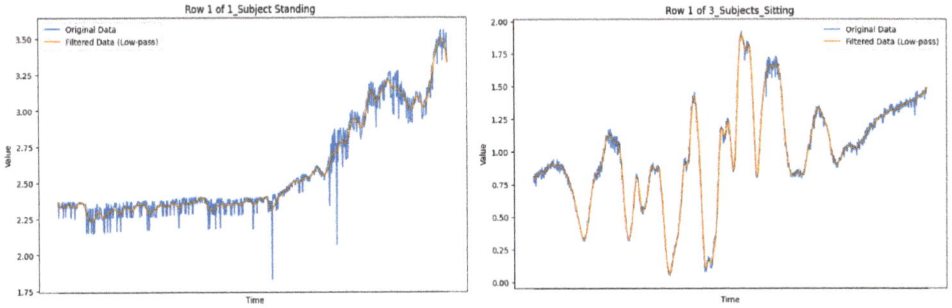

(a) (b)

Figure 3. Comparison of original and Butterworth-filtered CSI signals for single-user and multi-user activity sessions. (**a**) One subject standing, (**b**) three subjects sitting.

While the Butterworth filter reduces noise, it does not capture the non-stationary and transient nature of human motion. Therefore, the denoised signal $\tilde{x}(t)$ was further processed using the DWT. This technique decomposes the signal into time–frequency components across multiple scales, extracting rich hierarchical features.

Using the Haar wavelet $\psi(t)$ and decomposition level j, the DWT coefficients $W_{j,k}$ were computed as

$$W_{j,k} = \int \tilde{x}(t) \cdot \psi_{j,k}(t)\, dt, \tag{3}$$

where $\psi_{j,k}(t) = 2^{-j/2}\psi(2^{-j}t - k)$ represents the scaled and translated mother wavelet. A decomposition level of $J = 3$ was selected to balance detail extraction and computational cost. This produced approximation coefficients A_3 (low-frequency structure) and detail coefficients D_1, D_2, and D_3 (high-frequency transitions). These coefficients formed the basis for subsequent feature extraction and classification.

3.3. CSI Augmentation Techniques

Real-world CSI datasets for HAR often exhibit limitations in size and suffer from class imbalance. These characteristics pose significant challenges for training deep learning models, frequently leading to overfitting and reduced classification performance, particularly for underrepresented activity classes. To address these limitations and improve model generalisation, a data augmentation pipeline based on random transformation strategies was implemented. This approach aims to generate diverse training instances that effectively simulate the inherent variability of real-world CSI signals while preserving the key discriminative features associated with each activity, thereby enhancing both model robustness and its ability to generalise to unseen data [38].

Let $\mathbf{x} = (x_1, x_2, \ldots, x_T)$ denote a processed CSI data frame, where each $x_t \in \mathbb{R}^n$ represents the amplitude vector across n subcarriers at a specific time step t, and T is the total temporal window size of the data frame. The augmentation process then produces a transformed sequence $\mathbf{x}' = \mathcal{A}(\mathbf{x})$, where $\mathcal{A}$ represents a specific transformation operator applied to the original CSI data frame $\mathbf{x}$. In our augmentation pipeline, a combination of time-series augmentation methods informed by prior research in HAR and time-series analysis is employed: jittering, scaling, slice shuffling, and window warping. The specific implementations and parameters for these transformations were adapted from established techniques and findings in the literature [39,40].

3.4. CSI Augmentation Techniques

Real-world CSI datasets for HAR often suffer from limited size and class imbalance. These characteristics pose significant challenges for training deep learning models, frequently leading to overfitting and reduced classification performance, especially for underrepresented activity classes. To mitigate this, a data augmentation pipeline based on random transformation strategies is implemented. This approach generates diverse training instances that simulate real-world signal variability while preserving key discriminative features, thereby enhancing model generalisation and robustness [38].

Let $\mathbf{x} = (x_1, x_2, \ldots, x_T)$ denote a processed CSI data frame, where each $x_t \in \mathbb{R}^n$ represents the amplitude vector across n subcarriers at time step t, and T is the temporal window size. The augmentation process produces a transformed sequence $\mathbf{x}' = \mathcal{A}(\mathbf{x})$, where $\mathcal{A}$ is a transformation operator. Multiple time-series augmentation techniques are incorporated. This include jittering, scaling, slicing, and window warping, each designed to simulate different real-world signal distortions while maintaining temporal coherence [39,40]. Jittering introduces small Gaussian noise perturbations to simulate sensor noise. Scaling adjusts the amplitude dynamics to reflect variations in user strength or distance. Slicing randomly extracts sub-segments of the CSI window to improve robustness against partial observations, and window warping modifies the temporal progression to mimic speed variations in activity execution. Collectively, these augmentations expand the diversity of the training data, aiding the model in learning more invariant and generalisable representations.

Jittering: Gaussian noise is added to simulate sensor or environmental interference. Given a noise vector $\epsilon \sim \mathcal{N}(0, \sigma^2)$, the augmented sequence becomes

$$\mathbf{x}' = \mathbf{x} + \epsilon. \tag{4}$$

Scaling: A random scalar factor $\alpha \sim \mathcal{U}(a, b)$ adjusts the amplitude to emulate variations in movement intensity or proximity to the transmitter:

$$\mathbf{x}' = \alpha \cdot \mathbf{x}. \tag{5}$$

Slicing: To simulate temporal disorder, a segment $\mathbf{x}_{k:k+m}$ is repositioned in the sequence. This maintains class semantics while introducing variability:

$$\mathbf{x}' = \text{concat}(\mathbf{x}_{1:k}, \mathbf{x}_{k+m:T}, \mathbf{x}_{k:k+m}). \tag{6}$$

Window Warping: A non-linear warping function $\phi(t)$ temporally stretches or compresses a windowed segment to reflect changes in human motion speed:

$$\mathbf{x}'_t = \mathbf{x}_{\phi(t)}. \tag{7}$$

The effects are visualised in Figure 4. Each augmentation technique introduces controlled intra-class variability while preserving the core temporal structure essential for accurate recognition. This controlled diversity enhances the ability of the model to generalise to unseen activity patterns and user behaviours. To ensure label consistency, the augmentation techniques were applied within bounded transformations that retain the temporal and structural characteristics of the original signal, thereby preserving class identity across augmented samples.

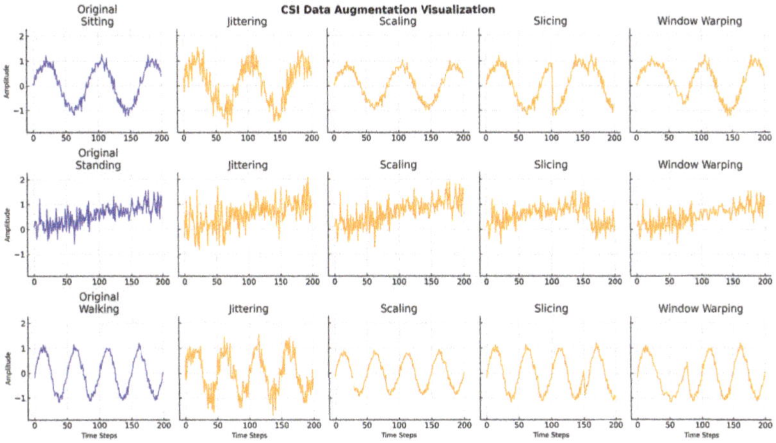

Figure 4. Augmentation impact of random-transformation techniques on CSI time-series for different activities. Each row displays the original and augmented signals using jittering, scaling, slicing, and window warping, respectively.

3.5. Feature Extraction

Our feature extraction strategy integrates time-domain, frequency-domain, and entropy-based measures to comprehensively represent both macroscopic motion trends and subtle signal variations crucial for HAR [41–43]. In total, 34 features are extracted from the preprocessed CSI signals to capture the underlying physical and spectral characteristics of human motion across a diverse range of activity classes.

Time-Domain Features: Statistical properties of the CSI signal within short temporal windows are computed to detect gross motion transitions. Metrics such as mean, variance, standard deviation, skewness, kurtosis, and root mean square (RMS) reflect signal magnitude and variability, essential for distinguishing static from dynamic states [42].

For instance, RMS indicates activity intensity, effectively differentiating walking (high RMS) from sitting (low RMS).

Frequency-Domain Features: Spectral characteristics using Fast Fourier Transform (FFT) techniques are used to capture periodicity and energy distribution. These include spectral entropy (quantifying frequency content unpredictability), spectral centroid (indicating dominant frequency band), and specific FFT coefficients, instrumental in identifying cyclic patterns in repetitive activities like walking, running, or cycling [43].

Entropy-Based Features: Permutation entropy and its weighted variant to quantify signal complexity and irregularity are incorporated, measuring the temporal unpredictability and structural complexity of CSI waveforms [41,42]. These are valuable for distinguishing subtle postural variations or transitions lacking strong spectral or amplitude signatures, such as differentiating standing from leaning based on their distinct temporal dynamics.

The integration of these features provides a holistic CSI signal representation, capturing magnitude, frequency distribution, and temporal complexity. A detailed breakdown is in Table 2. The feature set also includes advanced descriptors like wavelet energy, power bandwidth, and spectral distance, further enriching the feature space and supporting improved model generalisation across diverse activity contexts.

Table 2. CSI feature categories and descriptions.

Feature Category	Description
Time-Domain Statistical	Mean, Median, Std Dev, Min, Max, Kurtosis, Skewness, IQR, Variance, Root Mean Square
Temporal Dynamics	Mean Absolute Difference, Mean Difference, Median Absolute Difference, Sum of Absolute Differences
Signal Shape Characteristics	Peak-to-Peak Distance, Area Under Curve, Spectral Slope
Frequency Domain	FFT Mean Coefficient, Spectral Centroid (Weighted frequency mean), Spectral Entropy, Spectral Kurtosis
Signal Complexity	Permutation Entropy, Weighted Permutation Entropy, Spectral Variation (Normalised spectral std dev)
Energy/Power Features	Absolute Energy, Average Power, Wavelet Energy (Sum of squared DWT coefficients)
Statistical Distribution	Mean Absolute Deviation, Median Absolute Deviation, ECDF Percentile (25th percentile)
Spectral Relationships	Power Bandwidth (Integrated spectrum), Spectral Distance (Cumulative spectral differences)

3.6. The Proposed CNN + Transformer Model

HAR from CSI data involves mapping complex, high-dimensional time-series inputs to discrete activity classes. To guide the architectural design and learning approach, we first provide a mathematical formulation of the underlying classification task. Let $\mathcal{D} = \{(x^{(i)}, y^{(i)})\}_{i=1}^{N}$ be a set of N preprocessed and feature-extracted CSI samples, where $x^{(i)} \in \mathbb{R}^d$ denotes the d-dimensional input feature vector and $y^{(i)} \in \{1, 2, \ldots, K\}$ is the corresponding activity label among K possible classes. The goal is to learn a function $f_\theta : \mathbb{R}^d \to \{1, \ldots, K\}$ parameterised by θ, which minimises a classification loss over the dataset:

$$\min_\theta \frac{1}{N} \sum_{i=1}^{N} \mathcal{L}(f_\theta(x^{(i)}), y^{(i)}), \quad (8)$$

where $\mathcal{L}$ is the cross-entropy loss function appropriate for multi-class classification.

The preprocessing pipeline aims to enhance feature separability by suppressing irrelevant signal variations, including hardware-induced noise and emphasising activity-related patterns. Subcarrier averaging reduces dimensionality and smooths spatial fluctuations. Butterworth filtering attenuates high-frequency noise, preserving essential motion-induced signal changes. The DWT further decomposes signals into localised time–frequency representations, which increases the discriminative power of extracted features, particularly important for distinguishing between static (e.g., sitting, standing) and dynamic (e.g., walking) activities. This preprocessing improves the signal-to-noise ratio, enhancing inter-class distances and stabilising intra-class variance.

Our model architecture, depicted in Figure 5, uses a hybrid deep learning framework combining CNN and Transformer encoders for effective local and global feature extraction from time-series CSI data. This design captures the complex temporal features of HAR tasks by taking advantage of the CNN layers to learn local dependencies and the Transformer block for long-range contextual relationships [44,45]. See also Table 3 for the hyperparameter settings of the proposed CNN + Transformer model. The model consists of three components: a CNN layer for feature extraction, a Transformer block for relative positional encoding, and a classification head. This is denoted as

$$\mathbf{X} = \{x_0, x_1, x_2, \ldots, x_T\}, \quad x_t \in \mathbb{R}^d, \tag{9}$$

where each instance contains T time steps and d features per step. For univariate processing, the input is reshaped to $(T, 1)$.

CNN Feature Extractor Block. This block comprises three 1D convolutional layers. The first layer applies 32 filters with a kernel size of 3, followed by Batch Normalisation and MaxPooling1D with a pool size of 2. The second and third convolutional layers use 64 and 128 filters, respectively, and include similar normalisation and pooling. ReLU activation is applied throughout:

$$f(x) = \max(0, x), \tag{10}$$

The output is passed through Global Max Pooling and reshaped to $(1, 128)$ to match the input expected by the Transformer.

Transformer Encoder Block. To preserve temporal sequence information, vector-based relative positional encoding is applied:

$$\mathbf{X}_{\text{pos}} = \mathbf{X} + \mathbf{E}_{\text{pos}}, \quad \mathbf{E}_{\text{pos}} \in \mathbb{R}^{L \times d}, \tag{11}$$

where L is the sequence length. The Transformer comprises three encoder layers, each with a multi-head self-attention mechanism:

$$\text{Attention}(Q, K, V) = \text{softmax}\left(\frac{QK^\top}{\sqrt{d_k}}\right)V, \tag{12}$$

Each encoder includes residual connections, Layer Normalisation, and feedforward layers implemented with 1D convolutions of size $(256, d)$ using ReLU activation.

Classification Head. The Transformer output is passed through a Global Average Pooling layer and two dense layers with 256 and 128 units, respectively. ReLU is used along with Dropout (0.5 and 0.3) to reduce overfitting. The final output layer uses softmax activation:

$$\hat{y} = \text{softmax}(\mathbf{W}x + b), \tag{13}$$

This architecture provides an optimal balance between representational power and computational efficiency, making it particularly suitable for deployment in real-time or edge-based HAR systems [44].

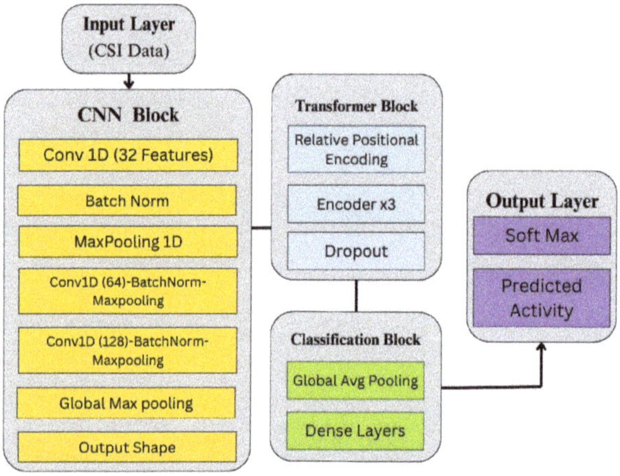

Figure 5. Architecture of the proposed time-series analysis model, incorporating CNN for feature extraction and a Transformer encoder for temporal representation, followed by a classification block.

Table 3. Hyperparameter settings for the CNN + Transformer model.

Component	Hyperparameter	Value
Architecture	Number of Conv1D Layers	3
	Conv1D Filter Sizes	32, 64, 128
	Kernel Size	3
	Pooling Type	MaxPooling1D, GlobalMaxPooling1D
	Batch Normalisation	Yes
Transformer	Encoder Layers	3
	Attention Heads	4
	Head Size	64
	Feedforward Dimension	256
	Dropout Rates	0.1 (Transformer), 0.5, 0.3 (Dense)
	Positional Encoding	Relative (vector-based)
Training	Optimiser	Adam
	Learning Rate	1×10^{-3}
	Batch Size	32
	Epochs	500
	Early Stopping Patience	10
	LR Schedule	Step decay at epochs 20 and 30
	Loss Function	Sparse Categorical Cross-entropy

3.7. *Performance Measurement Criteria*

To evaluate our CNN + Transformer model, accuracy and F1-score metrics are chosen to address the potential class imbalance prevalent in CSI-based HAR datasets. While accuracy represents the proportion of correct classifications, it can provide a skewed view in imbalanced scenarios. F1-score, the harmonic mean of precision and recall, and specificity (true negative rate) to obtain a more balanced performance assessment are also utilised. The mathematical definitions of these metrics are as follows:

$$\text{Accuracy} = \frac{TP + TN}{TP + TN + FP + FN} \tag{14}$$

$$\text{Precision} = \frac{TP}{TP + FP} \tag{15}$$

$$\text{Recall} = \frac{TP}{TP + FN} \tag{16}$$

$$\text{F1-Score} = 2 \cdot \frac{\text{Precision} \cdot \text{Recall}}{\text{Precision} + \text{Recall}} \tag{17}$$

Model generalisation was evaluated using 10-fold cross-validation. The performance results are then averaged across the ten folds to provide a reliable estimate of the model's ability to perform on unseen data.

4. Experiments and Results

This section details the experimental setup and presents the results obtained to evaluate the effectiveness and robustness of our proposed CSI-based HAR framework. A thorough analysis of the performance of the novel CNN + Transformer model is provided in comparison to several established baseline architectures. The experiments were structured to assess key aspects of our approach, including the impact of data augmentation, the model's performance in multi-user scenarios, and its overall classification accuracy across different activity classes.

The experiments were conducted in a Python 3.12 environment utilising the TensorFlow backend with Keras, with the Scikit-Learn, NumPy, and Pandas libraries for data manipulation and evaluation. Following the processing of the raw CSI data, the resulting dataset comprised instances representing the subcarriers across different channels. The original dataset contained 1777 instances. For each activity and user, 34 columns represented the extracted features, as detailed in Section 3.

4.1. Experiment I: Sensitivity Analysis of Augmented vs. Original CSI Data

To evaluate the impact of data augmentation on the statistical properties of the original CSI dataset, a sensitivity analysis is conducted comparing the distributions of extracted features, specifically, mean values across multiple multi-user activity configurations. The main objective of this experiment was to determine whether the augmentation process introduces statistically significant deviations in the distributional characteristics of CSI features. To this end, the following hypothesis is formulated:

- Null Hypothesis (H_0): The distributions of the original and augmented data are statistically identical, i.e., augmentation does not significantly alter feature distributions.
- Alternative Hypothesis (H_1): The distributions of the original and augmented data differ significantly.

To determine the appropriateness of parametric versus non-parametric testing, initially performed normality tests. The test was performed on both the original and augmented datasets using the Shapiro–Wilk (SW) [46] and Anderson–Darling (AD) tests [47]. For example, the SW test results for the two subjects (one sitting and one standing) class where W = 0.9842, $p = 0.2795$ for the original data and W = 0.9885, $p = 1.425 \times 10^{-8}$ for the augmented data. Similarly, the AD test returned $A^2 = 0.5591$ for the original and $A^2 = 7.0680$ for the augmented data both exceeding critical thresholds. These results suggest a violation of the normality assumption, especially for the augmented data. Therefore, non-parametric statistical tests were chosen.

The Mann–Whitney U test was used to examine whether there were statistically significant differences in the means of the two datasets. Levene's test was also used to assess the homogeneity of variances. As summarised in Table 4, the p-values from both tests exceeded 0.05 for all classes, indicating no statistically significant differences in central tendency or variance. Thus, we fail to reject the null hypothesis in all cases.

To complement these statistical findings, visualisations of the feature distributions were included. Figure 6 shows histograms for the two subjects (one sitting and one standing) and three subjects (two sitting and one standing) classes. While the augmented data (in red) displays broader tails, the distributions remain centred around the same mean as the original data (in blue), suggesting that augmentation preserves core statistical structure.

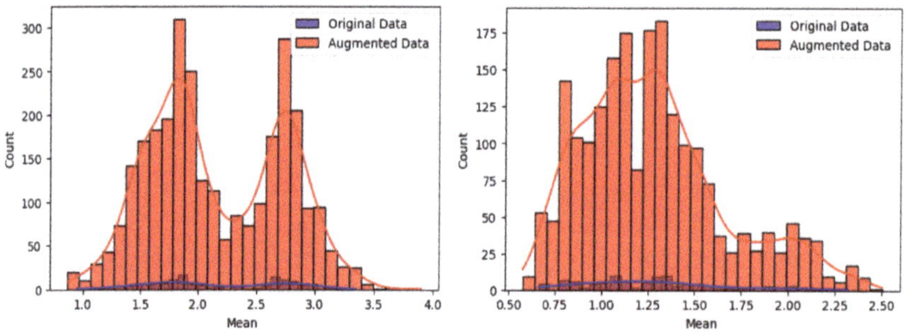

(a) (b)

Figure 6. Sensitivity analysis comparing the distribution of mean values between original and augmented CSI data for two multi-user activity scenarios: (**a**) two subjects performing, one sitting and one standing, and (**b**) three subjects performing, two sitting and one standing. Augmented data (red) show broader tails but remain centred similarly to original data (blue): (**a**) two subjects, one sitting and one standing (**b**) three subjects, two sitting and one standing.

Table 4. Mann–Whitney U and Levene's test results for original vs. augmented data.

Feature	Label	Mann–Whitney U	p-Value	Levene's W	p-Value	Interpretation
Mean	Empty	144,584.0	0.9139	0.1772	0.6739	Fail to reject H_0
Mean	1Subject-1Sit	206,671.5	0.9325	0.0449	0.8322	Fail to reject H_0
Mean	2Subjects-1Sit-1Stand	105,480.5	0.9384	0.0819	0.7747	Fail to reject H_0
Mean	3Subjects-2Sit-1Stand	105,100.5	0.9871	0.0858	0.7696	Fail to reject H_0
Mean	4Subjects-2Sit-2Stand	106,725.5	0.7811	1.0095	0.3151	Fail to reject H_0

In Figure 7, the boxplots for four activity configurations are presented, comparing spread, median, and outliers. The plots confirm that augmentation maintains the original data's distributional characteristics, with only minor variability introduced in higher-subject configurations.

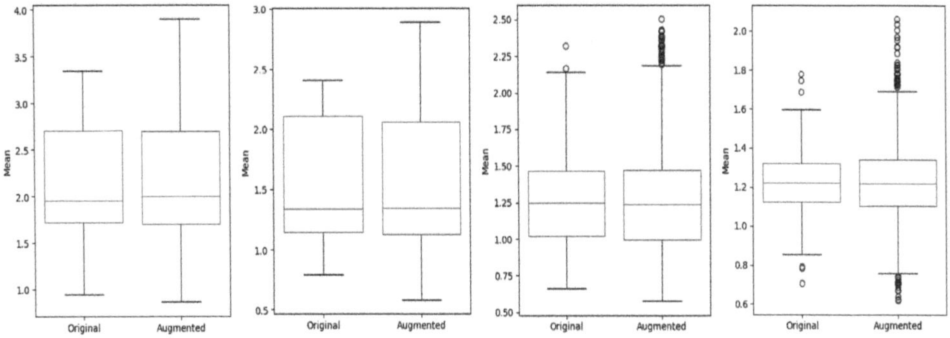

(a) (b) (c) (d)

Figure 7. Boxplot comparison of mean values between original and augmented CSI data across multi-user activity scenarios. Augmentation maintains central tendency and spread while introducing slight variations, especially with increased subject count: (**a**) one subject sitting (**b**) two subjects, one sitting and one standing; (**c**) three subjects, two sitting and one standing; (**d**) four subjects, two sitting and two standing.

4.2. Experiment II: Impact of Varying Augmentation Factors Across Models

This experiment investigates the influence of different data augmentation factors on the performance of the proposed CNN + Transformer model and three baseline hybrid architectures: CNN + BiLSTM, CNN + GRU, and CNN + LSTM. The data augmentation techniques detailed earlier to expand the models' decision boundaries were applied, aiming to enhance their generalisation capability on the original dataset and yield more efficient classifiers. A range of augmentation factors was experimented with to determine their optimal impact. For example, applying an augmentation factor of 3 increased the original dataset size from 1777 instances to 5331 instances (1777 multiplied by 3) for each augmentation method.

Table 5 presents the accuracy scores obtained for augmentation factors ranging from 0 to 10. The results demonstrate a consistent performance improvement from factor 1 to factor 5 across all evaluated models and activity phases, highlighting the benefit of moderate data augmentation. For example, the CNN + Transformer model's accuracy increased from 0.757 (no augmentation) to 0.939 at an augmentation factor of 5, while the CNN + GRU model's accuracy rose from 0.772 to 0.930 under the same conditions. It is noted that beyond an augmentation factor of 5, the performance gains begin to plateau, as illustrated by the CNN + LSTM model and accuracy increased only marginally from 0.927 at factor 5 to 0.959 at factor 10. This observation aligns with the principle of diminishing returns often associated with excessive data augmentation [38]. Furthermore, none of the models experienced a performance decline even at the highest tested augmentation factor of 10, underscoring the robustness of the specific augmentation techniques employed. The consistently lower performance observed at an augmentation factor of 0 (i.e., without any augmentation) further emphasises the critical role of data augmentation in enhancing the performance of deep learning models for HAR tasks, particularly when dealing with datasets that may be sparse or exhibit class imbalance.

Table 5. Experiment II results: accuracy across different augmentation factors for each model and phase.

Model	Aug. Factor	Phase 1	Phase 2	Phase 3	Phase 4	All Activities
CNN + Transformer	0	0.869	0.840	0.899	0.869	0.757
	1	0.963	0.927	0.957	0.885	0.817
	3	0.988	0.970	0.976	0.938	0.910
	5	0.994	0.979	0.987	0.959	0.939
	7	0.994	0.986	0.990	0.965	0.954
	10	0.994	0.989	0.991	0.973	0.963
CNN + BiLSTM	0	0.807	0.852	0.885	0.871	0.766
	1	0.968	0.925	0.957	0.874	0.805
	3	0.987	0.968	0.974	0.933	0.908
	5	0.992	0.977	0.986	0.955	0.937
	7	0.992	0.984	0.990	0.964	0.948
	10	0.995	0.985	0.992	0.972	0.960
CNN + GRU	0	0.762	0.729	0.832	0.881	0.772
	1	0.965	0.932	0.960	0.875	0.799
	3	0.985	0.969	0.979	0.935	0.906
	5	0.993	0.978	0.985	0.954	0.930
	7	0.993	0.985	0.989	0.963	0.952
	10	0.994	0.987	0.991	0.973	0.958
CNN + LSTM	0	0.746	0.729	0.841	0.869	0.761
	1	0.962	0.927	0.952	0.872	0.794
	3	0.984	0.966	0.974	0.933	0.901
	5	0.990	0.973	0.983	0.954	0.927
	7	0.993	0.982	0.988	0.965	0.949
	10	0.995	0.985	0.989	0.973	0.959

4.3. Experiment III: Multi-User Presence and Activity Detection

This experiment evaluated activity recognition performance in multi-user scenarios (ranging from one to four concurrent users, including a mixed-user setting). Table 6 presents classification results for each model. High performance was observed across all models in the single-user setting, with the CNN + Transformer achieving an F1-score of 0.997. As the number of users increased, a marginal decline in performance was noted, particularly in the four-user configuration.

The CNN + Transformer model demonstrated very good performance with an F1-score of 0.934 in the mixed multi-user scenario, highlighting its effective use of attention mechanisms for distinguishing activity signals. CNN + BiLSTM and CNN + GRU performed comparably in the two- and three-user settings, while CNN + LSTM showed a more noticeable performance drop in the four-user and mixed scenarios (F1-score: 0.926). These results underscore the necessity for advanced temporal and attention-based models to manage user concurrency, aligning with trends in ambient intelligence and ubiquitous computing [48].

Table 6. Experiment III results: multi-user presence and activity detection.

Model	Metric	One User	Two Users	Three Users	Four Users	Mixed 2/3/4 Users
CNN + Transformer	Accuracy	0.997	0.956	0.971	0.923	0.938
	Precision	0.997	0.956	0.970	0.923	0.935
	Recall	0.997	0.955	0.971	0.923	0.934
	F1-score	0.997	0.955	0.971	0.923	0.934
CNN + BiLSTM	Accuracy	0.995	0.953	0.971	0.916	0.935
	Precision	0.995	0.953	0.971	0.917	0.930
	Recall	0.995	0.953	0.970	0.917	0.930
	F1-score	0.995	0.953	0.971	0.917	0.930
CNN + GRU	Accuracy	0.996	0.952	0.971	0.921	0.933
	Precision	0.996	0.952	0.970	0.921	0.930
	Recall	0.996	0.952	0.970	0.920	0.929
	F1-score	0.996	0.952	0.970	0.920	0.928
CNN + LSTM	Accuracy	0.995	0.953	0.961	0.896	0.930
	Precision	0.994	0.953	0.960	0.896	0.926
	Recall	0.995	0.952	0.960	0.895	0.926
	F1-score	0.995	0.942	0.960	0.895	0.926

5. Discussion

The experimental results demonstrate the performance of the proposed CSI-based HAR approach across various setups, highlighting its capability to handle data diversity and complex multi-user environments. This can be largely attributed to the integrated pipeline of signal preprocessing, data augmentation, hybrid deep learning architecture, and comprehensive evaluation. The following key aspects of the system are further discussed:

5.1. Influence of Augmentation Factor on Performance

Experiment II explored the effect of varying augmentation factors, providing insights into how training diversity influences generalisation. All models showed improved accuracy with augmentation factors up to 5, with CNN + Transformer experiencing the highest increase from 0.757 to 0.939. This supports prior research indicating that moderate augmentation mitigates overfitting and enhances robustness [38,49]. Performance plateaued beyond factor 5, suggesting diminishing returns due to possible redundancy or over-perturbation [38]. Importantly, there was no decline in accuracy at factor 10, confirming the soundness of the augmentation strategy and its ability to preserve signal semantics. Specifically, the results also show the effectiveness of other techniques as jittering, slice shuffle, scaling and magnitude warping, in enhancing the overall performance. To further understand the contribution of individual augmentation techniques, additional experiments are conducted, the results of which are presented in Table 7. This table shows the performance of the CNN + Transformer model (at an augmentation factor of 5) with different combinations of our augmentation strategies.

Interestingly, while magnitude warping alone led to a noticeable drop in performance (Table 7), its inclusion within our complete augmentation pipeline contributed positively when combined with other techniques. This suggests that although aggressive or poorly controlled warping can distort temporal dynamics and impede learning, the combined effects, when balanced with jitter, scaling and slice shuffle, can enhance data variability without compromising the underlying signal integrity. This finding underscores the importance of carefully designing and balancing augmentation strategies rather than relying on any single transformation in isolation.

Table 7. Performance of CNN+Transformer with individual and cumulative augmentations (augmentation factor = 5) across all activity classes.

Model Variant	Accuracy (%)	F1-Score	Precision	Recall
CNN + Transformer + No Aug.	0.872	0.890	0.891	0.893
+ Magnitude_Warp	0.837	0.819	0.823	0.819
+ Magnitude_Warp + Slice_Shuffle	0.907	0.900	0.901	0.900
+ Magnitude_Warp + Slice_Shuffle + Scale	0.928	0.922	0.923	0.922
+ Magnitude_Warp + Slice_Shuffle + Scale +Jitters	0.939	0.933	0.940	0.934

5.2. Effectiveness of the Proposed Hybrid Model with Transformer Architecture

Experiments II and III further reinforced the effectiveness of the proposed CNN + Transformer model. The Transformer's self-attention mechanism offers an advantage in modelling temporal dependencies and isolating relevant features within complex signals. Unlike recurrent models (LSTM, GRU), it captures long-range dependencies without recurrence, which is crucial for multi-user activity recognition. In Experiment III, the CNN + Transformer achieved an F1-score of 0.934 in the mixed multi-user scenario, outperforming CNN + GRU (0.928), CNN + BiLSTM (0.930), and CNN + LSTM (0.926). These findings suggest that attention-based modelling enhances temporal resolution and activity discrimination, particularly in noisy multi-user environments. Additionally, its consistent performance across varying augmentation levels and user configurations highlights its generalisability and suitability for deployment in dynamic real-world conditions.

5.3. Performance Under HAR Multi-User Configuration

Experiment III focused on assessing the proposed framework's robustness in multi-user HAR settings, where concurrent activity signals introduce additional complexity due to overlapping motion patterns. Despite these challenges, all hybrid models demonstrated consistently high classification accuracy across two-user and three-user configurations, with only a moderate degradation observed under four-user and mixed-user scenarios. Among the models, the proposed CNN+Transformer performed best. This can be attributed to the global attention mechanism, which proved effective at disentangling simultaneous motion signals by leveraging contextual dependencies across time, enabling the model to distinguish activities even when users performed similar or overlapping actions. In contrast, purely sequential models with LSTM layers exhibited a more notable decline in performance as the number of users increased. This decline can be attributed to their limited ability to capture bidirectional and long-range relationships without explicit architectural modifications.

The confusion matrices shown in Figures 8–11 provide detailed insights into the per-activity classification performance under varying multi-user settings, revealing important patterns and challenges. In the two-user configuration (Figure 8), the proposed CNN + Transformer model exhibited strong discriminative ability, achieving high precision and recall across most activities. Dynamic activities such as walking were identified with particularly high accuracy, with minimal confusion between them. This is reflective of the distinct temporal patterns which the hybrid model's CNN and Transformer layers captured effectively.

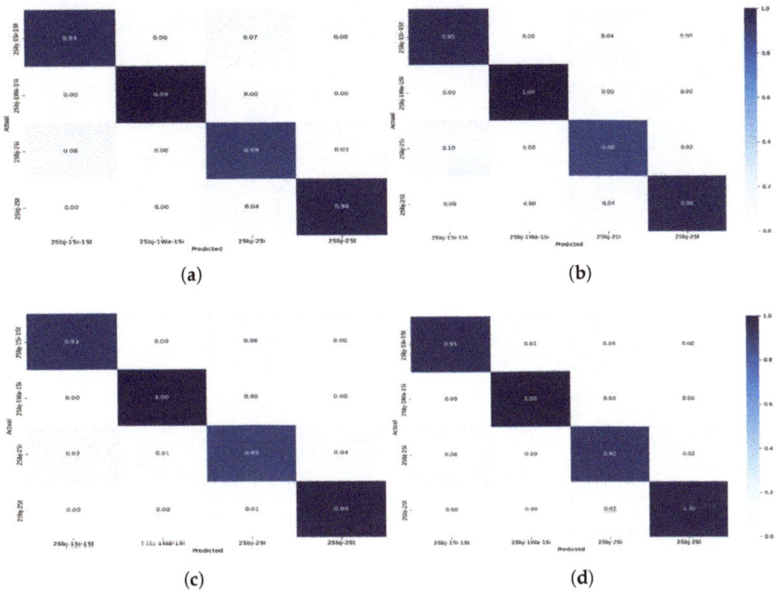

Figure 8. Confusion matrix for Experiment II showing the performance of the models for multi-users—2 subjects for different activities: (**a**) CNN + Transformer (**b**) CNN + GRU (**c**) CNN + BiLSTM (**d**) CNN + LSTM.

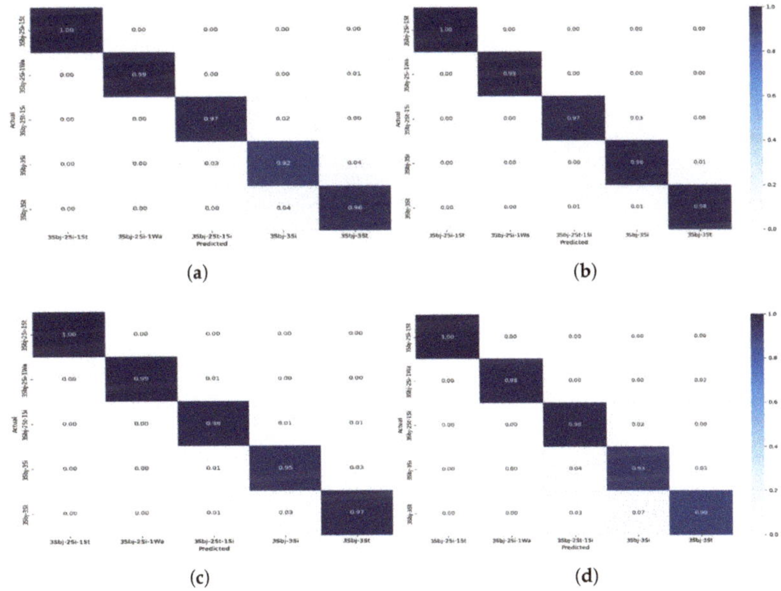

Figure 9. Confusion matrix for Experiment II showing the performance of the models for multi-users—3 subjects for different activities: (**a**) CNN + Transformer (**b**) CNN + GRU (**c**) CNN + BiLSTM (**d**) CNN + LSTM.

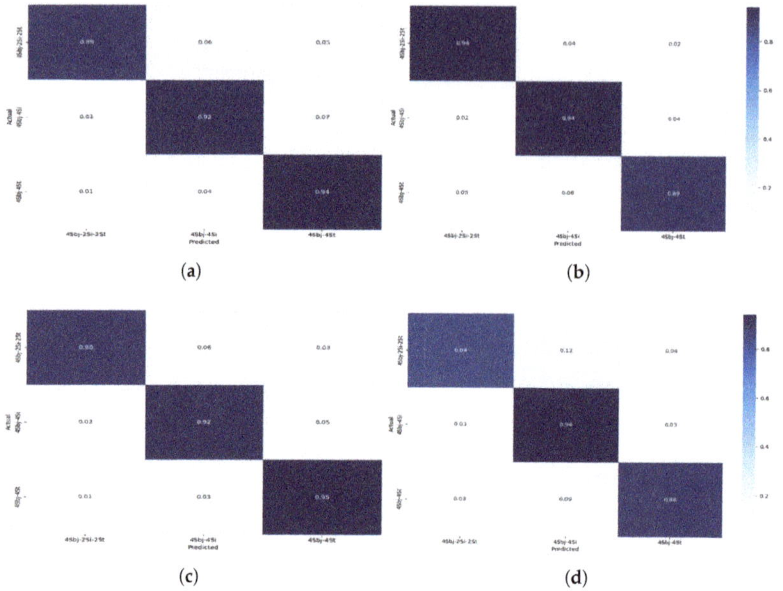

(a) (b) (c) (d)

Figure 10. Confusionmatrix for Experiment II showing the performance of the models for multi-users—4 subjects for different activities: (**a**) CNN + Transformer (**b**) CNN + GRU (**c**) CNN + BiLSTM (**d**) CNN + LSTM.

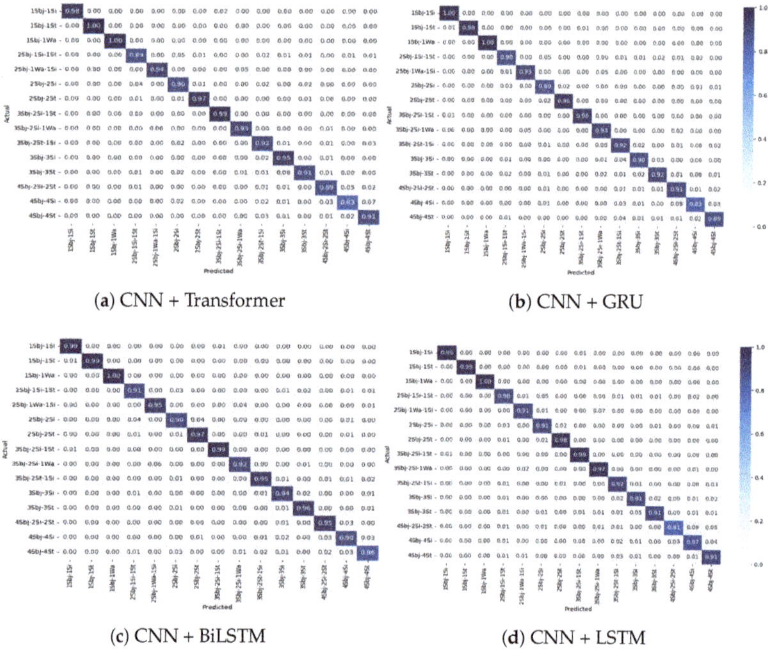

(**a**) CNN + Transformer (**b**) CNN + GRU

(**c**) CNN + BiLSTM (**d**) CNN + LSTM

Figure 11. Confusion matrix for Experiment II showing the performance of the models for multiple users—combined 2-3-4 subjects for different activities.

As the number of concurrent users increased to 3 (Figure 9), classification accuracy remained very good, although slight increases in confusion began to emerge. Specifically, while dynamic activities such as walking continued to be classified correctly for the majority of instances, a marginal rise in misclassification between standing and sitting became apparent. This can be attributed to the overlapping sensor signatures of these low-movement activities, which become increasingly indistinct when recorded from multiple users simultaneously.

The four-user scenario (Figure 10) further amplified these challenges. Static activities, such as standing and sitting, experienced a noticeable drop in classification precision. Standing was frequently misclassified as sitting, and sitting was sometimes confused with especially when two users or one user was involved. This degradation is likely due to the reduced motion variance across users performing sedentary activities at the same time, leading to highly similar sensor patterns that even the attention mechanism found difficult to differentiate. Despite this, the activities continued to be reliably classified, demonstrating the framework's robustness for dynamic activity detection even in dense user environments.

Under the mixed-user setting, where two, three, and four concurrent users were randomly present (Figure 11), the model maintained good performance, albeit with the most pronounced confusion rates observed across all settings. Again, misclassification was predominantly limited to low-motion activities. For example, confusion between standing and sitting reached its highest rate here, reflecting the real-world complexity when diverse user activities are interleaved. Notably, despite these challenges, the Transformer-based model was able to maintain separation between more kinetically distinct activities, such as walking, demonstrating the capability of capturing global temporal dependencies. These observations suggest that while the Transformer module effectively handles dynamic activity signals under user concurrency, there is room for enhancement when addressing static activities in overlapping scenarios.

To further assess model efficacy, an additional comparative experiment was conducted using classical machine learning classifiers KNN, SVM, and RF across the same multi-user configurations. The accuracy scores are visualised in Figure 12, with individual bars representing performance across 1-user, 2-user, 3-user, 4-user, and mixed 2-3-4 user setups. It is observed that, in contrast to classical models, CNN + Transformer performed best across all configurations, with performance only marginally affected as user concurrency increased. KNN and SVM, in particular, showed notable declines in accuracy as the number of users increased. This is primarily due to their limited ability to disambiguate overlapping signal sequences in the temporal domain. These results further demonstrate the proposed model's effectiveness and its suitability for multi-occupant applications where distinguishing between concurrent activity streams is critical.

Further comparative analysis based on Table 8 reinforces these observations. A standalone CNN model was tested, which achieved an accuracy of 89.3%, improving upon prior CNN-only approaches reported in the literature (85.7% [36]). The LSTM model provided a slight improvement to 90.0%, benefitting from its temporal sequence modelling capabilities. However, the proposed CNN+Transformer achieved the highest performance, with an accuracy of 93.9%, an F1-score of 93.3%, precision of 94.0%, and recall of 93.4%.

This significant gain can be attributed to the hybrid model's ability to integrate spatial feature extraction (via CNN) with long-range temporal dependency learning (via Transformer), offering a balanced and comprehensive representation of user activities. In particular, the high F1-score suggests that the model maintained a strong balance between precision and recall, essential in avoiding both false positives and false negatives in critical HAR applications.

Table 8. Comparison of classification performance across different model architectures, including standalone CNN, LSTM, and the proposed CNN + Transformer.

Model Variant	Accuracy	F1-Score	Precision	Recall
CNN [36]	0.857	–	–	–
CNN	0.893	0.891	0.893	0.892
LSTM	0.900	0.894	0.894	0.894
Proposed CNN + Transformer	0.939	0.933	0.940	0.934

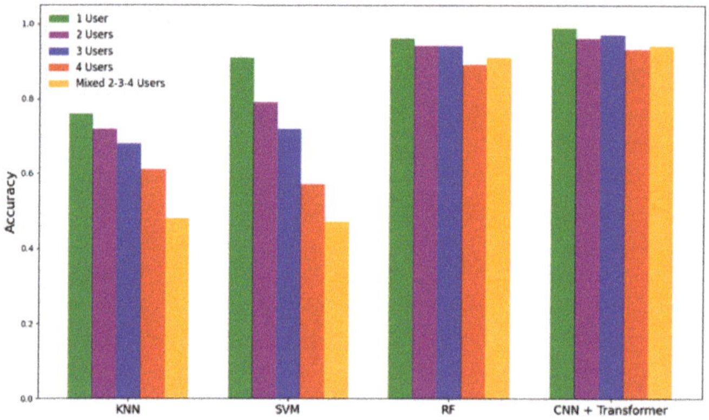

Figure 12. Comparisonof classification accuracy across different classifiers and proposed CNN+Transformer architecture under varying user configurations.

6. Conclusions

This paper presents a robust and scalable CSI-based HAR framework tailored for complex multi-user indoor environments. The method integrates multi-stage preprocessing, data augmentation, and a CNN + Transformer hybrid model, alongside other deep learning architectures, to effectively capture spatiotemporal CSI dependencies. Extensive experiments validate the effectiveness of the approach. Sensitivity analysis confirmed that augmentation preserves the underlying data distribution. Moderate augmentation, specifically at factor 5, improved model performance in all variants, with CNN + Transformer consistently outperforming others. The framework demonstrated high adaptability in multi-user experiments, maintaining strong classification accuracy even in dense user configurations. Overall, the proposed CSI-based HAR system exhibits notable improvements in robustness, accuracy, and scalability, forming a strong foundation for future intelligent activity recognition systems in ambient settings. Key limitations include non-adaptive augmentation, lack of explicit user-level separation, and the Transformer's computational demands. While user density and activity diversity are incorporated into the experimental protocol, the absence of external validation on an independent dataset limits the broader generalisability of the findings. Future work will focus on adaptive augmentation, finer-grained user identification, lightweight Transformer variants, and deployment across diverse real-world environments and populations. We also plan to include deeper multivariate analyses, such as principal component analysis and autocorrelation, to examine the latent structure and the validation of the current model on independently simulated CSI environments to better evaluate cross-environment robustness and strengthen the broader applicability of the proposed system.

Author Contributions: Conceptualisation, M.I.K., P.M., A.L., D.H. and I.K.I.; methodology, M.I.K.; software, M.I.K. and I.K.I.; validation, M.I.K., P.M. and I.K.I.; formal analysis, M.I.K., P.M., A.L., D.H. and I.K.I.; investigation, M.I.K.; resources, M.I.K., P.M. and I.K.I.; writing—original draft preparation,

M.I.K.; writing—review and editing, M.I.K., P.M., A.L., D.H. and I.K.I.; visualisation, M.I.K., P.M., A.L., D.H. and I.K.I.; supervision, I.K.I. All authors have read and agreed to the published version of the manuscript.

Funding: This research received no external funding.

Institutional Review Board Statement: Not applicable.

Informed Consent Statement: All the participating authors have signed and given informed consent statements.

Data Availability Statement: The dataset for this study is publicly available.

Conflicts of Interest: The authors declare no conflicts of interest.

References

1. Shalaby, E.; ElShennawy, N.; Sarhan, A. Utilizing deep learning models in CSI-based human activity recognition. *Neural Comput. Appl.* **2022**, *34*, 5993–6010. [CrossRef]
2. Ihianle, I.K.; Naeem, U.; Tawil, A.R.; Azam, M.A. Recognizing activities of daily living from patterns and extraction of web knowledge. In Proceedings of the 2016 ACM International Joint Conference on Pervasive and Ubiquitous Computing, Heidelberg, Germany, 12–16 September 2016; pp. 1255–1262. [CrossRef]
3. Lotfi, A.; Langensiepen, C.; Mahmoud, S.M.; Akhlaghinia, M.J. Smart homes for the elderly dementia sufferers: Identification and prediction of abnormal behaviour. *J. Ambient. Intell. Humaniz. Comput.* **2012**, *3*, 205–218. [CrossRef]
4. Jang, S.; Lee, H.; Kim, W.J.; Lee, J.; Woo, S.; Lee, S. Multi-scale structural graph convolutional network for skeleton-based action recognition. *IEEE Trans. Circuits Syst. Video Technol.* **2024**, *34*, 7244–7258. [CrossRef]
5. Naser, A.; Lotfi, A.; Mwanje, M.D.; Zhong, J. Privacy-Preserving, Thermal Vision With Human in the Loop Fall Detection Alert System. *IEEE Trans. Hum.-Mach. Syst.* **2023**, *53*, 164–175. [CrossRef]
6. Kumar, P.; Chauhan, S.; Awasthi, L.K. Human activity recognition (HAR) using deep learning: Review, methodologies, progress and future research directions. *Arch. Comput. Methods Eng.* **2024**, *31*, 179–219. [CrossRef]
7. Ankalaki, S. Simple to Complex, Single to Concurrent Sensor based Human Activity Recognition: Perception and Open Challenges. *IEEE Access* **2024**, *12*, 93450–93486. [CrossRef]
8. Doherty, A.; Yuan, H.; Plekhanova, T.; Walmsley, R.; Reynolds, A.; Maddison, K.; Bucan, M.; Gehrman, P.; Rowlands, A.; Ray, D.; et al. Self-supervised learning of accelerometer data provides new insights for sleep and its association with mortality. *NPJ Digit. Med.* *2024*, *7*, *86*. [CrossRef]
9. Tan, S.; Zhang, L.; Wang, Z.; Yang, J. MultiTrack: Multi-user tracking and activity recognition using commodity WiFi. In Proceedings of the 2019 CHI Conference on Human Factors in Computing Systems, Glasgow, UK, 4–9 May 2019; pp. 1–12. [CrossRef]
10. Szczurek, K.A.; Prades, R.M.; Matheson, E.; Rodriguez-Nogueira, J.; Di Castro, M. Multimodal multi-user mixed reality human–robot interface for remote operations in hazardous environments. *IEEE Access* **2023**, *11*, 17305–17333. [CrossRef]
11. Wang, L.; Gu, T.; Tao, X.; Chen, H.; Lu, J. Recognizing multi-user activities using wearable sensors in a smart home. *Pervasive Mob. Comput.* **2011**, *7*, 287–298. [CrossRef]
12. Rebuffi, S.A.; Gowal, S.; Calian, D.A.; Stimberg, F.; Wiles, O.; Mann, T.A. Data augmentation can improve robustness. In Proceedings of the 35th International Conference on Neural Information Processing Systems, Online, 6–14 December 2021; Volume 34, pp. 29935–29948.
13. Alomar, K.; Aysel, H.I.; Cai, X. Data augmentation in classification and segmentation: A survey and new strategies. *J. Imaging* **2023**, *9*, 46. [CrossRef]
14. Vaswani, A.; Shazeer, N.; Parmar, N.; Uszkoreit, J.; Jones, L.; Gomez, A.N.; Kaiser, Ł.; Polosukhin, I. Attention Is All You Need. In Proceedings of the 31st International Conference on Neural Information Processing Systems, Long Beach, CA, USA, 4–9 December 2017; Volume 30.
15. Saidani, O.; Alsafyani, M.; Alroobaea, R.; Alturki, N.; Jahangir, R.; Jamel, L. An efficient human activity recognition using hybrid features and transformer model. *IEEE Access* **2023**, *11*, 101373–101386. [CrossRef]
16. Ezzeldin, M.; Ghoneim, A.S.; Abdelhamid, L.; Atia, A. Multi-modal hybrid hierarchical classification approach with transformers to enhance complex human activity recognition. *Signal Image Video Process.* **2024**, *18*, 9375–9385. [CrossRef]
17. Ihianle, I.K.; Nwajana, A.O.; Ebenuwa, S.H.; Otuka, R.I.; Owa, K.; Orisatoki, M.O. A deep learning approach for human activities recognition from multimodal sensing devices. *IEEE Access* **2020**, *8*, 179028–179038. [CrossRef]
18. Pfeffer, M.A.; Ling, S.S.H.; Wong, J.K.W. Exploring the frontier: Transformer-based models in EEG signal analysis for brain-computer interfaces. *Comput. Biol. Med.* **2024**, *178*, 108705. [CrossRef]

19. Zhang, J.; Feng, L.; Liu, Z.; Wu, Y.; He, Y.; Dong, Y.; Xu, D. Diverse Intra-and Inter-Domain Activity Style Fusion for Cross-Person Generalization in Activity Recognition. In Proceedings of the 30th ACM SIGKDD Conference on Knowledge Discovery and Data Mining, Barcelona, Spain, 25–29 August 2024; pp. 4213–4222.
20. Chen, X.; Zhou, X.; Sun, M.; Wang, H. Temporal Contrastive Learning for Sensor-Based Human Activity Recognition: A Self-Supervised Approach. *IEEE Sens. J.* **2024**, *25*, 1839–1850. [CrossRef]
21. Xu, M.; Li, Y.; Han, K.; Zhao, Y.; Jiang, J.; Du, Y. A Conditional Diffusion Model Based WiFi Sensing Enhancement Method. In Proceedings of the 2024 IEEE 35th International Symposium on Personal, Indoor and Mobile Radio Communications (PIMRC), Valencia, Spain, 2–5 September 2024; pp. 1–6.
22. Xiao, C.; Jiang, X.; Du, X.; Yang, W.; Lu, W.; Wang, X.; Chetty, K. Boundary-enhanced time series data imputation with long-term dependency diffusion models. *Knowl.-Based Syst.* **2025**, *310*, 112917. [CrossRef]
23. Luo, F.; Khan, S.; Jiang, B.; Wu, K. Vision transformers for human activity recognition using WiFi channel state information. *IEEE Internet Things J.* **2024**, *11*, 28111–28122. [CrossRef]
24. Han, W.; Yu, J. Algorithm for interference filtering of Wi-Fi gesture recognition. *Int. J. Inf. Commun. Technol.* **2024**, *24*, 1–20. [CrossRef]
25. Zhao, R.; Liu, Z.; Song, T.; Jin, J.; Jin, G.; Fan, L. Hybrid CNN-transformer network for efficient CSI feedback. *Phys. Commun.* **2024**, *66*, 102477. [CrossRef]
26. Muaaz, M.; Chelli, A.; Gerdes, M.W.; Pätzold, M. Wi-Sense: A Passive Human Activity Recognition System Using Wi-Fi and Convolutional Neural Network and Its Integration in Health Information Systems. *Ann. Telecommun.* **2022**, *77*, 163–175. [CrossRef]
27. Elkelany, A.; Ross, R.; McKeever, S. WiFi-Based Human Activity Recognition Using Attention-Based BiLSTM. In Proceedings of the Artificial Intelligence and Cognitive Science (AICS 2022), Munster, Ireland, 8–9 December 2022; Communications in Computer and Information Science; Springer: Cham, Switzerland, 2023; Volume 1662, pp. 123–136. [CrossRef]
28. Shi, Z.; Wang, Y.; Jin, Y.; Liu, Y.; Chen, W. Environment-Robust WiFi-Based Human Activity Recognition Using Enhanced CSI and Deep Learning. *IEEE Internet Things J.* **2022**, *9*, 24643–24654. [CrossRef]
29. Qin, X.; Wang, J.; Chen, Y.; Lu, W.; Jiang, X. Domain Generalization for Activity Recognition via Adaptive Feature Fusion. *arXiv* **2022**, arXiv:2207.11221. [CrossRef]
30. Abuhoureyah, F.; Sim, K.S.; Wong, Y.C. Multi-User Human Activity Recognition Through Adaptive Location-Independent WiFi Signal Characteristics. *IEEE Access* **2024**, *12*, 112008–112024. [CrossRef]
31. Wang, Y.; Yao, L.; Wang, Y.; Zhang, Y. Robust CSI-Based Human Activity Recognition With Augment Few Shot Learning. *IEEE Sens. J.* **2021**, *21*, 24297–24308. [CrossRef]
32. Zhang, Y.; Chen, Y.; Wang, Y.; Liu, Q.; Cheng, A. CSI-Based Human Activity Recognition with Graph Few-Shot Learning. *IEEE Internet Things J.* **2022**, *9*, 4139–4151. [CrossRef]
33. Xiao, C.; Han, Y.; Yang, W.; Hou, Y.; Shi, F.; Chetty, K. Diffusion Model-Based Contrastive Learning for Human Activity Recognition. *IEEE Internet Things J.* **2024**, *11*, 33525–33536. [CrossRef]
34. Zhang, Y.; Zheng, Y.; Qian, K.; Zhang, G.; Liu, Y.; Wu, C.; Yang, Z. Widar3.0: Zero-Effort Cross-Domain Gesture Recognition With Wi-Fi. *IEEE Trans. Pattern Anal. Mach. Intell.* **2022**, *44*, 7083–7099. [CrossRef]
35. Shi, Z.; Zhang, J.A.; Xu, R.Y.; Cheng, Q. Environment-Robust Device-Free Human Activity Recognition With Channel-State-Information Enhancement and One-Shot Learning. *IEEE Trans. Mob. Comput.* **2020**, *21*, 540–554. [CrossRef]
36. Ashleibta, A.M.; Taha, A.; Khan, M.A.; Taylor, W.; Tahir, A.; Zoha, A.; Abbasi, Q.H.; Imran, M.A. 5g-enabled contactless multi-user presence and activity detection for independent assisted living. *Sci. Rep.* **2021**, *11*, 17590. [CrossRef]
37. Muszkats, J.P.; Seminara, S.A.; Troparevsky, M.I. (Eds.) *Applications of Wavelet Multiresolution Analysis*; Springer International Publishing: Berlin/Heidelberg, Germany, 2021.
38. Um, T.; Pfister, F.M.J.; Pichler, D.; Endo, S.; Lang, M.; Hirche, S.; Fietzek, U.; Kulić, D. Data augmentation of wearable sensor data for Parkinson's disease monitoring using convolutional neural networks. In Proceedings of the 19th ACM International Conference on Multimodal Interaction, Glasgow, UK, 13–17 November 2017; Volume 8, pp. 1–10.
39. Wen, Q.; Gao, J.; Sun, L.; Song, X.; Wang, H.; Yan, J.; Deng, Y. Time-series data augmentation for deep learning: A survey. *arXiv* **2020**, arXiv:2002.12478.
40. Le Guennec, A.; Malinowski, S.; Tavenard, R. Data augmentation for time series classification using convolutional neural networks. In Proceedings of the ECML/PKDD Workshop on Advanced Analytics and Learning on Temporal Data, Riva Del Garda, Italy, 19 September 2016.
41. Chen, Z.; Cai, C.; Zheng, T.; Luo, J.; Xiong, J.; Wang, X. RF-based human activity recognition using signal adapted convolutional neural network. *IEEE Trans. Mob. Comput.* **2021**, *22*, 487–499. [CrossRef]
42. Ihianle, I.K.; Machado, P.; Owa, K.; Adama, D.A.; Otuka, R.; Lotfi, A. Minimising redundancy, maximising relevance: HRV feature selection for stress classification. *Expert Syst. Appl.* **2024**, *239*, 122490. [CrossRef]
43. Chen, L.; Ahriz, I.; Le Ruyet, D. CSI-based probabilistic indoor position determination: An entropy solution. *IEEE Access* **2019**, *7*, 170048–170061. [CrossRef]

44. Ahmed, H.O.; Nandi, A.K. Convolutional-transformer model with long-range temporal dependencies for bearing fault diagnosis using vibration signals. *Machines* **2019**, *11*, 746. [CrossRef]
45. Thundiyil, S.; Shalamzari, S.S.; Picone, J.; McKenzie, S. Transformers for modelling long-term dependencies in time series data: A review. In Proceedings of the IEEE Signal Processing in Medicine and Biology Symposium (SPMB), Philadelphia, PA, USA, 2 December 2023; pp. 1–5.
46. Razali, N.; Wah, Y.B. Power comparisons of shapiro–wilk, kolmogorov–smirnov, lilliefors and anderson–darling tests. *J. Stat. Anal.* **2011**, *2*, 21–33.
47. Jäntschi, L.; Bolboacă, S.D. Computation of probability associated with Anderson–Darling statistic. *Mathematics* **2018**, *6*, 88. [CrossRef]
48. Cook, D.J.; Augusto, J.C.; Jakkula, V.R. Ambient intelligence: Technologies, applications, and opportunities. *Pervasive Mob. Comput.* **2013**, *5*, 277–298. [CrossRef]
49. Lupión, M.; Cruciani, F.; Cleland, I.; Nugent, C.; Ortigosa, P.M. Data augmentation for human activity recognition with generative adversarial networks. *IEEE J. Biomed. Health Inform.* **2024**, *28*, 2350–2361. [CrossRef]

sensors

MDPI

Review

A Comprehensive Review of Elbow Exoskeletons: Classification by Structure, Actuation, and Sensing Technologies

Callista Shekar Ayu Supriyono, Mihai Dragusanu * and Monica Malvezzi

Department of Information Engineering and Mathematics, University of Siena, 53100 Siena, Italy; c.supriyono@student.unisi.it (C.S.A.S.); monica.malvezzi@unisi.it (M.M.)
* Correspondence: mihai.dragusanu2@unisi.it

Abstract: The development of wearable robotic exoskeletons has seen rapid progress in recent years, driven by the growing need for technologies that support motor rehabilitation, assist individuals with physical impairments, and enhance human capabilities in both clinical and everyday contexts. Within this field, elbow exoskeletons have emerged as a key focus due to the joint's essential role in upper limb functionality and its frequent impairment following neurological injuries such as stroke. With increasing research activity, there is a strong interest in evaluating these systems not only from a technical perspective but also in terms of user comfort, adaptability, and clinical relevance. This review investigates recent advancements in elbow exoskeleton technology, evaluating their effectiveness and identifying key design challenges and limitations. Devices are categorized based on three main criteria: mechanical structure (rigid, soft, or hybrid), actuation method, and sensing technologies. Additionally, the review classifies systems by their supported range of motion, flexion–extension, supination–pronation, or both. Through a systematic analysis of these features, the paper highlights current design trends, common trade-offs, and research gaps, aiming to guide the development of more practical, effective, and accessible elbow exoskeletons.

Keywords: elbow exoskeleton; assistive; rehabilitation; augmentation; sensor; actuator

1. Introduction

The human upper limb, particularly the elbow joint, plays a critical role in performing a wide range of daily activities, from simple tasks like eating to complex functions in professional settings [1]. However, injuries, aging, neurological conditions, or physical impairments can severely affect the functionality of the elbow, limiting mobility and independence [2–4]. As the demand for assistive technologies grows, elbow exoskeletons have emerged as a promising solution for both the rehabilitation and augmentation of human motion. These wearable systems are specifically designed to assist users in performing elbow-related movements, supporting joint function and facilitating natural motion. Based on the natural biomechanics of the human elbow, these systems enable the mechanical transfer of power to produce two primary types of joint motions: flexion–extension and supination–pronation.

An exoskeleton is a wearable device designed to support and assist the human body by moving in harmony with its natural motions [5,6]. Numerous models of exoskeletons have been created and developed to serve various purposes, from rehabilitation to industrial applications. Elbow exoskeletons, as a subset of this technology, are created to provide support during elbow motions, either assisting with movement or aiding in rehabilitation processes.

Elbow exoskeletons are wearable devices including actuators, sensors, and control systems that facilitate smooth interaction between the user and the device. The actuators actuate or support natural limbs' and joints' movement, while sensors monitor system status, for example, joint angles, muscle activity, forces, and other key variables. Control algorithms then interpret this sensor feedback to provide the appropriate level of assistance or, in rehabilitation contexts, controlled resistance depending on the user's needs. As these devices evolve, their design has become increasingly sophisticated, incorporating advances in robotics, biomechatronics, and sensor technologies. According to Tiboni and colleagues' recent review [7], the elbow joint is the most considered in the design of devices for upper limb actuation.

This review paper aims to provide a comprehensive overview of the current state of elbow exoskeletons, with a focus on their design, actuation systems, sensor technologies, control strategies, and evaluation methods. We will examine the major actuation types, including pneumatic, hydraulic, cable-based, and electric systems, and their suitability for various applications. Additionally, we will explore the key sensors used for feedback and control, such as force sensors, torque sensors, EMG sensors, and IMUs. Finally, the paper will discuss the challenges faced in their development and the emerging trends in the field. The review concludes with a discussion on future directions, including the integration of artificial intelligence, soft robotics, and the commercialization of these technologies for broader use in clinical and industrial settings.

2. Methodology

To analyze the development trends of elbow exoskeleton technologies, we conducted a targeted literature search using Google Scholar (Google LLC, California, USA) as the sole database. We selected Google Scholar as the sole database for our literature search due to its comprehensive coverage of scholarly publications across a wide range of disciplines, including engineering, robotics, rehabilitation, and biomedical sciences. The initial search included publications related to upper-limb exoskeletons to provide broader context and ensure that no relevant elbow-focused research was missed. However, for the purposes of this study, we included only papers that specifically addressed elbow exoskeletons for our main analysis.

We used a combination of keywords including "elbow exoskeleton", "upper-limb exoskeleton", "rehabilitation", "assistive", "augmentation", "sensor", and "actuator" to identify relevant peer-reviewed journal articles and conference papers. Articles published between 2010 and 2025 were prioritized to capture both early developments and recent innovations. After removing duplicates and filtering out unrelated studies, we screened the remaining articles by title, abstract, and full text to ensure technical relevance and a specific focus on elbow assistance. The inclusion criteria emphasized academic rigor and topic relevance, leading us to select only peer-reviewed journal articles and conference papers for further analysis.

In total, 67 research papers were selected based on their technical depth, relevance, and contribution to the understanding of elbow exoskeleton design and development. From this pool, we identified and analyzed 17 individual elbow exoskeleton devices, chosen for their availability of detailed technical specifications and representation of diverse design approaches. Each device was evaluated across several key dimensions, including mechanical structure, degrees of freedom (DOFs), type of actuators, and the roles of integrated sensors.

An analysis of publication years revealed a clear trend: early research (2010–2015) focused primarily on mechanical design and proof-of-concept systems. From 2016 onward, the literature shows a growing emphasis on soft robotics, user adaptability, and wearable assistive systems. More recent studies increasingly address real-world applications, integration with sensors, and user-centered evaluation, indicating the field's gradual shift from laboratory prototypes toward clinical and commercial readiness.

Although many new exoskeleton systems have been introduced in recent years, our analysis was limited to those that explicitly target the elbow joint. This focused approach enabled us to identify and evaluate trends unique to this subfield within the broader landscape of wearable robotics. The reviewed literature spans the last 15 years, allowing us to trace the evolution of elbow exoskeleton technologies and gain insights into emerging research directions, design maturation, and the transition toward more refined, market-ready solutions. By analyzing how these devices have changed in structure and purpose over time, we aim to offer both a comparative assessment of current technologies and a contextual understanding of the field's development.

3. Anatomy of Human Elbow

The human body is divided into three main sections: the upper limbs, the trunk, and the lower limbs. The upper limb itself consists of three sections: the upper arm, forearm, and hand. Within these sections, we find important structures crucial for movement, such as the shoulder complex, elbow complex, wrist joint, and fingers. These structures work in harmony to provide the dexterity and flexibility necessary for complex tasks. The human upper limb features seven degrees of freedom (DOFs): three in the shoulder, two in the elbow, and two in the wrist. As noted by Gull and colleagues, most studies model the elbow as having only one degree of freedom, typically for flexion–extension. However, the forearm enables a second rotational movement supination–pronation which involves both the proximal and distal radioulnar joints, though it is often functionally associated with the elbow. While research often focuses on flexion–extension due to its simpler implementation, supination–pronation is equally important, particularly for tasks like eating and drinking, which require the rotation of the forearm [8].

3.1. Bones and Joint Structure

The elbow is a complex joint system composed of three bones: the humerus, radius, and ulna, which interact through three primary articulations: the humeroulnar (HU), humeroradial (HR), and proximal radioulnar (RU) joints. These interconnected joints enable two active degrees of freedom (DOFs): flexion–extension and pronation–supination, along with one passive DOF, varus–valgus (adduction–abduction) motion [9]. The humeroulnar joint primarily supports the hinge-like flexion and extension, while pronation and supination—the rotational movements of the forearm—are facilitated by the humeroradial and proximal radioulnar joints, rather than by the radius alone.

The distal humerus features the trochlea (medial side) and capitellum (lateral side), which articulate with the ulna and radius, respectively. This anatomical arrangement permits complex motion patterns involving rotation, sliding, and rolling across multiple planes. Consequently, describing the elbow as a simple hinge joint is a simplification; it is more accurately characterized as a multi-joint structure with coordinated biomechanical functions, critical for executing everyday activities requiring both strength and precision [10].

3.2. Muscles and Tendons

Key muscles involved in elbow movement include the biceps brachii, triceps brachii, and brachialis, among others. These muscles work together to control the motion of the elbow. The first one is the biceps brachii; responsible for elbow flexion, the biceps help bend the arm at the elbow joint. The second one is the triceps brachii; the triceps oppose the action of the biceps and are responsible for elbow extension, straightening the arm.

Then, the third one is the brachialis, a muscle located beneath the biceps, which assists in flexion of the elbow, particularly when the forearm is in a pronated position. Additional muscles, such as the pronator teres and supinator muscles, play key roles in forearm rotation, supination, and pronation [11].

3.3. Ligaments

The stability of the elbow joint is maintained by several key ligaments that counteract specific mechanical stresses during movement. The Ulnar Collateral Ligament (UCL) provides medial support by resisting valgus stress, which is the outward angulation of the forearm relative to the upper arm, a force commonly encountered during overhead throwing motions. On the lateral side, the Radial Collateral Ligament (RCL) resists varus stress, or inward angulation, helping to stabilize the elbow against forces that would push it outward. Additionally, the Annular Ligament encircles the head of the radius and holds it in place against the ulna, allowing smooth rotational movement during supination and pronation [12]. These ligaments play a critical role in maintaining joint integrity during both linear and rotational activities.

3.4. Movement, Range of Motion, and Force

The primary movement of the elbow joint is flexion and extension, which occurs along the sagittal plane and is primarily facilitated by the humeroulnar and humeroradial joints. The standard anatomical reference for elbow flexion begins at 0°, representing full extension where the arm is straightened alongside the body. However, as shown in Figure 1, some individuals may exhibit slight hyperextension, up to 11° beyond neutral, due to natural joint variability. The normal range of flexion extends up to approximately 154°, enabling common activities such as lifting and reaching [10].

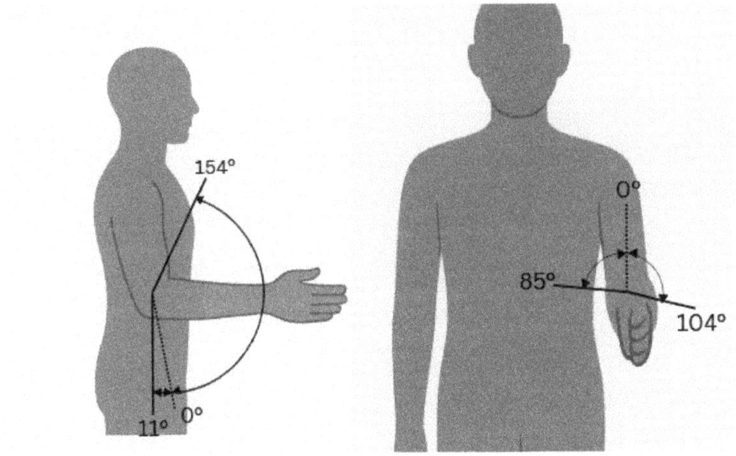

(**a**) Flexion–extension movement (**b**) Supination–pronation movement

Figure 1. Elbow movement scheme: (**a**) flexion–extension, (**b**) supination–pronation.

In addition to its hinge-like motion, the elbow joint complex comprising the humeroulnar, humeroradial, and proximal radioulnar joints supports pronation and supination, which are rotational movements of the forearm [9]. These occur between the radius and ulna, specifically at the proximal and distal radioulnar joints, and are crucial for tasks such as turning a doorknob or holding a cup. The typical range for pronation is 0° to 85°, while supination spans 0° to 104° [10]. Although biomechanically associated with the forearm, these motions are functionally coupled with elbow movement and are often considered in the design of elbow exoskeletons.

Regarding torque requirements, pronation and supination typically demand about 0.06 Nm [13], whereas flexion and extension require significantly more, approximately 2.7 Nm [14], highlighting the mechanical demands placed on assistive systems for the elbow. The range of motion (ROM) of the elbow joint is summarized in Table 1.

Table 1. Elbow joint range of motion (ROM) and torque.

Motion	ROM (Degrees)	Torque (Nm)	Reference
Flexion	0°–154°	∼2.7	[10,14]
Extension	0°–154°	∼2.7	[10,14]
Pronation	0°–85°	∼0.06	[10,13]
Supination	0°–104°	∼0.06	[10,13]

4. Elbow Exoskeleton Application

The concept of exoskeletons was first developed in the late 1960s for military purposes. The first successful prototype introduced in the 1960s was called Hardiman. At that time, the actuator system used was a hydraulic actuator, designed to provide strength assistance to the user [15]. Since this initial introduction, significant developments have been made in the design of elbow exoskeletons due to their potential, not only in military applications but also in improving users' quality of life and serving various other purposes, such as in industrial applications.

Elbow exoskeletons are commonly found in three main scenarios: assistive, rehabilitation, and augmentation [16].

4.1. Assistive Application

According to the World Health Organization (WHO), approximately 16.5 percent of the global population suffers from motor impairments, limiting their ability to engage in physical activities. To address this, lightweight and comfortable elbow exoskeletons have been designed for daily use as an assistive device [17]. These devices are also frequently used by elderly individuals with reduced physical strength to ease their daily routines [18]. In these scenarios, elbow exoskeletons serve as assistive devices, helping users perform daily activities more easily, such as lifting objects, reaching, or carrying groceries. The primary goal is to improve the quality of life for individuals with motor disabilities by providing them with the extra strength and stability they need to perform routine tasks with less effort.

4.2. Rehabilitation Application

In addition to being assistive devices, elbow exoskeletons can be used in rehabilitation. One example is in the case of stroke. Stroke, as we know, is one of the most dangerous illnesses and the second-leading cause of death worldwide. According to WHO, 15 million people suffer from stroke each year [19]. However, stroke is still a condition that can be managed and treated if immediate action is taken, and today, many stroke survivors can be found. Despite this, stroke remains a leading cause of upper limb impairment, with many survivors losing the ability to move their arms. For this reason, several elbow exoskeletons have been specifically designed to assist therapists in performing rehabilitative exercises, helping survivors regain mobility [20]. These exoskeletons are equipped with sensors and actuators that allow for controlled, repetitive motion, aiding in neuromuscular recovery. By using exoskeletons in therapy, patients can receive targeted assistance to restore motion, reduce the effects of muscle atrophy, and improve motor control, all while ensuring proper biomechanics during the recovery process [21].

4.3. Augmentation Application

Beyond the healthcare applications mentioned earlier, elbow exoskeletons also play an important role in the augmentation field. Building on the original idea first implemented in Hardiman [8], and with technological advancements, elbow exoskeletons are increasingly being used for augmentation purposes, such as assisting industrial workers with lifting and carrying heavy loads or aiding soldiers in military operations. This not only provides additional strength to the user but also protects them from both minor and severe injuries. Minor injuries, such as muscle fatigue, tendon strain, or joint discomfort, commonly arise from repetitive or sustained physical tasks. More severe injuries including musculoskeletal disorders, ligament tears, or spinal compression can result from improper lifting techniques, overexertion, or carrying heavy loads over time. Elbow exoskeletons help mitigate these risks by redistributing mechanical loads, limiting excessive joint movement, and supporting proper posture during strenuous activities [22–24]. In industrial settings, for example, workers often face physically demanding tasks that require heavy lifting or repetitive movements, leading to long-term physical strain. Elbow exoskeletons can mitigate the risk of injury by supporting the arm during lifting and improving endurance. Similarly, in military applications, exoskeletons are designed to assist soldiers by supporting load bearing tasks and reducing physical strain, which can help them to carry heavier equipment for extended periods and mitigate fatigue [?]. These devices help improve the overall performance of users in environments where physical exertion is high, making them valuable tools for a wide range of industries and sectors [16,26].

5. Elbow Exoskeleton Classification

Elbow exoskeletons can be classified into different types based on their mechanical structure and the nature of the assistance they provide, as shown in Figure 2. These classifications highlight the fundamental design differences and the types of assistance these devices offer to the user.

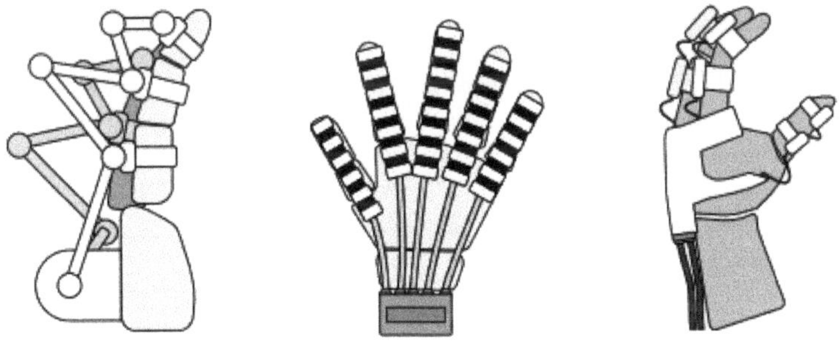

(**a**) Rigid exoskeleton (**b**) Soft exoskeleton (**c**) Hybrid exoskeleton

Figure 2. The drawing of three different mechanical structures of exoskeleton: (**a**) rigid exoskeleton, (**b**) soft exoskeleton, and (**c**) hybrid exoskeleton [27].

5.1. Rigid, Soft, and Hybrid Elbow Exoskeleton

Based on their mechanical structure, exoskeletons can be categorized into rigid, soft, or even hybrid exoskeletons [27].

Rigid exoskeletons provide strong structural support and precise control but tend to be heavier and more expensive due to material choices. These exoskeletons are often made from PLA, metal, carbon fiber, or other strong materials that offer higher levels of force output and support. They are designed to assist with tasks requiring greater strength and stability, making them ideal for rehabilitation and augmentation applications [1].

While rigid exoskeletons give strong support, soft exoskeletons prioritize comfort and flexibility. They are made from lighter, flexible materials like textiles or polymers, which are easier to wear and better integrated into the user's daily activities. These exoskeletons provide less mechanical force but offer greater adaptability to the human body, making them especially beneficial for assistive applications. Soft exoskeletons are generally lightweight, breathable, and more comfortable for prolonged use [28–31].

On the other hand, a hybrid exoskeleton is designed to assist human movement by providing support during activities while maintaining a balance between flexibility and structural stability. Unlike fully soft exoskeletons, which use soft materials (e.g., textile-based materials) for maximum comfortability, hybrid exoskeletons usually use a hard material for their structural support and use a soft material actuator for their actuation system [32–35].

5.2. Active and Passive Elbow Exoskeleton

In addition to the rigid–soft classification, exoskeletons can be categorized into active and passive systems. Active exoskeletons use powered actuators to actively assist the user's movements. These devices provide greater control and allow for precise, adjustable support, making them ideal for tasks that require significant strength or precision, such as lifting heavy objects or performing rehabilitation exercises. Active systems are commonly used in rehabilitation and augmentation settings, where user performance and strength are enhanced through powered assistance. In contrast, passive exoskeletons rely on springs, damping mechanisms, or other passive elements to assist motion. These systems do not have powered actuators and instead provide support through mechanical advantage, allowing users to move more easily without generating additional power. Passive exoskeletons are typically lighter, less expensive, and simpler in design. They are ideal for users who need less intensive support or for use in less physically demanding activities [36–38].

6. Elbow Exoskeleton Actuation System

In an active elbow exoskeleton, the actuator serves as the core driving element that generates motion and force to assist, augment, or rehabilitate the elbow joint.

Its primary function is to mimic or support the natural flexion and extension of the elbow. The choice of actuator significantly influences the exoskeleton's performance, comfort, and suitability for specific applications [7]. There are different types of actuators that have been used in exoskeletons' actuation: pneumatic, hydraulic, cable-based, electric, shape memory alloy, and Variable Stiffness Actuators. Specifically for elbow exoskeletons, hydraulic and shape memory alloy actuators are less frequent. For the sake of completeness, however, we included them in the description.

6.1. Pneumatic Actuator

Pneumatic actuators operate using compressed air to create movement and are known for their lightweight structure and rapid response. In elbow exoskeletons, this makes them particularly appealing for assistive settings where safety and compliance with the user's natural motion are important. Since air is compressible, pneumatic systems are generally softer and more forgiving, reducing the risk of injury. However, their reliance on external air sources like compressors or tanks limits their portability, and precise motion control is difficult due to the compressibility of air [39].

6.2. Hydraulic Actuator

Hydraulic actuators use pressurized fluids to produce high levels of force, offering exceptional power density and fine-grained control. However, their main drawbacks are their size, weight, and the complexity of fluid systems, which require pumps, reservoirs, and hoses. These systems can also leak, creating safety and maintenance issues. Due to these limitations, hydraulics are not ideal for mobile or wearable applications, but they shine in stationary, heavy-duty use cases [40].

6.3. Cable-Based

Cable-based actuators, such as Bowden cable systems or Twisted String Actuators (TSAs), use remotely placed motors to transmit force via flexible cables or strings, allowing the joint itself to remain lightweight and minimally encumbered. In TSA systems, a motor twists a pair of strings, causing them to shorten and generate linear motion that can be converted into joint rotation, making the setup compact and mechanically simple [41]. These systems are ideal for soft or wearable exoskeletons where low joint weight and flexibility are critical, such as in assistive daily-use or rehabilitation devices. However, they often suffer from mechanical losses due to friction, cable stretch, and hysteresis, especially in Bowden cables, and they require periodic maintenance to maintain performance [29]. Despite these drawbacks, their ability to offload weight from the joint and conform to the human body makes them a popular choice in ergonomic and user-friendly exoskeleton designs.

6.4. Electric Actuator

Electric actuators, like servo or brushless DC motors, convert electrical energy into mechanical motion and offer high precision, control, and reliability. They are commonly used in portable and battery-powered exoskeletons for both assistive and rehabilitative purposes, thanks to their ease of integration with digital control systems. However, delivering high torque directly at the elbow often requires motors that are relatively heavy and may need cooling solutions to prevent overheating. Despite these trade-offs, electric actuators are favored for applications that demand smooth, precise, and responsive movement in a compact and mobile format [42].

6.5. Shape Memory Alloy

Shape Memory Alloy (SMA) actuators are smart materials that can return to their original shape when heated. They work by changing shape in response to temperature, which creates movement. This makes them useful for small, lightweight, and quiet devices, like wearable exoskeletons. SMAs are especially good for soft and compact designs because they do not need motors or gears. However, they can be slow to cool down and may not be strong enough for heavy tasks [4,43].

6.6. Variable Stiffness Actuator

Variable Stiffness Actuators (VSAs) are specialized robotic actuators that can modify their mechanical stiffness independently from their position or torque control. Unlike conventional actuators with fixed stiffness, VSAs achieve stiffness changes through their mechanical design, avoiding the need for complex control loops and reducing the chance of instability. This feature enables rehabilitation devices using VSAs to adjust the level of assistance based on the patient's condition and gradually intensify therapy. The ability to vary stiffness improves the robot's flexibility, energy use, and safety during interaction with humans, making VSAs particularly beneficial in applications like rehabilitation robotics and prosthetics, where mimicking the natural joint stiffness can enhance motor function recovery and user comfort [44–46].

6.7. Actuators Comparison

Table 2 compares common actuator types used in elbow exoskeletons across five key performance categories: power density, control precision, weight, portability, and compliance. Power density reflects the actuator's force output relative to size and weight, crucial for wearable applications. Control precision measures how accurately the actuator can replicate natural elbow movements, essential for smooth and effective assistance. Weight and portability impact user comfort and device usability in mobile scenarios, with lighter and more portable actuators being preferable, like TSAs and SMAs. Compliance indicates how safely and comfortably the actuator interacts with the human body, with pneumatic, TSA, SMA, and VSA actuators offering higher compliance due to their inherent material properties or design flexibility. This comparison highlights the trade-offs involved in selecting actuators, where pneumatic and SMA actuators excel in compliance but may lack in power or control speed, while an electric actuator provides higher power and precision but varies in weight and compliance. Meanwhile, TSAs, Bowden cable-driven actuators, and VSAs aim to integrate the best of both worlds in terms of precision, adaptability, and safety.

Table 2. Comparison of actuator types used in elbow exoskeletons.

Actuator Type	Power Density	Control Precision	Weight	Portability	Compliance
Pneumatic	Medium	Moderate	Low	Low (requires compressor)	High (air compressibility)
Hydraulic	High	High	High (fluid + hardware)	Low (bulky pump/reservoir)	Low (fluid incompressibility)
Bowden Cable-Driven	Medium	Moderate to High	Low (motor remote)	High	Medium (some compliance)
TSA	Low to Medium	Moderate	Very Low	High	High (soft, compliant)
Electric (Motors)	High	High	Medium to High	High	Low to Medium
SMA	Low	Low to Moderate	Very Low	High	High (material properties)
VSA	Medium to High	High (stiffness and position control)	Medium (due to added stiffness mechanism)	Medium (depends on design)	High (adjustable stiffness improves compliance)

7. Elbow Exoskeleton Sensor Technologies

In an elbow exoskeleton, sensors play a crucial role in enabling intelligent interaction between the user and the device. They provide real-time data that allows the system to interpret user intention, monitor movement, control actuators, and ensure safety. Depending on the purpose of the exoskeleton, be it assistive, rehabilitative, or industrial, different types of sensors are integrated to gather information on muscle activity, joint motion, external forces, and environmental conditions. Among the commonly used sensors in elbow exoskeletons are force sensors, torque sensors, electromyography (EMG) sensors, and inertial measurement units (IMUs). Each of these serves a specific function in enhancing the responsiveness, adaptability, and effectiveness of the exoskeleton system.

7.1. Force Sensor

Force sensors are used to measure the amount of linear force being applied, either by the user or the exoskeleton itself. In elbow exoskeletons, load cells are often embedded at the attachment interfaces such as straps or rigid frame connections to monitor how much force is being exerted during movement or assistance [7]. This information is essential for modulating the actuator's output in real time, ensuring that the device provides the appropriate level of support or resistance. Force sensors also contribute to user safety by detecting unexpected loads that could indicate misuse or a malfunction.

7.2. Torque Sensor

Torque sensors provide measurements of rotational force at the joint. These sensors are particularly important in robotic exoskeletons where the control system needs to know how much torque the actuator is delivering or how much torque is being applied by the user [47]. By integrating torque sensors at the joint or motor, the system can precisely balance its assistance or resistance, leading to smoother, more natural movements.

7.3. EMG Sensor

EMG sensors detect the electrical activity produced by muscle contractions. Surface EMG sensors, which are non-invasive and placed on the skin, are commonly used on the biceps and triceps in elbow exoskeletons [32–34]. These sensors allow the system to interpret the user's muscle activation patterns, effectively reading their intention to move. This capability is particularly valuable in assistive and rehabilitative devices, where user-driven control enhances engagement and effectiveness.

7.4. IMU Sensor

IMUs combine accelerometers, gyroscopes, and sometimes magnetometers to measure orientation, acceleration, and angular velocity [48]. IMUs are lightweight and compact, making them ideal for wearable systems. They are particularly useful in scenarios where continuous motion monitoring is required, such as during rehabilitation exercises or physical assistance tasks.

7.5. Sensor Comparison

The sensor comparison (Table 3) categorizes each sensor type based on the quantity it measures such as force, torque, muscle activity, or motion and outlines its practical strengths and limitations. For instance, force and torque sensors offer accurate mechanical feedback but may add weight or require careful calibration. EMG sensors enable user-intent detection through muscle signals, though they are prone to signal noise. IMUs are lightweight and ideal for tracking motion, yet can suffer from drift over time. The Common Applications row shows how these characteristics align with specific use cases, such as rehabilitation, motion tracking, or adaptive control, providing a clear guide for selecting appropriate sensors based on system goals.

Table 3. Comparison of common sensors used in elbow exoskeletons.

Category	Force Sensor	Torque Sensor	EMG Sensor	IMU
Measured Quantity	Linear force	Rotational force (torque)	Muscle activation (bioelectrical signal)	Orientation, acceleration, angular velocity
Advantages	Simple integration, ensures safety	Precise joint control, real-time feedback	Captures user intent, supports voluntary control	Compact, good for motion tracking
Disadvantages	May lack motion detail	Adds bulk, needs careful calibration	Noisy signals, affected by skin/electrode contact	Drift over time, limited accuracy alone
Common Applications	Load monitoring	Joint torque measurement	Intent detection in rehabilitation	Gait and arm motion analysis

8. Existing Technologies of Elbow Exoskeleton

The development of elbow exoskeletons has advanced significantly, resulting in a variety of designs that differ in actuator mechanisms, sensor integration, degrees of freedom, and portability. Each configuration serves unique rehabilitation and assistive purposes. Table 4 presents a comprehensive list of elbow exoskeletons that are discussed in this paper, including their key features and specifications. Corresponding images of the devices are provided in Figure 3 to support a visual understanding of the designs.

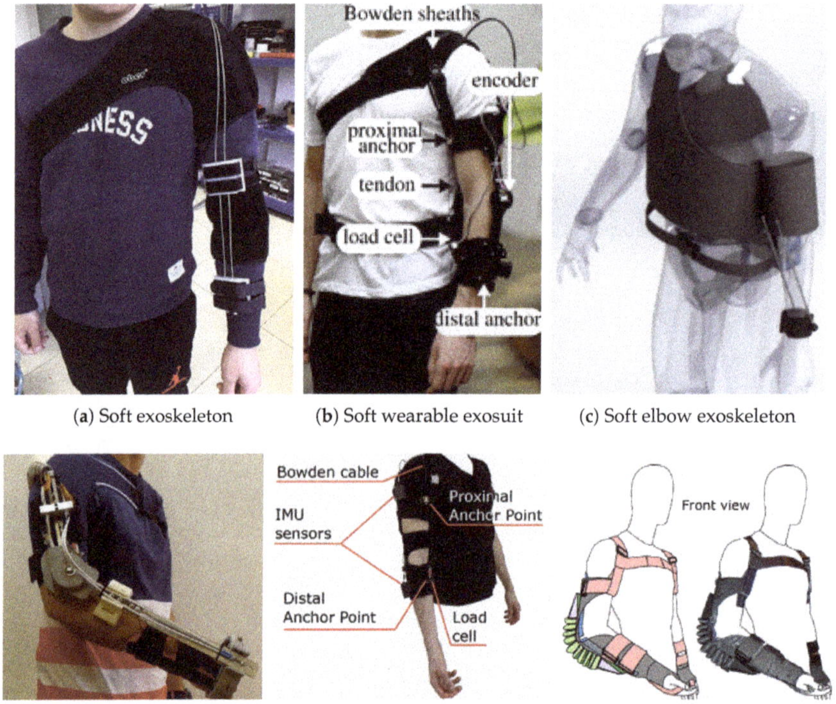

(**a**) Soft exoskeleton (**b**) Soft wearable exosuit (**c**) Soft elbow exoskeleton

(**d**) Elbow exoskeleton (**e**) Exosuit (**f**) Carry

Figure 3. Prototypes of the elbow exoskeletons. (**a**) Soft exoskeleton actuated by a cable-driven mechanism (Bowden cable), incorporating a force sensor for feedback control [29]. (**b**) The soft wearable exosuit utilizing a cable-driven actuator (Bowden cable), also integrated with a force sensor for motion assistance [30]. (**c**) A soft elbow exoskeleton employing a motor tendon actuator, equipped with an infrared sensor, capable of both flexion–extension and supination–pronation movements [31]. (**d**) An elbow exoskeleton actuated by shape memory alloy (SMA) wires, supporting both flexion–extension and supination–pronation [49]. (**e**) The lightweight exosuit with an inertial measurement unit (IMU) sensor, actuated via a Bowden cable for motion assistance [6]. (**f**) "Carry", a pneumatic elbow exoskeleton that uses force sensors to provide assistive support [39].

Table 4. Existing elbow exoskeleton devices.

Name	DoF	Application	Portability	Actuator	Sensor	Ref.
ExoSuit	FE	Assistive	Yes	TSA	Force Sensor, sEMG	[28]
Soft Elbow Exoskeleton	FE	Rehabilitation	Yes	Tendon-Sheath Actuator	sEMG, IMU	[2]
ULIX	FE, SP	Rehabilitation	No	Cable-Driven Actuator (Bowden Cable)	Position Sensor	[3]
Soft Exoskeleton	FE	Rehabilitation	Yes	Cable-Driven Actuator (Bowden Cable)	Force Sensor	[29]
Elbow Exoskeleton	FE	Assistive (Industrial Purposes)	Yes	Series Elastic Actuation	EMG Sensor	[32–34]
Elbow-sideWINDER	FE	Assistive (Industrial Purposes)	Yes	Cable-Driven Actuator (Bowden Cable)	Torque Sensor	[50]
Exoskeleton Arm	SP	Assistive	Yes	Cable-Driven Actuator (Bowden Cable)	Non Specified	[51]
Soft Wearable Exosuit	FE	Assistive	Yes	Cable-Driven Actuator (Bowden Cable)	Force Sensor	[30]
Exosuit	FE	Assistive	Yes	Cable-Driven Actuator (Bowden Cable)	IMU	[6]
NEUROExos	FE, SP	Rehabilitation	No	Electric Motor	Position, Torque Sensor	[52]
Elbow Exoskeleton	FE, SP	Rehabilitation	Yes	SMA	None Specified	[49]
Soft Elbow Exoskeleton	FE, SP	Assistive	No	Motor Tendon Actuator	Infrared Sensor	[31]
Carry	FE	Assistive (Industrial Purposes)	Yes	Pneumatic	Force Sensor	[39]
Soft Robotic Elbow Sleeve	FE	Assistive	Yes	Pneumatic	Force Sensor	[19]
Elbow Exoskeleton	FE	Experimental Purposes	No	TSA	Non Specified	[35]
Elbow Exoskeleton	FE, SP	Rehabilitation	No	VSA	Angle Sensor	[53]
DMLS-VSA Elbow Exoskeleton	FE	Rehabilitation	No	VSA	Force Sensor	[54]

Notes: FE = flexion–extension, SP = supination–pronation.

Introduced in 2020, the ExoSuit by Hosseini et al. [28] is a fully soft, assistive wearable device designed for flexion–extension tasks. It utilizes a TSA, in which an electric motor twists a string to generate linear tension. This compact and lightweight mechanism eliminates the need for bulky gears or pulleys, resulting in a low mechanical impedance system that reduces resistance and enhances user comfort. The ExoSuit is particularly well-suited for daily assistive use due to its modularity and gearless simplicity. It integrates surface electromyography (sEMG) sensors that monitor muscle activity in both the biceps and triceps, enabling adaptive, muscle-effort-sensitive control during both load application and removal. A similar TSA-based design was introduced earlier in 2013 by Popov et al. [35], featuring a rigid two-link structure mimicking human upper and forearm anatomy. This earlier design also benefits from the compactness and efficiency of the TSA, with the actuator connected via a coaxial pulley aligned with the elbow joint. However, its rigid structural materials may limit flexibility and long-term user comfort when compared to the fully soft construction of the ExoSuit.

The soft elbow exoskeleton, developed by Wu et al. [2] in 2023, is a soft-suit system designed for rehabilitation training, particularly targeting flexion–extension movements. It employs compliant tendon-sheath actuators driven by integrated servo motors, with real-time control implemented via a Matlab/xPC platform. The soft structure eliminates issues of joint misalignment, enhancing human–robot coordination and making the device comfortable and suitable for extended use. The system integrates sEMG sensors to monitor muscle activity in the biceps and triceps, along with IMUs to track motion, enabling intention-based adaptive assistance. Fastened with Velcro straps for a secure and wearable fit, this sensor-driven, soft-material design is particularly well-suited for long-term rehabilitation applications.

The Ultralow Impedance Exoskeleton (ULIX) [3], developed by Chen et al. in 2019, is a semi-rigid rehabilitation device designed to assist with elbow flexion–extension and forearm supination–pronation. It features a cable-driven differential transmission paired with series elastic actuators (SEAs), enabling high torque output while keeping the total worn mass under 0.9 kg. By decoupling the actuation hardware from the user via Bowden cable transmissions, the system significantly reduces inertia and enhances user comfort during rehabilitation tasks. The SEAs incorporate nonlinear torsional springs that provide low impedance during free movement and high stiffness under load, allowing for precise and responsive torque control. To further improve control fidelity, ULIX integrates dual encoders in each SEA to measure spring deflection and torque, along with an additional encoder on the forearm ring to compensate for control delays caused by cable slack and stiction. This dual-degree-of-freedom, sensor-rich design makes ULIX particularly well-suited for comprehensive upper-limb rehabilitation.

Several soft exoskeletons such as Soft Exoskeleton by Wei et al. (Figure 3a), Soft Wearable Exosuit by Xiloyannis et al. (Figure 3b), and Lightweight Exosuit by Missiroli et al. (Figure 3e) also utilize Bowden cable transmissions. The designs employ Bowden cable transmissions similar to the ULIX system but differ in their fully wearable and mobile configurations. These devices prioritize flexibility and user mobility by utilizing soft fabric structures, thereby enhancing comfort and wearability. In the 2018 design, designed by Wei et al., the motor is mounted remotely to minimize bulk at the joint, with force transmitted through Bowden cables [29]. Ergonomic considerations are central to the system, with carefully positioned anchor points on the textile interface and Velcro straps ensuring a secure yet comfortable fit. These exoskeletons are typically classified as soft elbow devices and vary in their sensor setups; some use force sensors, while others incorporate IMUs for motion detection enabling different modes of assistive support depending on the application [6,29,30].

Among EMG-responsive systems, the Elbow Exoskeleton (2023) by Emir Mobedi highlights the effectiveness of surface EMG sensors in detecting user intention. This device also focuses on improving ergonomics in industrial tasks involving repetitive and high-effort movements, building on prior work demonstrating the value of EMG-based control. It features a lightweight, cable-driven actuator using a series elastic actuation (SEA) system with a bungee element that mimics the damping and compliance of human muscles. Designed to support a single degree of freedom (elbow flexion/extension), the system incorporates a custom spool mechanism, an encoder for joint position tracking, a load cell for cable tension measurement, and an EMG interface for adaptive force control based on muscle activity [32–34].

The Elbow-sideWINDER, developed by Park et al. [50], is a semi-rigid exoskeleton designed to support elbow flexion–extension during dynamic tasks in industrial environments, particularly those involving confined spaces. It employs a tendon-driven actuation system using Bowden cables, which enables compact force transmission while minimizing inertia and bulk. Control is achieved through a Myo armband that integrates eight sEMG sensors and a three-axis accelerometer. These sensors estimate external loads based on muscle activity and track arm kinematics, respectively, feeding into a medium-level controller that dynamically adjusts assistive torque in real time. This streamlined, sensor-driven approach allows for effective load compensation with minimal hardware complexity, making the Elbow-sideWINDER well-suited for practical, real-world ergonomic applications [50].

The Exoskeleton Arm, developed by Dezman et al. in 2023, is a rigid, modular device designed specifically to support forearm supination–pronation in rehabilitation contexts. It employs Bowden cable actuation and introduces a novel guided-rod mechanism in place of traditional C-ring bearings, enabling efficient rotational movement while reducing overall volume and weight. This design allows the system to be used independently or as a supplementary module alongside flexion–extension exoskeletons. While Bowden cable slack and stretch remain technical challenges, the device's modularity makes it particularly well-suited for targeted rehabilitation where supination–pronation recovery is essential [51].

The NEUROExos, developed by Vitiello et al., is a rigid elbow exoskeleton designed for neurological rehabilitation, particularly post-stroke recovery, offering one degree of freedom focused on elbow flexion and extension. It employs a custom-designed smart series elastic actuator (SEA) that enables compliant and precise force control, critical for safe physical human–robot interaction. The SEA design facilitates impedance and admittance control strategies, allowing the device to adapt to patient-specific needs during therapy. The system integrates various sensors, including torque sensors within the actuator, position sensors (encoders), and force sensors, which together enable accurate joint torque measurement, motion tracking, and real-time monitoring of user–robot interaction forces. These features support adaptive therapy modes and ensure both safety and effectiveness in upper-limb rehabilitation [52].

Upper limb rehabilitation exoskeletons designed by Copaco et al. (Figure 3d) use special SMA actuators that are light (less than 1 kg) and quiet, making them comfortable to wear. These actuators work in pairs to control the elbow's bending (flexion–extension) and rotation (supination–pronation), which means the exoskeleton can move in multiple ways like a natural arm. The design is simple and adjustable, so patients can easily put it on, and it is made with low-cost parts including 3D-printed pieces. The device can either help move the arm (active mode) or just record movement data while the patient moves on their own (passive mode). Sensors inside the exoskeleton track the arm's position accurately, helping the actuators work smoothly. This combination of sensors, actuators, and multiple movement options makes the exoskeleton a useful and affordable tool for arm rehabilitation [49].

A range of innovative elbow exoskeletons has emerged in recent years, exploring both motor-tendon and pneumatic actuation methods for assistive and rehabilitation purposes. The Soft Elbow Exoskeleton (Figure 3c) features a dual-degree-of-freedom motor-tendon actuator system combined with infrared sensors [31]. In the pneumatic category, designs like the Robotic Elbow Sleeve [19] and the Carry exoskeleton (Figure 3f) provide high compliance and safe force delivery through air-powered actuators enclosed in textile sleeves. Specifically, the Carry system is designed for industrial and assistive tasks such as load holding and carrying, delivering up to 11 Nm of torque at 3.65 bar. Pressure sensors operating at 100 Hz enable responsive torque control, while the system demonstrates reductions in EMG activity, metabolic cost, and user fatigue. However, all pneumatic systems face limitations in portability and dynamic responsiveness due to reliance on external compressors, actuator filling/release cycles, and pressure constraints [39].

Recently, VSAs have become increasingly popular in the design of elbow exoskeletons, aiming to enhance rehabilitation by adapting to the complex and variable biomechanics of the human elbow. Two notable designs exemplify this trend: Yang et al. [53] developed a cable-driven elbow exoskeleton featuring a symmetric dual-motor VSA combined with a deviation compensation unit to accommodate the changing elbow stiffness and the shifting rotation axis during movement. Their system enables real-time stiffness adjustment and accurate alignment with the anatomical joint, improving comfort and safety in therapy. Meanwhile, Zhang et al. [54] introduced a novel dual-motor load-sharing VSA (DMLS-VSA) employing a planetary gear-based variable stiffness mechanism that allows both motors to simultaneously contribute to power output. This design achieves a broader and more precise stiffness range with faster response times through an innovative cascade PI control scheme, enhancing compliance and adaptability during human–robot interaction. Together, these advances reflect a shift toward more sophisticated, responsive, and anatomically aware VSA implementations in elbow exoskeletons, striving to improve rehabilitation effectiveness and patient safety.

While Table 4 focuses solely on elbow exoskeletons, there are also upper-limb exoskeletons designed to accommodate a wider range of degrees of freedom (DOFs), including shoulder and hand movements. In 2020, Yongtae et al. [36] developed an upper-limb exosuit intended for both industrial and rehabilitation applications. This exosuit is equipped with EMG sensors, a cable-driven actuation system using Bowden cables, and a voice recognition interface.

In 2021, Gull et al. introduced a four-DOF upper-limb exoskeleton designed to assist individuals with disabilities. This system aimed to provide effective motion support across multiple joints [55]. In 2022, Paterna et al. proposed a passive upper-limb exoskeleton utilizing pneumatic artificial muscles, specifically targeting industrial use cases to reduce physical strain during repetitive tasks [37].

Various actuation mechanisms have also been explored in recent designs. The Harmony exoskeleton, for instance, employs series elastic actuators (SEAs) and offers seven DOFs—comprising five active DOFs for the shoulder, one for the elbow, and one for the wrist—providing comprehensive upper-limb assistance [56]. In the same year, Park et al. developed a soft exosuit that uses shape memory alloys (SMAs) as actuators, offering a lightweight and compliant solution for upper-limb support [4].

In 2018, Liu et al. [44] presented a portable variable-stiffness elbow exoskeleton (PVSED) for home-based post-stroke rehabilitation. The device features six degrees of freedom (DOFs): three passive DOFs for human motion, two for adjustable frame length, and one active DOF at the elbow actuated by a motor with an integrated VSA. The VSA adjusts stiffness by shifting a pivot point, enabling customizable assistance based on impairment level. For precise closed-loop control, the system uses a GY-25 angle sensor (0.01° resolution), a six-axis force sensor (0.04 N resolution), and an MTx inertial sensor (0.05° resolution) to monitor joint movement and interaction force. Experiments showed that increasing joint stiffness reduced angular error, supporting effective assist-as-needed rehabilitation.

Two additional full upper-limb exoskeleton systems worth noting are ETS-MARSE and the EXOTIC Exoskeleton. ETS-MARSE is a seven-DOF exoskeleton designed for rehabilitation purposes, assisting movement across the shoulder, elbow, forearm, and wrist joints [21]. In contrast, the EXOTIC Exoskeleton provides five DOFs and features adjustable link lengths. Thøgersen et al. emphasized user safety in the EXOTIC design by incorporating mechanical stoppers, current limiters, an open-brace configuration, and a control system that only actuates upon user command. Additionally, the device is lightweight and includes a unique tongue-control interface for enhanced accessibility [17].

Elbow exoskeletons vary widely in their mechanical and control strategies. Soft, cable-driven systems dominate wearable, home friendly solutions, while rigid or pneumatic systems serve more specialized or clinical needs. Each system contributes uniquely to the evolving landscape of upper limb rehabilitation technologies.

9. Design, Engineering, and Adoption Challenges of Elbow Exoskeleton

Designing an elbow exoskeleton presents a unique blend of technical and practical challenges. While engineers must address complex biomechanical and mechanical constraints to create a device that is functional, comfortable, and safe, equally significant hurdles arise when it comes to real-world adoption. Factors such as user acceptance, cost, regulatory approvals, and workplace integration all influence whether these innovative devices can transition from prototypes to everyday tools. This section explores both the design and engineering obstacles and the adoption challenges of elbow exoskeletons.

9.1. Design and Engineering Challenges

The development of elbow exoskeletons involves not only the optimization of mechanical performance and control [55] but also a comprehensive consideration of human factors, usability, and practical deployment. The challenges are multifaceted, spanning actuator mechanics, signal processing, and user-centered design elements such as comfort, adjustability, and appearance.

This section integrates challenges identified across the literature with analysis from current exoskeleton technologies (see Section 8).

9.1.1. Actuator and Responsiveness

A critical engineering challenge lies in designing actuators that deliver sufficient torque for elbow flexion and extension while maintaining a compact, lightweight form factor. Pneumatic actuators, as demonstrated in the soft robotic elbow sleeve by Koh et al. [19], offer safe and compliant motion but require external air compressors, increasing overall system weight and reducing portability. Cable-driven systems, like those used in Elbow-sideWINDER [50] and ULIX [3], address portability by offloading motor mass to remote locations but introduce frictional losses and control complexity. TSA-based systems like ExoSuit [28] offer a compact and cost-effective solution, though they face nonlinear behavior and string fatigue over time [35,57].

9.1.2. Comfort and Wearability

For exoskeletons intended for prolonged use, especially in rehabilitation, comfort is paramount. Rigid or bulky components can cause discomfort, fatigue, or even misalignment with human joints. Designs must minimize contact pressure, use breathable and soft materials, and consider weight distribution. Soft wearable systems such as those by Wu and Chen [2] and Xiloyannis et al. [30] show promise.

9.1.3. Weight and Device Placement

Weight distribution affects both usability and safety. Devices must avoid placing excessive weight on the forearm or shoulder. Poor placement can lead to strain, reduced range of motion, or unnatural joint alignment. In soft robotic designs, there is a push toward decentralizing components (e.g., compressors, batteries) to the waist or back, as seen in TSA- and Bowden-based systems [2,28,50]. This improves ergonomics but might introduce cabling and connection management issues.

9.1.4. Safety and User Protection

Safety is a non-negotiable aspect, especially in rehabilitation. Devices must prevent hyperextension, respond appropriately to involuntary user motion, and fail gracefully in case of malfunction. Similarly, in the Elbow Exoskeleton designed by Ismail et al. [31] and Upper Limb Exoskeleton designed by Thorgesen et al. [17], user safety is a primary consideration during both wear and operation.

9.1.5. Sensor Accuracy and Stability

Effective control systems require stable and accurate sensor inputs. sEMG signals, while promising for intent detection, suffer from signal variability, placement sensitivity, and susceptibility to noise. This challenge requires robust filtering, threshold calibration, and session-specific tuning. Alternatives like joint torque sensors (e.g., in Elbow-sideWINDER [50]) and IMUs (e.g., [2,6]) provide consistent motion data but introduce complexity in mechanical integration and signal drift mitigation.

9.1.6. Cost and Accessibility

Many current exoskeleton prototypes are expensive to produce, limiting accessibility outside research or hospital settings. High costs stem from custom components, high precision actuators, and integrated electronics. Future engineering must focus on low-cost materials, modular assembly, and open-source electronics to enable community rehabilitation and assistive use at scale. Lightweight fabrication techniques like 3D printing and textile-based integration offer promising avenues [28,49].

9.1.7. Adjustability and Fit

One size does not fit all. The customizability of joint alignment, strap tension, and arm dimensions is crucial, especially for systems targeting diverse populations such as elderly individuals or stroke patients. Many designs still lack simple, tool-free adjustment mechanisms. Modular architectures or self-aligning joints, like those proposed in NEUROExos [52], provide a solution, albeit at the cost of added complexity.

9.1.8. Ease of Use and Setup

The devices should be easy to don and doff independently. Primarily to avoid time-consuming setup, especially requiring a therapist's assistance (rehabilitation application), future systems must aim for plug-and-play usability, minimal calibration, and, ideally, self-guided instructions. Systems like [2] show progress in this area with user-friendly interfaces.

9.1.9. Design Appearance

Appearance may seem secondary but plays a significant role in user adherence, especially for wearables used outside clinical settings. Devices that resemble medical or industrial equipment may deter consistent use due to social stigma or aesthetic discomfort. Incorporating slim profiles, textile coverings, or clothing-like integration (as in soft systems [2,6,30]) may improve adoption and comfort, especially in social or work environments.

9.2. Adoption and Real-World Implementation Challenges

Despite the growing body of research on exoskeletons, their adoption in real-world settings remains limited due to a combination of scientific, technical, behavioral, economic, and institutional barriers.

9.2.1. Limited Long-Term Evidence and Field Validation

One of the primary issues is the lack of long-term field studies that demonstrate the sustained effectiveness and safety of exoskeletons in everyday work environments. While laboratory-based research has shown promising results particularly in reducing work-related musculoskeletal disorders (WMSDs), these findings often do not translate easily into complex, real-world contexts. Organizations are hesitant to adopt exoskeletons without robust longitudinal data that confirm their benefits over time and across varied use cases [58,59].

9.2.2. User Acceptability and Behavioral Resistance

User acceptability is another significant barrier. In both rehabilitation and occupational settings, there is concern that exoskeletons may reduce the user's sense of agency, relegating them to a more passive role. This resistance can be psychological as much as physical, particularly when the technology is perceived as uncomfortable, intrusive, or incompatible with the natural movements of the human body [59,60].

9.2.3. Lack of Stakeholder Integration

Institutionally, the adoption process is often fragmented. Key stakeholders including workers, health and safety personnel, human resources, unions, and policymakers are not always adequately involved in the selection, evaluation, or implementation phases. This disconnect leads to a lack of shared understanding and commitment, which is critical for successful integration [59].

9.2.4. Economic and Organizational Factors

Economic and organizational barriers such as high initial costs, unclear return on investment, and limited reimbursement models contribute to hesitancy, particularly in sectors like healthcare and public services where procurement processes are complex and budget-driven. Compounding these challenges is a lack of policy guidance and public awareness about the broader societal applications of exoskeletons beyond industrial use. While robotics have become more common in manufacturing, surgery, and logistics, their social and rehabilitative applications are still emerging, often without sufficient support from government policies or institutional strategies. This reflects a broader issue where research and technological development are not yet fully aligned with practical implementation needs [60,61].

To enable wider adoption, research must expand beyond technical performance to include user experience, workplace dynamics, policy design, and long-term impact assessments ensuring that the integration of exoskeletons is not only technologically sound but also socially and economically sustainable.

10. Future Direction and Trends

As elbow exoskeleton technology advances, new frontiers are emerging that aim to enhance user comfort, functionality, and accessibility across both clinical and daily life settings. Driven by interdisciplinary innovation across robotics, materials science, and neuroscience, the future of elbow exoskeletons will likely be defined by smart adaptability, seamless human–robot interaction, and integration into everyday rehabilitation and assistive routines.

10.1. *Toward Fully Wearable and Portable System*

One of the clearest trends is the miniaturization and portability of components. Future exoskeletons will increasingly abandon stationary or bulky support systems, such as external air compressors used in pneumatic actuators, in favor of self-contained, battery-powered units. Innovations like lightweight fabric-based actuators or twisted string systems have the potential to replace traditional rigid motors and bulky pneumatics while maintaining comparable torque outputs. Similar to several exoskeleton devices that have been developed, such as the soft actuated glove [62] and the MGlove-TS [63], which are exoskeletons for the hand and wrist, TSA has demonstrated good and promising performance, particularly in the field of rehabilitation. The use of TSA in these devices creates a more flexible and lightweight environment compared to other types of actuators [64,65].

10.2. *Smart and Adaptive*

A shift toward intention aware exoskeletons is evident in recent work, such as the soft elbow exoskeleton that uses sEMG-based control to interpret muscle signals for active assistance alongside IMU data [2]. Future systems are expected to leverage machine learning algorithms to classify and adapt to individual movement patterns, fatigue levels, and rehabilitation goals over time. Furthermore, the integration of multimodal sensing such as pressure sensors, torque sensors, and various biosignals will enable context-aware behavior, allowing the exoskeleton to dynamically adjust support levels in real time. This closed-loop, adaptive control approach promises to enhance user comfort and safety while minimizing the need for manual recalibration.

Although these sensors have not yet been implemented in the elbow exoskeletons discussed in this paper (Section 8), recent advances in soft skin sensor technologies present exciting opportunities for future integration. A notable example is the three-axis Hall effect-based sensor developed by Tomo et al. [66], which features a silicone-encased array capable of detecting pressure and shear forces in three dimensions. With its soft, conformal construction, multi-axis sensitivity, and built-in temperature compensation, this sensor is particularly well-suited for providing accurate and comfortable real-time force feedback critical for safe and responsive exoskeleton control.

Additionally, skin-interfaced wearable sensor systems such as those reviewed by Ray et al. [67] offer stretchable and conformal platforms capable of monitoring joint motion, strain, and physiological signals during physical activity. These systems are currently used in fields like sports science and performance monitoring, where continuous real-time feedback is essential. Their potential integration into elbow exoskeleton cuffs could enable seamless biomechanical and physiological data acquisition without compromising comfort or mobility. Recent developments have also introduced soft, stretchable sensors that support in situ sweat analysis and biochemical monitoring, further expanding the possibilities for holistic, real-time feedback. If applied to future exoskeleton designs, these technologies could significantly improve personalization, adaptiveness, and health awareness in wearable assistive devices.

10.3. Cost-Effective Manufacturing

Despite the promising clinical results, most elbow exoskeletons are limited to research labs or specialized clinics due to high costs and limited scalability. A future trend will be focused on low-cost, modular designs using 3D printing, open-source control electronics, and readily available materials. Modular exoskeleton kits that can be custom fitted or 3D printed on demand could democratize access, particularly in underserved or remote healthcare settings. The use of low-cost actuators is also a viable solution; in this regard, TSA offer a more cost-effective alternative compared to other actuator types [63].

11. Discussion and Conclusions

Elbow exoskeletons have emerged as essential tools in modern rehabilitation and assistive technologies. Their ability to support, augment, or restore arm movement makes them valuable across diverse applications from clinical recovery programs and daily assistive use to industrial support tasks. This review has highlighted the broad spectrum of mechanical structures, actuation systems, sensor integrations, and control strategies that define the current landscape of elbow exoskeleton development.

A prominent trend in recent years is the growing interest in cable-driven actuation mechanisms, particularly Bowden cables and TSA. While Bowden cable systems are widely adopted for their flexibility and remote actuation capabilities, TSA remains relatively underutilized in elbow exoskeletons despite its promising attributes. TSA systems offer a compact, lightweight, and low-impedance alternative that enhances user comfort and could become more prevalent as research into soft, adaptive devices advances.

Another notable observation is that most elbow exoskeletons currently focus exclusively on flexion–extension movement. This is likely due to the mechanical complexity involved in incorporating both flexion–extension and supination–pronation within a single device. Designing systems that accommodate these combined degrees of freedom remains a significant engineering challenge, often requiring trade-offs in size, weight, and usability.

A recurring theme across the reviewed systems is the trade-off between precision and usability. Rigid exoskeletons often achieve superior control accuracy and torque delivery but may compromise comfort, mobility, and long-term wearability. In contrast, soft-material and cable-driven designs enhance ergonomics and user experience but sometimes fall short in delivering the responsiveness or force required for intensive rehabilitation scenarios. Balancing functional performance with human-centered design remains a critical focus for future innovations.

Despite notable progress, technical challenges persist. These include improving the accuracy of user intention detection (particularly via EMG), ensuring reliable power autonomy for untethered use, enhancing the stability of sensor readings, and optimizing actuator efficiency. Furthermore, the variability among users such as anatomical differences, varying degrees of impairment, and personalized therapy needs calls for adaptable, modular solutions that can be fine-tuned to individual users. The integration of machine learning and intelligent control systems offers promising pathways to address these complexities.

In conclusion, elbow exoskeletons are transitioning rapidly from experimental prototypes to practical, user-centric solutions. The convergence of soft robotics, advanced sensing technologies, and personalized control algorithms is driving the field toward more accessible and effective systems. By embracing interdisciplinary collaboration, focusing on affordability, and maintaining a strong commitment to user-centered design, future elbow exoskeletons can achieve seamless human–machine integration. These advancements hold the potential to restore independence, improve rehabilitation outcomes, and significantly enhance the quality of life for individuals with upper limb impairments around the world.

Author Contributions: Conceptualization, C.S.A.S. and M.D.; methodology, C.S.A.S.; formal analysis, C.S.A.S., M.D. and M.M.; investigation, C.S.A.S., M.D. and M.M.; writing—original draft preparation, C.S.A.S., M.D. and M.M.; writing—review and editing, M.M.; visualization, C.S.A.S., M.D. and M.M.; supervision, M.M. All authors have read and agreed to the published version of the manuscript.

Funding: This work was supported by the European Union by the Next Generation EU project ECS17 THE—Tuscany Health Ecosystem (PNRR MUR M4 C2 Inv. 1.5, CUP B63C22000680007, Spoke 9: Robotics and Automation for Health).

Institutional Review Board Statement: Not applicable.

Informed Consent Statement: Not applicable.

Data Availability Statement: The data presented in this study are available on request from the corresponding author.

Conflicts of Interest: The authors declare no conflicts of interest.

Abbreviations

The following abbreviations are used in this manuscript:

EMG	Electromyography
IMU	Inertial Measurement Unit
DOF	Degree of Freedom
UCL	Ulnar Collateral Ligament
RCL	Radial Collateral Ligament
WHO	World Health Organization
PLA	Polylactide
TSA	Twisted String Actuator
SMA	Shape memory alloy
sEMG	Surface Electromyography
SEA	Series elastic actuator
VSA	Variable Stiffness Actuator

References

1. Pehlivan, A.U.; Sergi, F.; Erwin, A.; Yozbatiran, N.; Francisco, G.E.; O'Malley, M.K. Design and Validation of the RiceWrist-S Exoskeleton for Robotic Rehabilitation after Incomplete Spinal Cord Injury. *Robotica* **2014**, *32*, 1415–1431. [CrossRef]
2. Wu, Q.; Chen, Y. Adaptive cooperative control of a soft elbow rehabilitation exoskeleton based on improved joint torque estimation. *Mech. Syst. Signal Process.* **2023**, *184*, 109748. [CrossRef]
3. Chen, T.; Casas, R.; Lum, P.S. An Elbow Exoskeleton for Upper Limb Rehabilitation with Series Elastic Actuator and Cable-Driven Differential. *IEEE Trans. Robot.* **2019**, *35*, 1464–1474. [CrossRef]
4. Park, S.J.; Park, C.H. Suit-type Wearable Robot Powered by Shape-memory-alloy-based Fabric Muscle. *Sci. Rep.* **2019**, *9*, 9157. [CrossRef]
5. Sambhav, R.; Jena, S.; Chatterjee, A.; Bhasin, S.; Santapuri, S.; Kumar, L.; Muthukrishnan, S.P.; Roy, S. An Integrated Dynamic Closed Loop Simulation Platform for Elbow Flexion Augmentation Using an Upper Limb Exosuit Model. *Front. Robot. AI* **2022**, *9*, 768841. [CrossRef]
6. Missiroli, F.; Lotti, N.; Xiloyannis, M.; Sloot, L.H.; Riener, R.; Masia, L. Relationship Between Muscular Activity and Assistance Magnitude for a Myoelectric Model Based Controlled Exosuit. *Front. Robot. AI* **2020**, *7*, 595844. [CrossRef]
7. Tiboni, M.; Borboni, A.; Vérité, F.; Bregoli, C.; Amici, C. Sensors and actuation technologies in exoskeletons: A review. *Sensors* **2022**, *22*, 884. [CrossRef] [PubMed]
8. Gull, M.A.; Bai, S.; Bak, T. A Review on Design of Upper Limb Exoskeletons. *Robotics* **2020**, *9*, 16. [CrossRef]
9. Kincaid, B.L.; An, K.N. Elbow joint biomechanics for preclinical evaluation of total elbow prostheses. *J. Biomech.* **2013**, *46*, 2331–2341. [CrossRef]
10. Perrelli, M.; Lago, F.; Garofalo, S.; Bruno, L.; Mundo, D.; Carbone, G. A critical review and systematic design approach for innovative upper-limb rehabilitation devices. *Robot. Auton. Syst.* **2025**, *183*, 104835. [CrossRef]
11. Javed, O.; Maldonado, K.A.; Ashmyan, R. Anatomy, Shoulder and Upper Limb, Muscles. 2020. Available online: https://www.ncbi.nlm.nih.gov/books/NBK482410/ (accessed on 18 May 2015).

12. Olsen, B.S.; Michael, T.V.; Søjbjerg, J.O.; Helmig, P.; Sneppen, O. Lateral collateral ligament of the elbow joint: Anatomy and kinematics. *J. Shoulder Elb. Surg.* **1996**, *5*, 103–112. [CrossRef]
13. Dragusanu, M.; Guinet, N.; Suthar, B.; Baldi, T.L.; Prattichizzo, D.; Malvezzi, M. A 3 Degrees-of-Freedom Lightweight Flexible Twisted String Actuators (TSAs)-Based Exoskeleton for Wrist Rehabilitation. *IEEE Robot. Autom. Lett.* **2025**, *10*, 6520–6527. [CrossRef]
14. Eastman, J.; White, H.; Evans, J.; Augsburger, S.; Wallace, J.; Riley, S.; Iwinski, H. What is the minimum torque required to obtain passive elbow end range of motion? *Gait Posture* **2022**, *93*, 235–239. [CrossRef]
15. Anam, K.; Al-Jumaily, A.A. Active Exoskeleton Control Systems: State of the Art. *Procedia Eng.* **2012**, *41*, 988–994. [CrossRef]
16. Bardi, E.; Gandolla, M.; Braghin, F.; Resta, F.; Pedrocchi, A.L.G.; Ambrosini, E. Upper limb soft robotic wearable devices: A systematic review. *J. Neuroeng. Rehabil.* **2022**, *19*, 87. [CrossRef] [PubMed]
17. Thøgersen, M.B.; Mohammadi, M.; Gull, M.A.; Bengtson, S.H.; Kobbelgaard, F.V.; Bentsen, B.; Khan, B.Y.; Severinsen, K.E.; Bai, S.; Bak, T.; et al. User Based Development and Test of the EXOTIC Exoskeleton: Empowering Individuals with Tetraplegia Using a Compact, Versatile, 5-DoF Upper Limb Exoskeleton Controlled through Intelligent Semi-Automated Shared Tongue Control. *Sensors* **2022**, *22*, 6919. [CrossRef]
18. Guatibonza, A.; Solaque, L.; Velasco, A.; Peñuela, L. Assistive Robotics for Upper Limb Physical Rehabilitation: A Systematic Review and Future Prospects. *Chin. J. Mech. Eng.* **2024**, *37*, 69. [CrossRef]
19. Koh, T.H.; Cheng, N.; Yap, H.K.; Yeow, C.H. Design of a Soft Robotic Elbow Sleeve with Passive and Intent-Controlled Actuation. *Front. Neurosci.* **2017**, *11*, 597. [CrossRef]
20. Waheed, Z.A.; Humaidi, A.J.; Sadiq, M.E.; Al-Qassar, A.A.; Hasan, A.F.; Al-Dujaili, A.Q.; Ajel, A.R.; Abbas, S.J. Control of Elbow Rehabilitation System Based on Optimal-Tuned Backstepping Sliding Mode Controller. *J. Eng. Sci. Technol.* **2023**, *18*, 584–603.
21. Rahman, M.H.; Rahman, M.J.; Cristobal, O.L.; Saad, M.; Kenné, J.P.; Archambault, P.S. Development of a whole arm wearable robotic exoskeleton for rehabilitation and to assist upper limb movements. *Robotica* **2015**, *33*, 19–39. [CrossRef]
22. Butler, T.; Gillette, J.C. Exoskeletons Used as a PPE for Injury Prevention. *Prof. Saf.* **2019**, *64*, 32–37 .
23. Nnaji, C.; Okpala, I.; Gambatese, J.; Jin, Z. Controlling safety and health challenges intrinsic in exoskeleton use in construction. *Saf. Sci.* **2023**, *157*, 105943. [CrossRef]
24. Butler, T.; Wisner, D. Exoskeleton Technology: Making Workers Safer and More Productive, Vol. All Days, Professional Development Conference and Exposition. 2017. Available online: https://onepetro.org/ASSPPDCE/proceedings-pdf/ASSE17/All-ASSE17/ASSE-17-579/1233834/asse-17-579.pdf (accessed on 1 March 2025).
25. Proud, J.K.; Lai, D.T.H.; Mudie, K.L.; Carstairs, G.L.; Billing, D.C.; Garofolini, A.; Begg, R.K. Exoskeleton Application to Military Manual Handling Tasks. *Hum. Factors* **2022**, *64*, 527–554. [CrossRef] [PubMed]
26. Taal, S.R.; Sankai, Y. Practical Design of Full Body Exoskeletons - Stretching the Limits of Weight and Power. In Proceedings of the Third International Conference on Biomedical Electronics and Devices, Barcelona, Spain, 11–14 February 2010; SciTePress—Science and Technology Publications: Setúbal, Portugal , 2010; pp. 133–138. [CrossRef]
27. Achilli, G.M.; Amici, C.; Dragusanu, M.; Gobbo, M.; Logozzo, S.; Malvezzi, M.; Tiboni, M.; Valigi, M.C. Soft, Rigid, and Hybrid Robotic Exoskeletons for Hand Rehabilitation: Roadmap with Impairment-Oriented Rationale for Devices Design and Selection. *Appl. Sci.* **2023**, *13*, 11287. [CrossRef]
28. Hosseini, M.; Meattini, R.; San-Millan, A.; Palli, G.; Melchiorri, C.; Paik, J. A sEMG-Driven Soft ExoSuit Based on Twisted String Actuators for Elbow Assistive Applications. *IEEE Robot. Autom. Lett.* **2020**, *5*, 4094–4101. [CrossRef]
29. Wei, W.; Qu, Z.; Wang, W.; Zhang, P.; Hao, F. Design on the Bowden Cable-Driven Upper Limb Soft Exoskeleton. *Appl. Bionics Biomech.* **2018**, *2018*, 1925694 . [CrossRef]
30. Xiloyannis, M.; Annese, E.; Canesi, M.; Kodiyan, A.; Bicchi, A.; Micera, S.; Ajoudani, A.; Masia, L. Design and Validation of a Modular One-To-Many Actuator for a Soft Wearable Exosuit. *Front. Neurorobot.* **2019**, *13*, 39. [CrossRef]
31. Ismail, R.; Ariyanto, M.; Perkasa, I.A.; Adirianto, R.; Putri, F.T.; Glowacz, A.; Caesarendra, W. Soft Elbow Exoskeleton for Upper Limb Assistance Incorporating Dual Motor-Tendon Actuator. *Electronics* **2019**, *8*, 1184. [CrossRef]
32. Mobedi, E.; Kim, W.; Momi, E.D.; Tsagarakis, N.G.; Ajoudani, A. A Soft Assistive Device for Elbow Effort-Compensation. In Proceedings of the 2021 IEEE/RSJ International Conference on Intelligent Robots and Systems (IROS), Prague, Czech Republic, 27 September–1 October 2021; pp. 9540–9547. [CrossRef]
33. Mobedi, E.; Kim, W.; Leonori, M.; Tsagarakis, N.G.; Ajoudani, A. Design and Control of an Assistive Device for Elbow Effort-Compensation. *IEEE/ASME Trans. Mechatronics* **2023**, *28*, 3446–3457. [CrossRef]
34. Mobedi, E.; Hjorth, S.; Kim, W.; De Momi, E.; Tsagarakis, N.G.; Ajoudani, A. A Power-Aware Control Strategy for an Elbow Effort-Compensation Device. *IEEE Robot. Autom. Lett.* **2023**, *8*, 4330–4337. [CrossRef]
35. Popov, D.; Gaponov, I.; Ryu, J. A preliminary study on a twisted strings-based elbow exoskeleton. In Proceedings of the IEEE World Haptics Conference Proceedings, Daejeon, Republic of Korea, 14–17 April 2013; pp. 473–484. [CrossRef]
36. Kim, Y.G.; Little, K.; Noronha, B.; Xiloyannis, M.; Masia, L.; Accoto, D. A voice activated bi-articular exosuit for upper limb assistance during lifting tasks. *Robot. Comput.-Integr. Manuf.* **2020**, *66*, 101995. [CrossRef]

37. Paterna, M.; Gisolo, S.M.; Benedictis, C.D.; Muscolo, G.G.; Ferraresi, C. A passive upper-limb exoskeleton for industrial application based on pneumatic artificial muscles. *Mech. Sci.* **2022**, *13*, 387–398. [CrossRef]
38. Huysamen, K.; Bosch, T.; de Looze, M.; Stadler, K.S.; Graf, E.; O'Sullivan, L.W. Evaluation of a passive exoskeleton for static upper limb activities. *Appl. Ergon.* **2018**, *70*, 148–155. [PubMed]
39. Nassour, J.; Zhao, G.; Grimmer, M. Soft pneumatic elbow exoskeleton reduces the muscle activity, metabolic cost and fatigue during holding and carrying of loads. *Sci. Rep.* **2021**, *11*, 12556. [CrossRef]
40. Lee, D.; Song, B.; Park, S.Y.; Baek, Y.S. Development and Control of an Electro-Hydraulic Actuator System for an Exoskeleton Robot. *Appl. Sci.* **2019**, *9*, 4295. [CrossRef]
41. Palli, G.; Hosseini, M.; Melchiorri, C. Experimental Evaluation of Guided Twisted Actuation. *IFAC-PapersOnLine* **2016**, *49*, 380–385. [CrossRef]
42. Kapsalyamov, A.; Hussain, S.; Jamwal, P.K. State of the Art Assistive Powered Upper Limb Exoskeletons for Elderly. *IEEE Access* **2017**, *8*, 178991–179001. [CrossRef]
43. Park, S.J.; Choi, K.; Rodrigue, H.; Park, C.H. Fabric muscle with a cooling acceleration structure for upper limb assistance soft exosuits. *Sci. Rep.* **2022**, *12*, 11398. [CrossRef]
44. Liu, Y.; Guo, S.; Hirata, H.; Ishihara, H.; Tamiya, T. Development of a powered variable-stiffness exoskeleton device for elbow rehabilitation. *Biomed. Microdevices* **2018**, *20*, 64. [CrossRef]
45. Cestari, M.; Sanz-Merodio, D.; Arevalo, J.C.; Garcia, E. An Adjustable Compliant Joint for Lower-Limb Exoskeletons. *IEEE/ASME Trans. Mechatronics* **2015**, *20*, 889–898. [CrossRef]
46. Liu, L.; Hong, Z.; Penzlin, B.; Misgeld, B.J.E.; Ngo, C.; Bergmann, L.; Leonhardt, S. Low Impedance-Guaranteed Gain-Scheduled GESO for Torque-Controlled VSA with Application of Exoskeleton-Assisted Sit-to-Stand. *IEEE/ASME Trans. Mechatronics* **2021**, *26*, 2080–2091. [CrossRef]
47. Kim, J.H.; Shim, M.; Ahn, D.H.; Son, B.J.; Kim, S.Y.; Kim, D.Y.; Baek, Y.S.; Cho, B.K. Design of a Knee Exoskeleton Using Foot Pressure and Knee Torque Sensors. *Int. J. Adv. Robot. Syst.* **2015**, *12*, 112. [CrossRef]
48. Neťuková, S.; Bejtic, M.; Malá, C.; Horáková, L.; Kutílek, P.; Kauler, J.; Krupička, R. Lower Limb Exoskeleton Sensors: State-of-the-Art. *Sensors* **2022**, *22*, 9091. [CrossRef]
49. Copaci, D.; Martin, F.; Moreno, L.; Blanco, D. SMA Based Elbow Exoskeleton for Rehabilitation Therapy and Patient Evaluation. *IEEE Access* **2019**, *7*, 31473–31484. [CrossRef]
50. Park, D.; Natali, C.D.; Sposito, M.; Caldwell, D.G.; Ortiz, J. Elbow-sideWINDER (Elbow-side Wearable INDustrial Ergonomic Robot): design, control, and validation of a novel elbow exoskeleton. *Front. Neurorobot.* **2023**, *17*, 1168213. [CrossRef]
51. Dežman, M.; Asfour, T.; Ude, A.; Gams, A. Exoskeleton Arm Pronation/Supination Assistance Mechanism With A Guided Double Rod System. In Proceedings of the 2019 IEEE-RAS 19th International Conference on Humanoid Robots (Humanoids), Toronto, ON, Canada, 15–17 October 2019; pp. 559–564. [CrossRef]
52. Vitiello, N.; Lenzi, T.; Roccella, S.; De Rossi, S.M.; Cattin, E.; Giovacchini, F.; Vecchi, F.; Carrozza, M.C. NEUROExos: A Powered Elbow Exoskeleton for Physical Rehabilitation. *IEEE Trans. Robot.* **2013**, *29*, 220–235. [CrossRef]
53. Yang, L.; Zhang, F.; Fu, Y. A cable-driven elbow exoskeleton with variable stiffness actuator for upper limb rehabilitation. *Robotica* **2025**, *43*, 662–679. [CrossRef]
54. Zhang, M.; Li, H.; Shi, K.; Song, A. Design, Modeling, and Control of a Variable Stiffness Actuator with Dual-Motor Load Sharing for Elbow Exoskeletons. *IEEE/ASME Trans. Mechatronics* **2025**, 1–11 . [CrossRef]
55. Gull, M.A.; Thoegersen, M.; Bengtson, S.H.; Mohammadi, M.; Andreasen Struijk, L.N.; Moeslund, T.B.; Bak, T.; Bai, S. A 4-DOF Upper Limb Exoskeleton for Physical Assistance: Design, Modeling, Control and Performance Evaluation. *Appl. Sci.* **2021**, *11*, 5865. [CrossRef]
56. Kim, B.; Deshpande, A.D. An upper-body rehabilitation exoskeleton Harmony with an anatomical shoulder mechanism: Design, modeling, control, and performance evaluation. *Int. J. Robot. Res.* **2017**, *36*, 414–435. [CrossRef]
57. Popov, D.; Gaponov, I.; Ryu, J. Bidirectional Elbow Exoskeleton Based on Twisted-String Actuators. In Proceedings of the IEEE/RSJ International Conference on Intelligent Robots and Systems (IROS) Proceedings, Tokyo, Japan, 3–7 November 2013; pp. 5853–5858. [CrossRef]
58. Botti, L.; Bacchetta, A.; Oliva, M.; Melloni, R. Exoskeletons at Work: Opportunities, Suggestions for Implementation and Future Research Needs. In *Human Aspects of Advanced Manufacturing, Proceedings of the AHFE International Conference*; Karwowski, W., Trzcielinski, S., Eds.; AHFE Open Access: Orlando, FL, USA, 2023; Volume 80. [CrossRef]
59. Crea, S.; Beckerle, P.; De Looze, M.; De Pauw, K.; Grazi, L.; Kermavnar, T.; Masood, J.; O'Sullivan, L.W.; Pacifico, I.; Rodriguez-Guerrero, C.; et al. Occupational exoskeletons: A roadmap toward large-scale adoption. Methodology and challenges of bringing exoskeletons to workplaces. *Wearable Technol.* **2021**, *2*, e11. [CrossRef] [PubMed]
60. Turchetti, G.; Vitiello, N.; Trieste, L.; Romiti, S.; Geisler, E.; Micera, S. Why Effectiveness of Robot-Mediated Neurorehabilitation Does Not Necessarily Influence Its Adoption. *IEEE Rev. Biomed. Eng.* **2014**, *7*, 143–153. [CrossRef] [PubMed]

61. Östlund, B.; Malvezzi, M.; Frennert, S.; Funk, M.; Gonzalez-Vargas, J.; Baur, K.; Alimisis, D.; Thorsteinsson, F.; Alonso-Cepeda, A.; Fau, G.; et al. Interactive robots for health in Europe: Technology readiness and adoption potential. *Front. Public Health* **2023**, *11*, 979225 . [CrossRef]
62. Dragusanu, M.; Troisi, D.; Suthar, B.; Prattichizzo, D.; Malvezzi, M. Development of a Soft Actuated Glove Based on Twisted String Actuators for Hand Rehabilitation. In Proceedings of the 2024 10th IEEE RAS/EMBS International Conference for Biomedical Robotics and Biomechatronics (BioRob), Heidelberg, Germany, 1–4 September 2024; pp. 1702–1708. [CrossRef]
63. Dragusanu, M.; Troisi, D.; Suthar, B.; Hussain, I.; Prattichizzo, D.; Malvezzi, M. MGlove-TS: A modular soft glove based on twisted string actuators and flexible structures. *Mechatronics* **2024**, *98*, 103141. [CrossRef]
64. Dragusanu, M. Hand/Wrist Exoskeleton. In *Design of Soft–Rigid Devices for Rehabilitative and Assistive Robotics*; Springer Nature: Cham, Switzerland, 2025; pp. 21–96. [CrossRef]
65. Dragusanu, M.; Saeed, A.; Guinet, N.; Troisi, D.; Prattichizzo, D.; Malvezzi, M. Development of the Modular Finger Elements of an Actuated Glove for Hand Rehabilitation. In *Advances in Italian Mechanism Science*; Quaglia, G., Boschetti, G., Carbone, G., Eds.; Springer Nature : Cham, Switzerland, 2024; pp. 563–570. [CrossRef]
66. Tomo, T.P.; Somlor, S.; Schmitz, A.; Jamone, L.; Huang, W.; Kristanto, H.; Sugano, S. Design and Characterization of a Three-Axis Hall Effect-Based Soft Skin Sensor. *Sensors* **2016**, *16*, 491. [CrossRef]
67. Ray, T.; Choi, J.; Reeder, J.; Lee, S.P.; Aranyosi, A.J.; Ghaffari, R.; Rogers, J.A. Soft, skin-interfaced wearable systems for sports science and analytics. *Curr. Opin. Biomed. Eng.* **2019**, *9*, 47–56.

sensors

MDPI

Article

Application of Surface Electromyography (sEMG) in the Analysis of Upper Limb Muscle Activity in Women Aged 50+ During Torqway Riding

Sylwia Agata Bęczkowska *, Iwona Grabarek and Zuzanna Zysk

Faculty of Transport, Warsaw University of Technology, 00-662 Warsaw, Poland; iwona.grabarek@pw.edu.pl (I.G.); zuzanna.zysk@pw.edu.pl (Z.Z.)
* Correspondence: sylwia.beczkowska@pw.edu.pl

Abstract: The aim of this study was to analyze the activation of selected upper limb muscles. For the purposes of this article, we present results concerning the following muscles: triceps brachii, anterior and posterior deltoid, and trapezius in women aged 50 and above during simulated riding of the Torqway device, using surface electromyography (sEMG). The primary objective was to compare muscle activity across two movement phases: active and passive. Accordingly, the following research hypotheses were formulated: muscle activity (measured by RMS values) will be significantly higher during the active phase compared to the passive phase, and MPF (mean power frequency) values will decrease over time, indicating the onset of muscle fatigue. Additionally, the potential of surface electromyography was assessed as a diagnostic tool for evaluating ergonomics and muscle effort in the context of designing personalized mobility devices for older adults. As the study of the Torqway device represents a pioneering research effort, this publication makes a significant contribution to the biomechanical analysis of new forms of active mobility supported by wearable sensor technologies.

Keywords: active transport; sensors; sEMG analysis; muscle synergy; sustainable mobility; physical activity; rehabilitation

1. Introduction

The growing demand for sustainable and health-promoting transport solutions has led to an increased interest in personal mobility devices that support physical activity, particularly among aging populations.

The endeavor to change society's mindset regarding transportation choices is a long-term process. The first step is a shift in attitude towards public transportation, followed by the utilization of individual means of transportation, such as bicycles or scooters. To enrich the range of individual transportation options, designers propose new solutions with an ecological emphasis, but primarily solutions that contribute to enhancing physical fitness, especially among individuals aged 60+ [1–4].

Interest and willingness to use such vehicles must be preceded by credible research demonstrating their benefits, as well as their impact on users' physical condition, particularly on the muscular system [5,6].

One of the currently used techniques for assessing muscle activity is surface electromyography (sEMG), which focuses on measuring and analyzing myoelectric signals using surface electrodes [7–9]. Surface electromyography (sEMG) enables the assessment of muscle loading and fatigue based on the analysis of electrical activity of stimulated muscles.

 https://doi.org/10.3390/s25144280

Muscle fatigue is typically defined as a reduction in the muscle's ability to generate force. More precisely, it is a reversible decline in the muscle's capacity to produce force over time due to sustained or repetitive activation. In surface EMG analysis, fatigue is often characterized by an increase in signal amplitude (RMS) and a decrease in mean power frequency (MPF), reflecting altered motor unit recruitment and conduction velocity [10,11]. From an sEMG perspective, fatigue is often associated with an increase in RMS values and a decrease in MPF, although this interpretation requires caution.

The sEMG signal is influenced by both internal (personal) and external factors. Internal factors include the conduction speed of muscle fiber action potentials, switching and synchronization of individual motor units, as well as anatomical factors such as subcutaneous layer thickness (fat tissue content) and the proportion of muscle fibers of a particular type. External factors are associated with the applied external force, duration of load maintenance, type of measuring electrodes used, and electrical resistance between the electrode and the skin. Additionally, the sEMG signal depends on geometric factors affecting muscle length changes (in the case of analyzed studies resulting from changes in body position and the technique of riding the examined device). Among the factors influencing the sEMG signal, the physical activity of the subjects should also be highlighted. The signals received result from physiological changes in the state of muscle fiber cell membranes [1,10–12]. In contrast to classical neurological sEMG, where the artificial response of muscles to external electrical stimulation is examined under static conditions, kinesiological sEMG allows for the examination of neuromuscular activity during tasks related to posture, functional movements, work, and treatment/training [13–16]. In addition to basic physiological and biomechanical research, kinesiological sEMG serves as an assessment tool in scientific studies within the scope of physiotherapy/rehabilitation, sports, training, ergonomics, as well as human body interaction with industrial products and work conditions [17–19].

This versatile tool has become an indispensable element in the fields of medicine, rehabilitation, sports, and ergonomic research. Consequently, research on human muscle activity during individual transportation was conducted at the Faculty of Transport of the Warsaw University of Technology using the aforementioned method. The research was commissioned by TORQWAY, a company implementing the construction of a hybrid personal mobility device for standing movement called "Torqway" as part of the European Union's Horizon 2020 research and innovation program, project number: 778154 (SMEI H2020) [20]. Torqway is an invention patented in Poland in 2011. It was primarily created for sports and recreational purposes. Promoting sustainable mobility involves not only reducing dependence on fossil fuels but also encouraging transportation solutions that enhance users' health and reduce the environmental footprint. Active transport modes, such as walking, cycling, and human-powered vehicles, play a vital role in achieving urban sustainability goals. Devices like the Torqway bridge the gap between mobility support and physical activity, making them particularly valuable for older populations.

Torqway is suitable for use wherever pedestrians and cyclists move: on bike paths and promenades, on forest trails and in residential areas, in park avenues and city squares, as well as on scenic routes outside the city.

What distinguishes it from scooters, Segways, or electric scooters is the fact that its use engages the muscles of the upper and lower limbs as well as the torso. It is a hand-powered vehicle that allows for movement in a standing position, similar to a Segway. Moving the levers forward and backward while riding generates a unidirectional rotational movement of the wheel axle, causing the vehicle to move forward. Activity on the Torqway combines elements of Nordic walking and using an orbital-type device. Since the device is easy to operate, it can be used by children, adults, and seniors. The broad range of potential users significantly distinguishes Torqway from other individual means of transportation

(Figure 1). Currently, a hybrid version is also available, which can be used by physically weak individuals.

Figure 1. Torqway personal mobility device. Source: Adapted from https://antyweb.pl/polacy-z-torunia-stworzyli-torqway-to-bedzie-wiekszy-hit-niz-segway (accessed on 20 May 2025).

The length and frequency of lever movement depend on the user's preference. The resistance of the lever is moderated. The research included an evaluation of the user's body movement kinematics, the results of which were published in [21], and an analysis of muscle tension, presented in this article. The aim of this study was to evaluate muscle activation patterns and potential fatigue in selected upper limb muscles—namely the triceps brachii, anterior and posterior deltoid, and trapezius—in women aged 50 and above during simulated Torqway riding using surface electromyography (sEMG). The analysis focused on two movement phases: active and passive. Accordingly, the following research hypotheses were formulated: muscle activity (measured by RMS values) will be significantly higher during the active phase compared to the passive phase, and MPF (mean power frequency) values will decrease over time, indicating the onset of muscle fatigue. Additionally, the potential of surface electromyography was assessed as a diagnostic tool for evaluating ergonomics and muscle effort in the context of designing personalized mobility devices for older adults. As the study of the Torqway device represents a pioneering research effort, this publication makes a significant contribution to the biomechanical analysis of new forms of active mobility supported by wearable sensor technologies.

The present research is situated within the emerging paradigm of sensor-integrated biomechanics and dynamic physiology, where the use of wearable technologies, such as surface electromyography (sEMG), plays a transformative role in evaluating human performance. By bridging engineering and biological systems, wearable sensors allow for a high-resolution capture of neuromuscular activity during real-world functional tasks. As emphasized in recent research, such integration enables a deeper understanding of subtle dynamics of movement and posture, which are critical to optimizing physical activity and designing inclusive mobility solutions. This study contributes to this growing field by applying sEMG to assess human–device interaction with a manually powered mobility platform.

2. Materials and Methods

A laboratory-based experimental protocol was conducted to evaluate upper limb muscle activity in women aged 50+ during simulated use of the Torqway personal mobility device. sEMG data were recorded across two movement phases: active and passive. The selection of muscles and measurement parameters was based on their functional involvement in operating the device.

2.1. *Study Design and Participants*

The research participants consisted of eleven women aged 50 and above, following the project's assumptions. Participant recruitment was carried out among female residents of the Mazovian Voivodeship through announcements distributed via organizations promoting physical activity. Women aged 50 and above were eligible for inclusion. The inclusion criteria were as follows: overall good health, no medical contraindications to moderate physical activity, and the ability to move independently. Exclusion criteria included neurological or cardiac conditions, balance disorders, prior upper limb injuries, or implanted electronic devices (e.g., pacemakers). The sample size (n = 11) was determined based on the pilot nature of the study and the availability of participants meeting the inclusion criteria. Due to the exploratory character of the project and organizational constraints, no formal power analysis was conducted; however, the adopted sample size was sufficient to perform preliminary analyses of muscle activity differences between the examined movement phases. The characteristics of the research participants are presented in Table 1. The research was preceded by obtaining approval from the Ethics Committee: Komisja Etyki i Bioetyki Uniwersytetu Kardynała Stefana Wyszyńskiego w Warszawie. Additionally, each study participant was examined by a physician and signed a consent form to participate in the experiment.

Table 1. Characteristics of the research participants.

Tested Person	Age	Height (cm)	Weight (kg)	BMI
k1	54	165	72	26.45
k2	54	164	79	29.37
k3	52	153	62	26.49
k4	59	162	69	26.29
k5	62	165	63	23.14
k6	50	167	90	32.27
k7	57	166	69	25
k8	50	170	57	19.7
k9	52	164	57	21.2
k10	58	161,5	62	23.92
k11	50	170	72	24.91

The average age was 54.36 years. Due to the relatively small size of the research participants, participants were selected to ensure homogeneity in terms of physical fitness and build.

2.2. *Test Environment and Equipment*

The experimental research was carried out at the Faculty of Transport of the Warsaw University of Technology. The following section will present the results concerning the electromyographic analysis of the activity of selected muscles while the subject was riding on a Torqway. The analysis was based on parameters characterizing the sEMG signal, determined in the time domain (RMS amplitude) and in the frequency domain (mean power frequency, MPF). Another results of the analysis of body movement kinematics were published in [21].

Description of the Torqway Device

The Torqway is a manually powered personal mobility device designed to promote upper limb activity. It stands approximately 150 cm tall and weighs around 25 kg. The vehicle is propelled through a lever mechanism, requiring the user to push and pull the handlebars in a coordinated manner. Each lever movement contributes directly to the rotation of the drive axle, ensuring that there is no idle motion. Turning is achieved by shifting foot pressure: pressing the left platform turns the vehicle left, and pressing the right platform turns it right. The device reaches speeds of up to 12 km/h and can be operated in a standing position.

2.3. *Surface Electromyography (sEMG) Measurement*

The sEMG signal was recorded using Noraxon MR software version 3.10.64 [22]. Bipolar surface electrodes were placed according to SENIAM guidelines on the following muscles of the dominant side: triceps brachii, anterior and posterior deltoid, and trapezius. The inter-electrode distance was set at 20 mm. Data were sampled at a frequency of 2000 Hz, band-pass filtered (20–450 Hz), and rectified. RMS (Root Mean Square) and MPF (mean power frequency) indicators were extracted for further analysis to quantitatively assess muscle activity and fatigue [23]. The electrode module, shown in Figure 2, consists of several key components used for collecting electromyographic (sEMG) data.

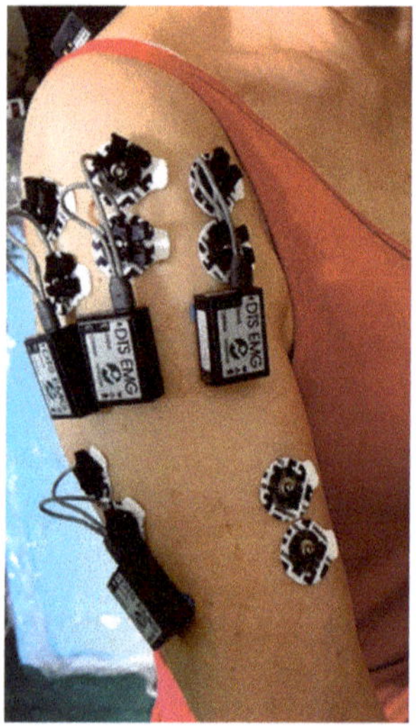

Figure 2. Placement of measurement sensors on the upper limb.

2.4. *Estimation of Time and Frequency-Domain sEMG Signal Parameters*

The first step of the analysis was to determine the Root Mean Square (RMS) amplitude for the signal recorded at rest (RMSrel) and during muscle activation under conditions similar to maximum load (RMSref). Then, based on the signal recorded during Torqway device riding, RMS amplitude and mean power frequency (MPF) were determined. To calculate RMS and MPF parameters, the sEMG signal was divided into windows of 1 s length. The sampling frequency of the sEMG signal was 1500 Hz; thus, a 1 s time window contained 1500 consecutive signal values. From each window, one RMS parameter value and one MPF parameter value were calculated. To normalize the amplitude, for each of the muscles studied, RMS values calculated from the sEMG signal recorded during Torqway riding (RMStg) were divided by the RMS values calculated from the reference signal recorded during muscle activation under conditions similar to maximum load (RMSref), and then multiplied by 100. The normalization of the sEMG signal amplitude is represented by Equation (1).

$$RMS = \frac{RMStg}{RMSref} \cdot 100 \ [\% \ ref] \tag{1}$$

Normalization of the RMS parameter values aimed to minimize the influence of individual factors (such as electrical resistance of the skin–electrode connection or signal attenuation by subcutaneous layers) on the amplitude of the sEMG signal.

Electromyographic signal analysis was performed using MATLAB ver. 2019. For each muscle and for both movement phases (active and passive), a set of time- and frequency-domain indicators was extracted.

In the frequency domain, a fast Fourier transform (FFT) with a segment length of 1024 points and Hamming windowing was applied. Two indicators were extracted: mean power frequency (MPF) and median frequency (MDF). MPF was calculated as follows (Equation (2)):

$$MPF = \frac{\int_0^\infty fS(f)df}{\int_0^\infty S(f)df} \quad (2)$$

In summary, the integration of time- and frequency-domain analysis enabled a comprehensive evaluation of muscle function during the simulated propulsion task. The RMS parameter provided a quantitative measure of muscle activation intensity, while MPF and MDF allowed for the identification of spectral changes potentially associated with fatigue. This dual approach facilitated a more precise assessment of both the immediate neuromuscular response and time-related adaptations, supporting the overall aim of the study to characterize upper limb muscle performance during the use of a manually powered mobility device.

2.5. Statistical Analysis

To confirm the results regarding muscle activity during the use of the Torqway device, a statistical analysis of the data collected during the study was conducted. The focus was on comparing the values of RMS and MPF parameters in different phases of muscle activity (active and passive) and assessing the variability of these parameters over time. The statistical analysis aimed to verify hypotheses regarding significant differences in muscle activity between phases and potential signs of muscular fatigue. The following statistical tests were applied in the analysis: dependent samples *t*-test—to compare RMS and MPF between the active and passive phases; repeated measures ANOVA—to assess the variability of parameters over time; and Pearson correlation—to analyze the relationship between variables, such as BMI and muscular fatigue.

Normalization of RMS values was carried out according to Formula (1). Calculation of the average MPF power frequency was performed according to Formula (2).

The *t*-test for dependent samples was used to analyze differences between the active and passive phases. Its mathematical form is as follows:

$$t = \frac{\overline{d}}{\frac{s_d}{\sqrt{n}}}$$

where

$\overline{d}$—mean difference between pairs;
s_d—standard deviation of the differences;
n—number of pairs of observations.

An analysis of variance was used to assess differences between measurements at different times:

$$F = \frac{MS_{within}}{MS_{between}}$$

where

MS_{within}—mean square within groups;

$MS_{between}$—mean square between groups.

3. Experimental Studies

3.1. Muscles Tested

In the experimental procedure, surface sEMG signals were collected from twelve muscles. However, for the purpose of this article, we focused the analysis and interpretation of the results on four upper-body muscles—triceps brachii (TB), anterior deltoid (DA), posterior deltoid (DP), and upper trapezius (TR). These muscles were selected due to their consistent signal quality and functional involvement during the operation of the Torqway device. The remaining muscles, although recorded, showed less significant or inconsistent activation patterns under the tested conditions and will be considered in future publications. It was assumed that riding the Torqway device occurs symmetrically; therefore, only the muscles on the right side of the body were included in the studies. The selected muscles for activity assessment represent different muscle groups of the upper and lower body, which are involved in maintaining posture, controlling limb movements, and stabilizing the body during dynamic activities such as riding the Torqway. This approach was also guided by expert interviews with rehabilitation specialists who worked on the project. The muscles examined are presented in Figure 3.

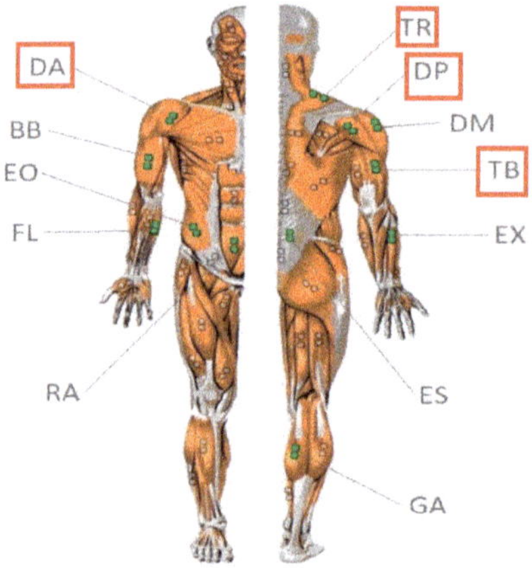

Figure 3. Muscle abbreviations. Source: Own elaboration based on https://hermanwallace.com/download/The_ABC_of_EMG_by_Peter_Konrad.pdf. (accessed on 25 May 2025). Where: Triceps brachii (TB), Anterior deltoid (DA), Posterior deltoid (DP), Upper trapezius (TR).

3.2. Experimental Procedure

After placing the sensors, the sEMG signal was recorded for each of the examined muscles both at rest (referred to as the "relaxed" signal) and during muscle activation under conditions similar to maximum load (referred to as the "reference" signal). To allow interindividual comparison and reduce the influence of skin impedance and subcutaneous tissue on the EMG signal amplitude, normalization was performed with respect to the maximum voluntary contraction (MVC) for each muscle. MVC tests were conducted under standardized, isometric conditions for each muscle group separately. Participants were verbally encouraged to exert maximal effort for each test, and each contraction lasted 3–5 s, with 1–2 min of rest between attempts to prevent fatigue. In the article, the standardization and subsequent normalization to MVC were described only for four muscles: triceps brachii (TB), anterior deltoid (DA), posterior deltoid (DP), and upper trapezius (TR).

For consistency and reproducibility across participants, the following joint positions and resistance setups were used during MVC testing:

- Triceps brachii (TB):
  Elbow flexed at 90°, shoulder in neutral position. Participants performed an isometric elbow extension against manual resistance applied at the distal forearm.
- Anterior deltoid (DA):
  Shoulder flexed to 90°, elbow extended, palm facing down. The participant resisted a downward force applied just above the wrist to produce isometric shoulder flexion.
- Posterior deltoid (DP):
  Shoulder abducted to 90° in the horizontal plane (reverse fly position), elbow flexed at 90°. The participant exerted isometric horizontal abduction against resistance applied at the lateral elbow.
- Upper trapezius (TR):
  Shoulder in neutral position, participant elevated (shrugged) the shoulder isometrically against manual downward pressure applied to the acromion process.

To ensure data quality, three MVC attempts were performed per muscle. The trial with the highest RMS amplitude was used as the reference value for normalization. The EMG signals recorded during Torqway riding were then expressed as a percentage of this maximum value (%MVC), enabling relative comparisons across participants and conditions.

Subsequently, the sEMG signal was recorded during simulated Torqway riding (participants performed movements similar to natural Torqway riding, but the device was mounted on a stationary research stand). During the experimental trials, movement speed was controlled using a metronome set to 50 repetitions per minute to ensure consistency across participants. Force output was standardized by calibrating the resistance applied to the Torqway levers based on pre-test measurements. The pace of movement was maintained throughout the 10 min test sessions by providing verbal reminders to participants, ensuring uniformity in the experimental conditions. The 10 min duration of the simulated Torqway riding session was selected to provide a balance between ecological validity, participant comfort, and the ability to detect neuromuscular changes such as muscle fatigue. Previous studies on dynamic upper-body exercise, such as arm ergometry or Nordic walking [...], have demonstrated that moderate-duration efforts of 8–12 min are sufficient to induce observable changes in EMG parameters, particularly in older adults.

Additionally, a longer duration could risk excessive fatigue or disengagement in participants unaccustomed to prolonged physical activity. The 10 min timeframe enabled participants to perform the repetitive motion at a controlled cadence (50 cycles/min) for a total of approximately 500 cycles, which was deemed sufficient to elicit physiological adaptation or early fatigue indicators (e.g., increased RMS or decreased MPF).

While not intended to induce maximal exhaustion, the protocol duration was designed to simulate a typical short-distance usage scenario in a real-world context (e.g., travel through a park or urban zone), ensuring both functional relevance and practical feasibility for future interventions.

The procedure for conducting experimental studies for representative participants is illustrated in Figure 4. All 11 participants completed the full 10 min test without interruptions or procedural modifications [24–26].

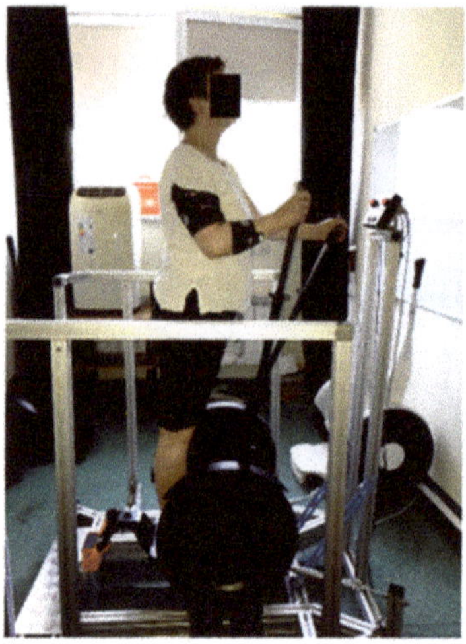

Figure 4. Participants on the stationary experimental setup.

In the context of the study evaluating muscle activity during the use of the Torqway device, understanding the active and passive phases of muscle engagement is crucial for interpreting the results accurately. These phases are distinguished based on the nature of muscle activation during the cycling motions performed on the Torqway. The active phase was defined as periods in which the Root Mean Square (RMS) value of the triceps brachii exceeded 25% of the participant-specific maximum RMS (RMSmax), maintained for a minimum duration of 300 milliseconds. These thresholds were used to identify segments of voluntary muscular effort corresponding to propulsion movements while using the Torqway. The passive phase was defined as periods during which the RMS signal remained below the 25% RMSmax threshold, indicating minimal or no voluntary muscle activation. This typically included short recovery intervals between propulsion cycles. Phase classification was applied to all recorded muscle groups and was verified using synchronized video recordings to ensure consistency between signal-based segmentation and observed lever movements.

A marked increase in sEMG signal amplitude indicates an active phase, while a drop in amplitude indicates a transition to the passive phase.

By employing these methods, researchers can reliably categorize the muscle activity recorded during the experiment, providing insights into the muscle engagement patterns across different phases of Torqway usage. Understanding the active and passive phases is fundamental to the study's objectives. It allows researchers to analyze how muscle activation varies with task demands, thereby providing insights into the biomechanics of using the Torqway device. This information can inform future improvements in design, optimize training protocols, and enhance the understanding of muscle dynamics in the context of novel transportation devices.

In electromyographic testing, it is necessary to determine a reference signal against which the values of signals recorded in specific tests are compared. Such a reference signal is the signal from the maximum muscle tension test. In a procedure in which the reference value is the maximum level of activation during contractions, the sEMG signal recorded during voluntary and spontaneous maximal contraction, expressing maximum muscle tension under isometric conditions, was used. The best results were obtained during the execution of isolated movement in a single joint, with static resting in the intermediate position of the range of motion.

4. Results

Following the analysis of the sEMG signal for each examined muscle and participant, 600 values of the RMS parameter and MPF parameter were obtained (each subsequent second of Torqway riding corresponds to one parameter value). The RMS and MPF parameter values derived from the sEMG signal underwent second-degree polynomial approximation, resulting in a trend line depicting parameter changes over the entire measurement duration. The analysis was performed using Noraxon's MR3.14 software.

4.1. Analysis of Time-Dependent Muscle Activation

Torqway riding involves cyclic movements, distinguishable into "active" and "passive" phases of muscle activity. Another direction of sEMG signal analysis was to determine the initial and final RMS amplitude values based on the raw sEMG signal. For this purpose, characteristic segments of the signal from the first and last few tens of seconds of Torqway riding were selected (as close to the beginning and end of the measurement as possible, usually from the first and last twenty seconds of measurement). The method of determining initial and final RMS amplitude values based on the raw sEMG signal is illustrated in Figure 5.

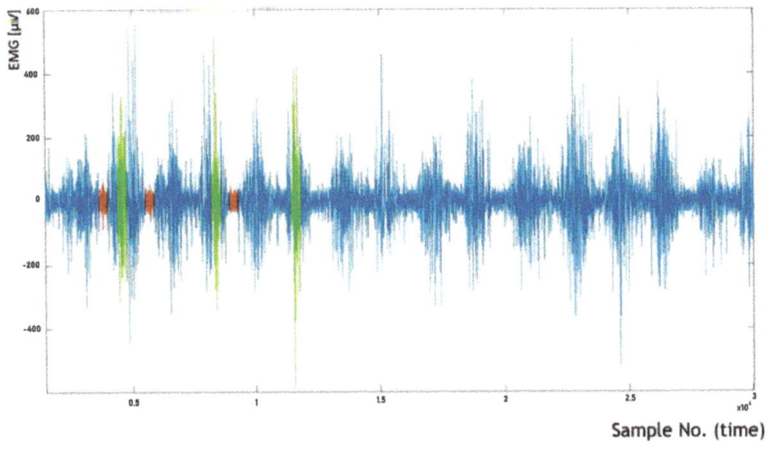

Figure 5. The method of determining the initial and final RMS amplitude values based on the raw sEMG signal (the first 20 s of recording are shown in the figure).

Riding on the Torqway involves cyclic movements, where an "active" and "passive" phase of muscle work can be distinguished (as depicted in Figure 5; the active phase corresponds to segments with higher signal amplitude, while the passive phase corresponds to segments with lower amplitude). From both the initial and final segments of the signal, three segments corresponding to the active phase (marked in green) and three segments corresponding to the passive phase (marked in red) were selected. The length of each selected segment is 500 samples, which corresponds to a time interval of 1/3 of a second.

For each selected segment, the RMS amplitude was determined (which was also normalized). Subsequently, the RMS values from the three selected segments were averaged separately for the active and passive phases, and separately for the initial and final segments. As a result, one RMS parameter value was obtained for each of the following:

- The active phase from the initial seconds of riding (referred to as BH);
- The passive phase from the initial seconds of riding (BL);
- The active phase from the final seconds of riding (EH);

- The passive phase from the final seconds of riding (EL).

The determined initial and final RMS amplitude values based on the raw sEMG signal, corresponding to segments BH, BL, EH, and EL, enable both the assessment of changes in the RMS signal amplitude during the test duration and the determination of muscle tension levels during the active phase compared to the passive phase during Torqway riding, which can serve as a measure of muscle activation degree.

Below are selected results related to the following muscles: TB, DA, DP, and TR, which showed increased activity during driving.

It is worth emphasizing that if the muscle were fatigued, one would expect a simultaneous increase in the RMS amplitude of the sEMG signal and a decrease in the average MPF frequency. The following figures (from Figures 6–17) display the results of the analyses for selected muscles.

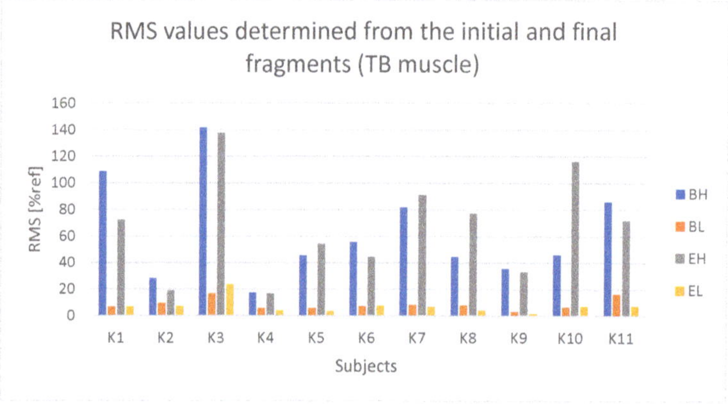

Figure 6. RMS parameter values determined based on the initial and final segments of raw sEMG signal from the triceps brachii muscle (TB) for all participants (BH—active phase from the first seconds of riding, BL—passive phase from the first seconds of riding, EH—active phase from the last seconds of riding, EL—passive phase from the last seconds of riding).

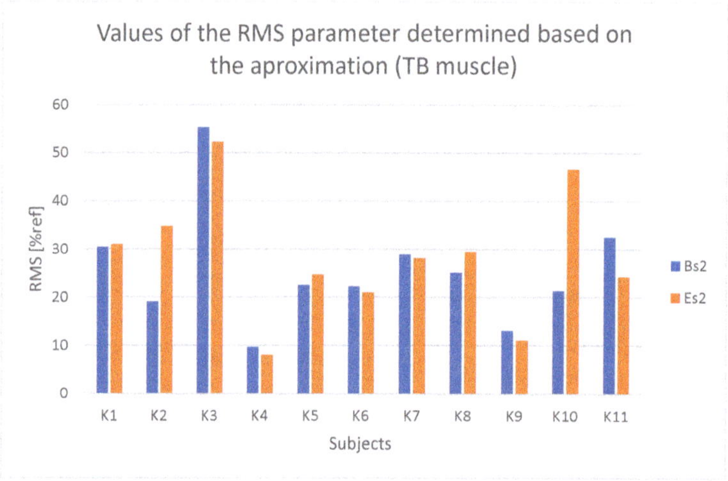

Figure 7. Values of the RMS parameter determined based on the approximation of the course from the triceps brachii muscle (TB) for all participants (Bs2—initial parameter value, Es2—final parameter value).

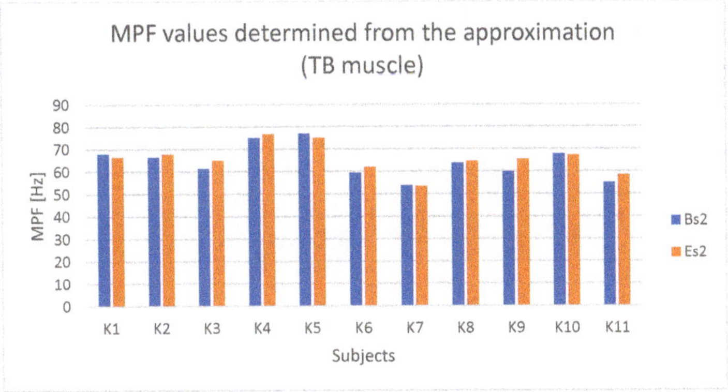

Figure 8. Values of the MPF parameter determined based on the approximation of the course from the triceps brachii muscle (TB) for all participants (Bs2—initial parameter value, Es2—final parameter value).

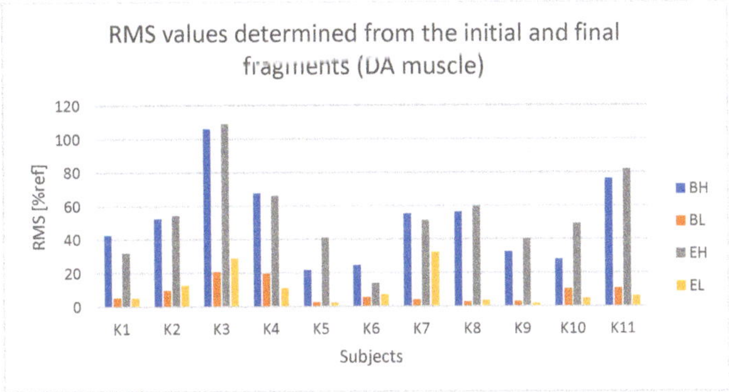

Figure 9. Values of the RMS parameter determined based on the initial and final segments of the raw sEMG signal from the anterior deltoid muscle (DA) for all participants (BH—active phase from the first seconds of the ride, BL—passive phase from the first seconds of the ride, EH—active phase from the last seconds of the ride, EL—passive phase from the last seconds of the ride).

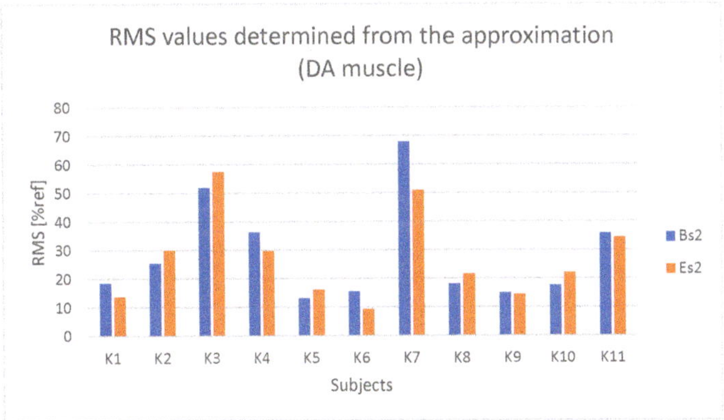

Figure 10. Values of the RMS parameter determined based on the approximation of the curve from the anterior deltoid muscle (DA) for all participants (Bs2—initial value of the parameter, Es2—final value of the parameter).

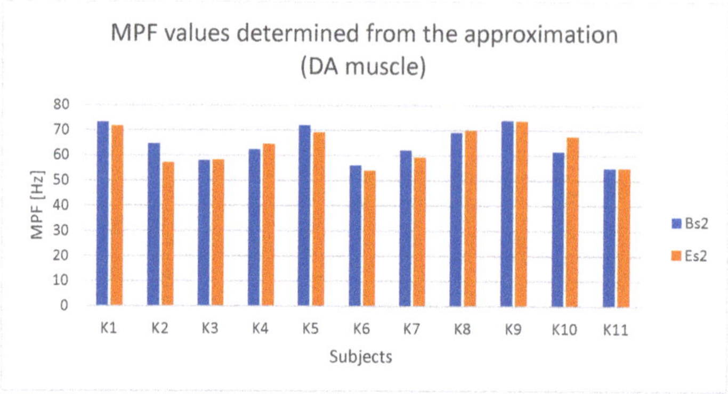

Figure 11. Values of the MPF parameter determined based on the approximation of the curve from the anterior deltoid muscle (DA) for all participants (Bs2—initial value of the parameter, Es2—final value of the parameter).

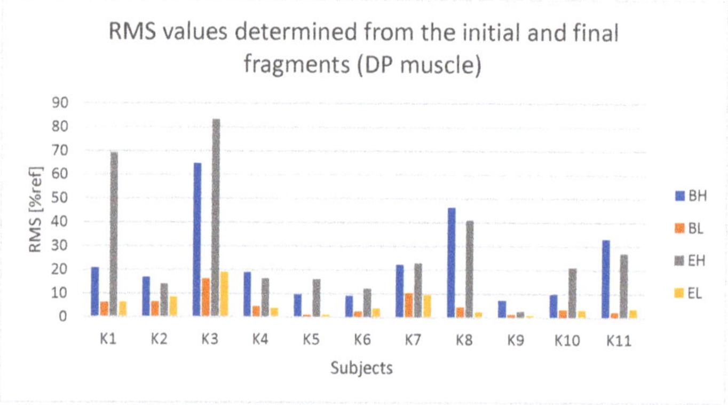

Figure 12. RMS parameter values determined from the initial and final fragments of the raw sEMG signal from the DP (posterior deltoid) muscle for all subjects (BH—active phase from the first seconds of driving, BL—passive phase from the first seconds of driving, EH—active phase from the last seconds of driving, EL—passive phase from the last seconds of driving).

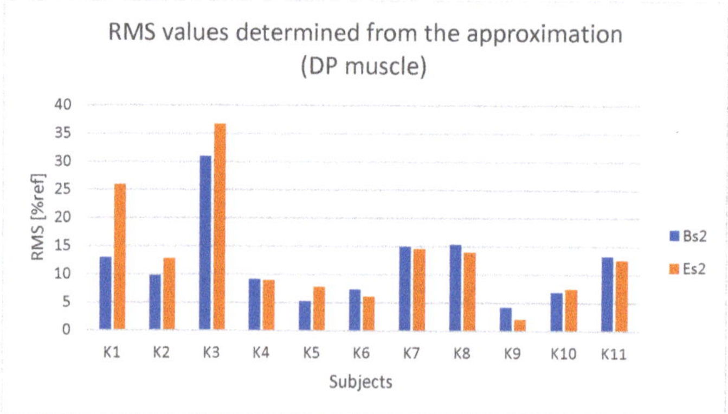

Figure 13. RMS parameter values determined based on the approximation of the DP (posterior deltoid) muscle signal for all examined subjects (Bs2—initial parameter value, Es2—final parameter value).

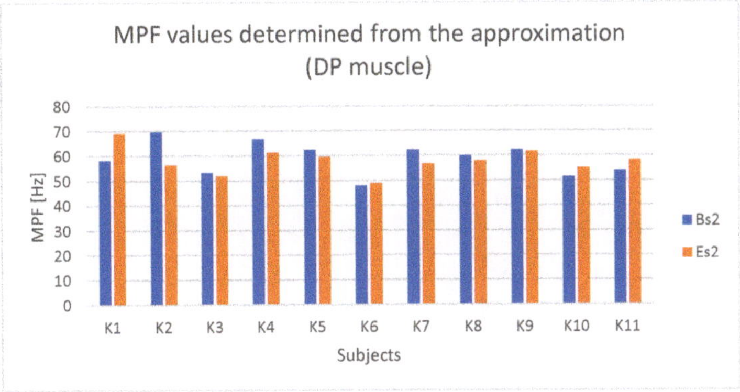

Figure 14. Values of the MPF parameter determined based on the approximation of the DP (posterior deltoid) muscle signal for all examined subjects (Bs2—initial parameter value, Es2—final parameter value).

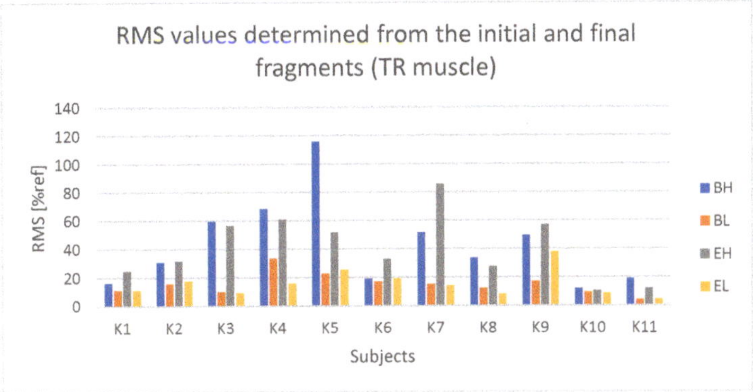

Figure 15. Values of the RMS parameter determined based on the initial and final segments of the raw sEMG signal from the TR (upper trapezius) muscle for all examined subjects (BH—active phase from the first seconds of riding, BL—passive phase from the first seconds of riding, EH—active phase from the last seconds of riding, EL—passive phase from the last seconds of riding).

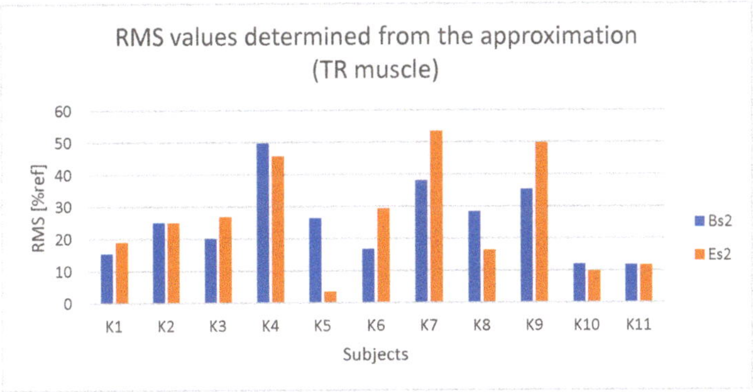

Figure 16. Values of the RMS parameter determined based on the approximation of the TR (upper trapezius) muscle signal for all examined subjects (Bs2—initial value of the parameter, Es2—final value of the parameter).

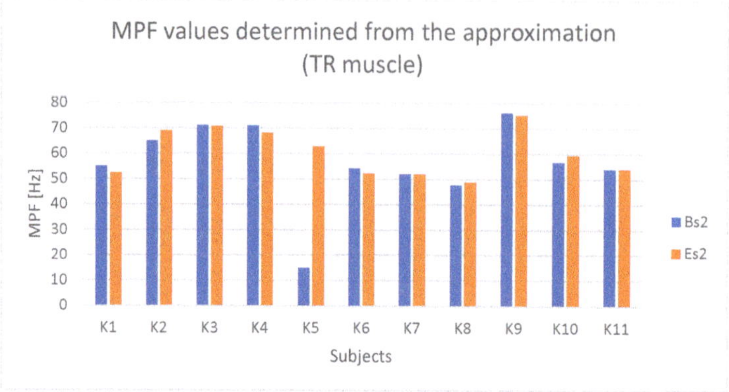

Figure 17. Values of the MPF parameter determined based on the approximation of the TR (upper trapezius) muscle signal for all examined subjects (Bs2—initial value of the parameter, Es2—final value of the parameter).

For the triceps brachii muscle (TB), in all participants except for K2 and K4, there are noticeably higher values during the active phase of movement (BH and EH) compared to the passive phase (BL and EL). However, it should be noted that in participants K2 and K4, differences between the active and passive phases are also present, although not as pronounced as in the other participants.

Based on Figures 7 and 8, a slight trend indicating fatigue of the triceps brachii muscle can be observed in the case of participants K1, K5, and K10.

In the case (Figure 9) of the anterior deltoid muscle (DA), higher values are observed during the active phase (BH and EH) compared to the passive phase (BL and EL). During the active phase, the amplitude for most participants ranged from about 40% to 80% of the reference value (% ref).

Based on Figures 10 and 11, a relationship indicating fatigue of the anterior deltoid muscle (DA) can be observed in the case of participants K2 and K5.

The results concerning the posterior deltoid muscle (DP), similar to the DM muscle, indicate lower muscle activation (% ref) compared to the forearm and arm muscles (Figure 12). However, there is still a noticeable difference between the active (BH and EH) and passive (BL and EL) phases.

Based on Figures 13 and 14, a relationship indicating fatigue of the DP muscle can be observed for subjects K2, K3, and K5.

In the case of the TR (upper trapezius) muscle (Figure 15), higher values were observed during the active phase (BH and EH) compared to the passive phase (BL and EL) for most examined subjects, although these differences were not as pronounced as in the previously analyzed muscles. During the active phase, the amplitude for most subjects ranged from 30% to 60% of the reference value (% ref).

Based on Figures 16 and 17, a relationship indicating the occurrence of fatigue in the TR muscle can be observed in the case of subjects K1, K3, K6, and K9.

Based on the obtained results, it can be concluded that for all analyzed muscles, significantly higher values occur during the active phase compared to the passive phase. This indicates a considerable activation of muscles during Torqway riding.

The analysis regarding the occurrence of muscle fatigue did not provide unequivocal results. A summary of cases where changes in sEMG signal parameters indicating muscle fatigue (simultaneous increase in RMS amplitude and decrease in mean MPF) were observed for the analyzed muscles is presented in Table 2. Studies confirming the relationship between muscle fatigue and changes in sEMG signal parameters, such as an increase in RMS amplitude and a decrease in mean frequency (MPF), have appeared in the literature for many years. References can be made, for example, to Sung, Lee [27], and Chowdhury et al. [28].

Table 2. Summary of cases where changes in sEMG signal parameters indicating muscle fatigue were observed during Torqway riding.

Muscle/ Person	TB	DA	DP	TR
K1	x			x
K2		x	x	
K3			x	x
K4				
K5	x	x	x	
K6				x
K7				
K8				
K9				x
K10	x			
K11				

The relationship indicating the occurrence of muscle fatigue is most often observed in the case of individual K5. However, when discussing the involvement of muscles (DA, TB, TR) in the context of Torqway riding, we emphasize that while these muscles were indeed activated, their levels of engagement varied. Specifically, although the DP muscle showed lower activation compared to the primary movers, it still contributed to the overall activity during both the active and passive phases. This variability underscores the different roles that various muscle groups play during the exercise, where some muscles serve primarily for stabilization and support, while others are more engaged in generating movement. However, Table 3 presents the activation levels of analyzed muscles in the studied project at the Faculty of Transport, only those discussed in the article. It shows the percentage values of the RMS parameter (% ref), determined based on the initial segments of the raw sEMG signal for both the active and passive phases. The results are presented in the BH/BL configuration (BH—active phase from the first seconds of riding, BL—passive phase from the first seconds of riding) to better illustrate the examined issue.

Table 3. A summary presenting the activation levels of the analyzed muscles—percentage values of the RMS parameter (% ref), determined based on the initial segments of the raw sEMG signal for the active and passive phases of movement; the results are presented in the BH/BL configuration (BH—active phase from the first seconds of riding, BL—passive phase from the first seconds of riding).

Muscle/ Person	TB	DA	DP	TR
K1	109/ 7	42/ 5	21/ 6	16/ 11
K2	28/ 9	52/ 10	17/ 6	31/ 16
K3	142/ 17	106/ 21	65/ 16	59/ 10
K4	17/ 6	68/ 20	19/ 5	68/ 33
K5	46/ 6	22/ 2	10/ 1	116/ 23

Table 3. *Cont.*

Muscle/ Person	TB	DA	DP	TR
K6	56/ 7	25/ 6	9/ 3	19/ 17
K7	82/ 8	55/ 4	22/ 10	52/ 15
K8	45/ 8	56/ 3	46/ 4	34/ 12
K9	36/ 3	33/ 3	7/ 1	49/ 17
K10	46/ 6	28/ 10	10/ 3	12/ 9
K11	86/ 17	76/ 11	33/ 2	19/ 4

4.2. Statistical Results

A statistical analysis was conducted to compare the normalized values of RMS and MPF parameters in the active and passive phases for selected upper limb muscles (Table 4). A paired *t*-test was applied to evaluate the significance of differences between the phases, while repeated measures ANOVA was used to assess the variability of parameters over time. The table below presents the mean ± standard deviation values for each phase, as well as the results of the statistical tests for the following muscles: triceps brachii (TB), anterior deltoid (DA), trapezius (TR), and posterior deltoid (DP). These results indicate significantly higher muscle activity during the active phase and demonstrate signs of muscle fatigue over the duration of the test.

Table 4. Statistical analysis active and passive phases for selected upper limb muscles.

Muscle	RMS Active (M ± SD)	RMS Passive (M ± SD)	Test *t* (*p*-Value)	MPF Active (M ± SD)	MPF Passive (M ± SD)	ANOVA (F, *p*)
TB	109 ± 7	28 ± 9	t(10) = 5.62, $p < 0.001$	120 ± 8	95 ± 10	F(1,10) = 12.34, $p = 0.003$
DA	106 ± 21	52 ± 10	t(10) = 4.92, $p < 0.005$	115 ± 9	92 ± 12	F(1,10) = 9.87, $p = 0.007$
TR	116 ± 23	31 ± 16	t(10) = 6.21, $p < 0.001$	112 ± 7	90 ± 11	F(1,10) = 11.45, $p = 0.004$
DP	98 ± 15	40 ± 12	t(10) = 4.35, $p < 0.005$	110 ± 9	88 ± 13	F(1,10) = 10.12, $p = 0.005$

The statistical comparison of the analyzed muscles shows a clear and consistent increase in RMS values during the active phase compared to the passive phase, which confirms higher neuromuscular involvement during physical effort using the Torqway device. Concurrently, the observed decrease in MPF values during the active phase reflects the onset of muscle fatigue, particularly in the triceps brachii and trapezius muscles. The statistically significant differences ($p < 0.005$ in all cases) support the hypothesis that prolonged use of Torqway induces measurable fatigue and can effectively engage upper limb muscles. These findings highlight the potential of Torqway as a tool for active mobility, inclusive physical activity, and even therapeutic training in rehabilitation or senior recreation settings.

5. Discussion

The paper discusses the results of muscle activation during Torqway riding, focusing on four upper limb muscles—the anterior deltoid (DA), posterior deltoid (PD), triceps brachii (TB), and trapezius (TR). These results indicate significant activation of these muscles in the active phase compared to the passive phase in individuals simulating Torqway riding.

The stationary tests were designed to minimize the risk of injury during actual riding due to insufficient training time before the tests. Additionally, a requirement set by the client was the characteristic of the study group, i.e., women aged 50 and older. The experimental studies were conducted at the Faculty of Transport of the Warsaw University of Technology using the Noraxon system.

Our study focused on evaluating muscle activity and fatigue during the use of the Torqway device, specifically by analyzing the Root Mean Square (RMS) and Median Power Frequency (MPF) of surface electromyographic signals (sEMG). The key findings from our research indicate that the RMS values, which reflect overall muscle activation levels, showed a significant increase during the exercise session. This suggests heightened muscle activity as participants engaged in repetitive movements with the Torqway device. Notably, the initial and final phases of the exercise cycle exhibited the most considerable differences in RMS values, reflecting changes in muscle engagement and potential fatigue over time.

The MPF values, which provide insights into the frequency characteristics of the sEMG signal, demonstrated a notable decrease towards the end of the exercise session. This decline is consistent with previous findings indicating that muscle fatigue is associated with a shift towards lower frequency components in the sEMG signal. The combined analysis of RMS and MPF provided a comprehensive view of muscle performance, revealing that as muscles fatigue, their activation patterns and frequency characteristics undergo significant changes.

However, sEMG alone cannot confirm fatigue definitively. Alternative explanations, such as motor unit synchronization or improved neuromuscular recruitment, are possible. No direct measures of torque or force were used, limiting interpretation.

Our study focused on specific segments of the exercise cycle, particularly the initial and final seconds, to capture the dynamic changes in muscle activity. This segmentation allowed for a detailed analysis of how muscle performance evolves during repetitive tasks. The methodological approach involved rigorous filtering of sEMG signals to remove motion artifacts, ensuring the accuracy and reliability of the data. By employing techniques such as low-pass filtering and visual inspection, we minimized the impact of noise and external disturbances on our measurements.

The insights gained can inform the design of training programs and rehabilitation protocols that aim to optimize muscle function and reduce the risk of injury. Future research could expand on these findings by exploring different exercise modalities, participant demographics, and incorporating advanced statistical analyses to further validate and extend our conclusions. While the study provides valuable insights into muscle activation patterns during the use of a personal mobility device, several limitations must be acknowledged. First, the sample size was relatively small (N = 11), and all participants were women aged 50 and above. This demographic limitation, although intentional, restricts the generalizability of the findings to broader populations, including younger users or men. Second, the tests were conducted in a stationary setting to minimize the risk of injury and maintain consistency, which may not fully capture the biomechanical dynamics of real-world riding scenarios.

Furthermore, although EMG data were collected from twelve muscles, the analysis focused on four upper-body muscles showing the highest and most consistent activation.

This selection approach, while methodologically justified, may overlook synergistic or stabilizing roles of other muscles during riding.

Future studies should consider expanding the participant pool to include individuals of different ages, genders, and fitness levels to examine the variability in muscle engagement. Real-world testing conditions should also be incorporated to validate the results under dynamic environments. Additionally, combining sEMG with other sensor modalities, such as inertial measurement units (IMUs), pressure sensors, or motion tracking, could provide a more holistic biomechanical profile of user–device interaction. Longitudinal studies assessing changes in muscle performance, fatigue, or rehabilitation outcomes over time would also enhance understanding of the long-term impact of Torqway usage.

A hypothesis was formulated that it is possible to assess muscle activity in individuals using the Torqway personal mobility device through surface electromyography (sEMG). Torqway is a device that uniquely combines the most desirable features of electric vehicles, bicycles, and Nordic walking. Therefore, the research hypothesis that the personal mobility device activates the upper limb muscles discussed in the study can be confirmed. To confirm the hypothesis, the authors first reviewed studies utilizing the sEMG measurement technique. Since Torqway is an innovative device, these were pioneering studies, and there is no literature reference to research on this vehicle. However, there are studies on measuring upper limb muscle activity when using Nordic walking poles, which clearly indicate the activation of upper limb muscles. In studies by Zhang and Liu [29], the authors demonstrated that upper limb muscle activity significantly increased due to Nordic walking, especially the triceps brachii, similar to the studies on Torqway. In another study by Wang and Li [30], the effects of walking with and without Nordic walking poles on the activation of upper and lower limb muscles were compared. Their results indicate that using Nordic walking poles significantly increases the activation of both upper and lower limb muscles. Ribeiro, Tomeleri, and Schoenfeld [31] demonstrated that using similar types of devices, such as elliptical trainers, also significantly increases the activation of the upper and lower limb muscles. Romano, Sardella, and Zanetti [32] further confirmed the increased muscle activation during Nordic walking compared to traditional walking. Huang and Yu [33] specifically examined older adults and found significant muscle activation with Nordic walking, supporting the applicability of these findings to the Torqway. Therefore, the muscle activity observed during studies on the Torqway can be compared to these findings.

The presented literature studies expand our understanding of muscle activity during various forms of walking or moving on the Torqway and can be useful for conceptualizing the results of our study, which also focuses on analyzing muscle activation in response to specific stimuli associated with using recreational devices.

Furthermore, it is important to highlight the wide application of the sEMG method for such studies. It is most commonly used in athlete research or fields such as medicine and ergonomics, where it is necessary to demonstrate the activity of individual muscles or their fatigue. The results of studies conducted in this area are described in [1,2,6,9,10,16,21,22,34–42]. For example, scientific works [43,44] have shown that sEMG can be an effective tool for assessing movement patterns and muscle load under various physical conditions. In rehabilitation, sEMG is used to monitor therapy progress and design personalized exercise programs [45–47]. Studies indicate [48–51] that sEMG can also be useful for assessing muscle function, identifying muscle asymmetries, and conducting muscle training to restore full functionality after injuries or surgeries. In sports, sEMG is used to analyze movement techniques, assess muscle load, and monitor muscle fatigue [49,50]. In the field of ergonomic literature [21,52–55], studies suggest that sEMG can help identify risk factors for musculoskeletal injuries and assist in designing work environments that provide optimal ergonomic conditions.

This method also allows for the assessment of muscle function under various conditions, such as changes in body temperature, ambient temperature, or neuromuscular training. In the area of human–computer interaction, sEMG is used to control user interfaces using muscle signals, which can be an effective alternative to traditional control interfaces, especially for individuals with mobility limitations. Additionally, sEMG is used in diagnostics, treatment, sports training, and designing ergonomic technical objects, as described in [40–42].

In biomechanical studies, sEMG is often used to analyze muscle activity during various activities, such as walking, running, jumping, weightlifting, and riding different individual transportation means. From the perspective of the studies presented in the article, the results of these experiments are significant, focusing on muscle activation during riding on various individualized transportation means. This issue is addressed in works [1,2,18,31], and the presented research results have confirmed the effectiveness of this method. It is worth noting that the results described in this article pertain to pioneering studies of a patented personal mobility device developed under the Horizon 2020 program. The use of sEMG techniques by the authors to assess the suitability of the Torqway in terms of user fit and the potential benefits from activating selected muscle groups during riding represents an innovative research approach that undoubtedly requires further continuation. Further research could include the demographic diversity of participants, long-term studies on rehabilitation effectiveness, comparative analysis with other devices, and real-world usage conditions of the personal mobility device.

It is also worth mentioning the technical and measurement limitations of this method. Surface electromyography is susceptible to environmental interference, such as electromagnetic interference generated by electrical equipment, lighting, or other medical devices, which can affect measurement accuracy. Therefore, the authors thoroughly analyzed raw data and eliminated gross errors. Additionally, the sEMG signal must pass through the skin, subcutaneous tissue, and muscle tissue, which can lead to signal attenuation or distortion. Despite these limitations, the selected methods and measurement tools allowed for demonstrating muscle activity and justifying the use of the Torqway for both recreational and rehabilitation purposes.

These findings align with the broader goals of this Special Issue focused on sustainable transport and mobility. The Torqway, as a form of active, low-emission mobility, presents an innovative response to the challenges of overloaded conventional transportation systems, increasing emissions, and the need to adapt urban spaces for elderly users and individuals with limited mobility. Its compact design, zero emissions, and potential to engage upper limb musculature make it suitable for promoting active transport and recreational mobility in urban and touristic areas, supporting the achievement of Sustainable Development Goals related to transport, public health, and social inclusion.

From a technological standpoint, the study illustrates how electromyographic sensing and time–frequency data analytics can serve as practical tools for evaluating personalized transport solutions. Future work may extend this approach by integrating multimodal sensors (e.g., inertial measurement units, pressure sensors, motion tracking systems) to provide a more comprehensive biomechanical profile. Moreover, the ability to quantify muscle fatigue and activity in real-time supports potential applications in adaptive user interfaces, intelligent feedback systems, and rehabilitation robotics, which are central to the evolving landscape of human-centered transport innovation. Although our findings revealed increased RMS and decreased MPF values during the active phase of Torqway riding, which are typically associated with neuromuscular fatigue, it is important to consider alternative physiological explanations. These changes in sEMG parameters could also reflect improved motor unit recruitment strategies, increased voluntary drive, or motor learning adaptations over time, particularly as participants became more familiar with the movement pattern.

Furthermore, RMS and MPF changes can be influenced by factors unrelated to true fatigue. For example, increased motor unit synchronization, changes in skin impedance (e.g., due to perspiration), and variations in electrode placement or signal filtering may affect signal interpretation. While we minimized motion artifacts and maintained signal consistency, these confounding factors cannot be entirely excluded.

It is also important to note that no direct measures of muscular force, torque output, or perceived fatigue were collected during the experiment. Thus, although RMS and MPF are valuable indicators, they should not be viewed as definitive proof of muscular fatigue. Future studies should include complementary assessments—such as dynamometry, biochemical markers, or subjective fatigue ratings—to provide a more robust characterization of fatigue.

We acknowledge this limitation and recommend that future research incorporate multimodal indicators to improve the specificity and validity of sEMG-based fatigue assessment in personalized transport applications.

6. Conclusions

The study demonstrated that upper limb muscle activity is significantly higher during the active propulsion phase compared to the passive phase while using the Torqway. The observed decline in MPF supports the presence of early fatigue signs. These findings suggest the Torqway can be an effective tool for promoting physical activity and rehabilitation in older adults. Further field research is recommended, involving real-world testing of the device in urban and touristic settings, to better evaluate its impact on mobility, public health, and user quality of life. The findings highlight the relevance of wearable sEMG in advancing sensor-based assessment frameworks for sustainable and inclusive transport. The integration of such sensing technologies can pave the way for personalized ergonomic evaluation, real-time fatigue monitoring, and user-responsive mobility systems, supporting the broader vision of smart and health-oriented urban environments.

7. Limitations

One of the limitations of this study is the lack of direct measurement of subcutaneous fat thickness, which is known to affect the amplitude and quality of surface EMG signals. While participants' BMI was recorded and used to ensure general physical homogeneity, variations in localized subcutaneous tissue could still have introduced interindividual differences in signal attenuation. Future studies should consider the inclusion of ultrasound or caliper-based fat measurements to improve the precision and interpretability of EMG data. Additionally, the study did not include direct measurements of muscle force output (e.g., torque, peak force) or subjective fatigue ratings (e.g., Borg scale), which limits the interpretation of fatigue based solely on sEMG parameters. Without complementary biomechanical or perceptual indicators, RMS and MPF changes cannot be unequivocally attributed to neuromuscular fatigue. Future research should integrate multidimensional fatigue assessment, including dynamometry, biochemical markers, and user-reported outcomes, to confirm physiological interpretations.

Author Contributions: Conceptualization, S.A.B., I.G. and Z.Z.; methodology, S.A.B., I.G. and Z.Z.; software, S.A.B., I.G. and Z.Z.; validation, S.A.B., I.G. and Z.Z.; formal analysis, S.A.B., I.G. and Z.Z.; investigation, S.A.B., I.G. and Z.Z.; resources, S.A.B., I.G. and Z.Z.; data curation, S.A.B., I.G. and Z.Z.; writing—S.A.B., I.G. and Z.Z.; writing—review and editing, S.A.B., I.G. and Z.Z.; visualization,

S.A.B., I.G. and Z.Z.; supervision, S.A.B., I.G. and Z.Z.; project administration, S.A.B., I.G. and Z.Z. All authors have read and agreed to the published version of the manuscript.

Funding: This research was funded by Horyzont 2020, nr: 778154 (SMEI H2020).

Institutional Review Board Statement: The study was conducted in accordance with the Declaration of Helsinki and approved by or Ethics Committee of Komisja Etyki i Bioetyki Uniwersytetu Kardynała Stefana Wyszyńskiego w Warsaw (protocol code 16.05.2018r.).

Informed Consent Statement: Informed consent was obtained from all subjects involved in the study.

Data Availability Statement: The original contributions presented in the study are included in the article; further inquiries can be directed to the corresponding author. Data are available upon request.

Acknowledgments: During the preparation of this manuscript, the authors used ChatGPT (OpenAI, GPT-4, June 2025) for language editing and assistance in refining the structure of the text. The authors have reviewed and edited the output and take full responsibility for the content of this publication.

Conflicts of Interest: The authors declare no conflicts of interest.

References

1. Zhang, X.; Huang, H.; Zhang, X.; Yu, L.; Liu, H. Electromyographic Analysis of Lower Limb Muscles during Riding a Self-Balancing Electric Scooter. *Sensors* **2020**, *20*, 4624. [CrossRef]
2. Wang, W.; Li, J.; Li, Y.; Zhang, J. Electromyographic Analysis of Lower Limb Muscles during Riding a Segway PT. *Sensors* **2019**, *19*, 5534. [CrossRef]
3. Ribeiro, A.S.; Schoenfeld, B.J.; Souza, M.F.; Tomeleri, C.M.; Souza, D.; Venturini, D.; Barbosa, D.S.; Cyrino, E.S. Traditional and pyramidal resistance training systems improve muscle quality and metabolic biomarkers in older women: A randomized crossover study. *Exp. Gerontol.* **2019**, *127*, 110723. [CrossRef]
4. Rimaud, D.; Messonnier, L.; Castells, J.; Devillard, X.; Calmels, P.; Saboul, D. Electromyographic assessment of muscle activity between genders during unilateral weight-bearing tasks using adjusted distances. *J. Electromyogr. Kinesiol.* **2017**, *34*, 14–21. [CrossRef]
5. Romano, R.; Sardella, F.; Zanetti, A.; Guccione, A.A. Electromyographic analysis of vastus medialis obliquus and vastus lateralis muscles during open kinetic chain and closed kinetic chain exercises in patients with patellofemoral pain syndrome: A case–control study. *J. Electromyogr. Kinesiol.* **2018**, *43*, 61–67. [CrossRef]
6. Silva, D.C.; Silva, Z.; Sousa, G.d.C.; Silva, L.F.; Marques, K.d.V.; Soares, A.B.; Cerqueira, E.P.; Liberti, E.A.; Bérzin, F. Electromyographic evaluation of upper limb muscles involved in armwrestling sport simulation during dynamic and static conditions. *J. Electromyogr. Kinesiol.* **2009**, *19*. [CrossRef]
7. Maarsingh, E.J.; Oud, M.; van Eykern, L.A.; Hoekstra, M.O.; van Aalderen, W.M. Electromyographic monitoring of respiratory muscle activity in dyspneic infants and toddlers. *Respir. Physiol. Neurobiol.* **2006**, *150*, 191–199. [CrossRef]
8. Arghadeh, R.; Alizadeh, M.H.; Minoonejad, H.; Sheikhhoseini, R.; Asgari, M.; Jaitner, T. Electromyography of shoulder muscles in individuals without scapular dyskinesis during closed kinetic chain exercises on stable and unstable surfaces: A systematic review and meta-analysis. *Front. Sports Act. Living* **2024**, *6*. [CrossRef]
9. Zhang, X.; Huang, H.; Zhang, X.; Yu, L.; Liu, H. Electromyographic Analysis of Upper Limb Muscles during Riding a Self-Balancing Electric Unicycle. *Sensors* **2020**, *20*, 7111. [CrossRef]
10. De Luca, C.J. The Use of Surface Electromyography in Biomechanics. *J. Appl. Biomech.* **1997**, *13*, 135–163.
11. Mills, K.R. The basics of electromyography. *J. Neurol. Neurosurg. Psychiatry* **2005**, *76*, ii32–ii35. [CrossRef] [PubMed]
12. Mizrahi, J. *Advances in Applied Electromyography*; IntechOpen: London, UK, 2011; ISBN 978-953-307-382-8. Available online: https://www.intechopen.com/books/359 (accessed on 20 April 2024).
13. Preston, D.C.; Shapiro, B.E. *Electromyography and Neuromuscular Disorders*, 4th ed.; Elsevier: Amsterdam, The Netherlands, 2020; ISBN 9780323661805.
14. Papagiannis, G.I.; Triantafyllou, A.I.; Roumpelakis, I.M.; Zampeli, F.; Garyfallia Eleni, P.; Koulouvaris, P.; Papadopoulos, E.C.; Papagelopoulos, P.J.; Babis, G.C. Methodology of surface electromyography in gait analysis: Review of the literature. *J. Med. Eng. Technol.* **2019**, *43*, 59–65. [CrossRef]
15. Hellig, T.; Johnen, L.; Mertens, A.; Nitsch, V.; Brandl, C. Investigation of observational methods assessing workload of static working postures based on surface electromyography. *Work* **2019**, *62*, 185–195. [CrossRef] [PubMed]
16. Kinali, G.; Kara, S.; Yıldırım, M.S. Electromyographic analysis of an ergonomic risk factor: Overhead work. *J. Phys. Ther. Sci.* **2016**, *28*, 1924–1927. [CrossRef]

17. Ficek, K.; Gołas, A.; Pietraszewski, P.; Strózik, M.; Krzysztofik, M. The Effects of a Combined Pre- and Post-Operative Anterior Cruciate Ligament Reconstruction Rehabilitation Program on Lower Extremity Muscle Imbalance. *Appl. Sci.* **2022**, *12*, 7411. [CrossRef]
18. Lee, K. EMG-Triggered Pedaling Training on Muscle Activation, Gait, and Motor Function for Stroke Patients. *Brain Sci.* **2022**, *12*, 76. [CrossRef]
19. Pilkar, R.; Momeni, K.; Ramanujam, A.; Ravi, M.; Garbarini, E.; Gail, F. Forrest; Use of Surface EMG in Clinical Rehabilitation of Individuals With SCI: Barriers and Future Considerations. *Front. Neurol.* **2020**, *11*, 578559. [CrossRef]
20. Horyzont 2020 Projekt. Available online: https://torqway.com/pl (accessed on 13 April 2025).
21. Bęczkowska, S.A.; Grabarek, I.; Zysk, Z.; Gosek-Ferenc, K. Physical Activity and Ecological Means of Transport—Functional Assessment Methodology. *Int. J. Environ. Res. Public Health* **2022**, *19*, 9211. [CrossRef]
22. Noraxom.com. Available online: https://www.noraxon.com/ (accessed on 20 April 2024).
23. Seniam.com. Available online: http://www.seniam.org/ (accessed on 20 April 2024).
24. Alizadehkhaiyat, O.; Fisher, A.C. Electromyographic analysis of shoulder muscle activation during push-up variations on stable and unstable surfaces. *Phys. Ther. Sport* **2007**, *8*, 146–155.
25. Liu, J.Z.; Brown, R.W.; Yue, G.H. A dynamical model of muscle activation, fatigue, and recovery. *Biophys. J.* **2002**, *82*, 2344–2359.
26. Warth, R.; Millett, P. *Physical Examination of the Shoulder: An Evidence-Based Approach*; Springer: New York, NY, USA, 2015. [CrossRef]
27. Sung, Y.; Lee, D. Surface Electromyography Analysis for Evaluating Muscle Fatigue in Upper Extremity Muscles. *J. Electromyogr. Kinesiol.* **2020**, *55*, 102476. [CrossRef]
28. Chowdhury, R.H.; Reaz, M.B.I.; Bin Mohd Ali, M.A.; Bakar, A.A.; Chellappan, K.; Chang, T.G. Surface Electromyography Signal Processing and Classification Techniques. *Sensors* **2021**, *21*, 2909. [CrossRef]
29. Zhang, X.; Liu, H. Electromyographic Analysis of Upper Limb Muscles during Nordic Walking. *J. Electromyogr. Kinesiol.* **2020**, *53*, 102400. [CrossRef]
30. Wang, W.; Li, Y. Comparative Analysis of Muscle Activation during Walking with and without Nordic Walking Poles. *Sensors* **2021**, *21*, 1234. [CrossRef]
31. Kamavuako, E.N.; Englehart, K.B. On the usability of intramuscular EMG for prosthetic control: A Fitts' law approach. *J. NeuroEng. Rehabil.* **2015**, *12*, 51. [CrossRef]
32. Del Vecchio, A.; Holobar, A.; Falla, D. Large-scale detection of variability in fascicle conduction velocity reveals motor unit recruitment strategies. *J. Physiol.* **2019**, *597*, 523–540. [CrossRef]
33. Kallenberg, L.A.; Hermens, H.J. Motor unit firing rate patterns during voluntary muscle force generation: A simulation study. *J. Electromyogr. Kinesiol.* **2018**, *41*, 104–112. [CrossRef]
34. Gazzoni, M.; Celadon, N.; Mastrapasqua, D. Surface EMG applications in the assessment of neuromuscular function. *J. Electromyogr. Kinesiol.* **2017**, *35*, 1–15. [CrossRef]
35. De Luca, C.J. The use of surface electromyography in biomechanics. *J. Appl. Biomech.* **2019**, *35*, 86–101. [CrossRef]
36. Merletti, R.; Botter, A.; Troiano, A. Technology and instrumentation for detection and conditioning of the surface electromyographic signal: State of the art. *Clin. Biomech.* **2009**, *24*, 122–134. [CrossRef]
37. Merletti, R.; Parker, P.A. (Eds.) *Electromyography-Physiology, Engineering, and Noninvasive Applications*; John Wiley & Sons: Hoboken, NJ, USA, 2004; ISBN 0-471-67580-6.
38. Earp, J.E.; Newton, R.U.; Cormie, P.; Blazevich, A.J. Knee angle-specific EMG normalization: The use of polynomial based EMG-angle relationships. *J. Electromyogr. Kinesiol.* **2013**, *23*, 238–244. [CrossRef]
39. Mahaudens, P.; Banse, X.; Mousny, M.; Detrembleur, C. Gait in adolescent idiopathic scoliosis: Kinematics and electromyographic analysis. *Eur. Spine J.* **2009**, *18*, 512–521. [CrossRef]
40. Shanbehzadeh, S.; Mohseni Bandpei, M.A.; Ehsani, F. Knee muscle activity during gait in patients with anterior cruciate ligament injury: A systematic review of electromyographic studies. *Knee Surg. Sport. Traumatol. Arthrosc.* **2017**, *25*, 1432–1442. [CrossRef]
41. Mohseni-Bandpei, M.A.; Rajabzadeh, F.; Hamedinia, M.R.; Zarghami, M.; Motealleh, A. Electromyographic analysis of the effect of adding vibration to physical therapy for the management of low back pain. *J. Bodyw. Mov. Ther.* **2017**, *21*, 715–722. [CrossRef]
42. Herrington, L.; Waterman, R.; Smith, L. Electromyographic analysis of shoulder muscles during press-up variations and progressions. *J Electromyogr. Kinesiol.* **2015**, *25*. [CrossRef]
43. Qian, Y.; Zhang, H.; Xie, H.; Zheng, Y. Electromyographic Analysis of Thigh Muscles during Unconventional Bicycle Riding. *Sensors* **2020**, *20*, 3910. [CrossRef]
44. Shenoy, S. EMG in sports rehabilitation. *Br. J. Sport. Med.* **2010**, *44*, i10. [CrossRef]
45. Felici, F.; Vecchio, A.D. Surface Electromyography: What limits its use in exercise and sport physiology? *Front. Neurol.* **2020**, *11*, 578504. [CrossRef]

46. de Sire, A.; Demeco, A.; Marotta, N.; Moggio, L.; Palumbo, A.; Iona, T.; Ammendolia, A. Anterior Cruciate Ligament Injury Prevention Exercises: Could a Neuromuscular Warm-Up Improve Muscle Pre-Activation before a Soccer Game? A Proof-of-Principle Study on Professional Football Players. *Appl. Sci.* **2021**, *11*, 4958. [CrossRef]
47. Paiva, A.; Catarino, A.; Carvalho, H.; Postolache, O.; Postolache, G.; Ferreira, F. Design of a Long Sleeve T-Shirt with ECG and EMG for Athletes and Rehabilitation Patients. In *Innovation, Engineering and Entrepreneurship. HELIX 2018*; Machado, J., Soares, F., Veiga, G., Eds.; Lecture Notes in Electrical Engineering; Springer: Cham, Switzerland, 2018; Volume 505, ISBN 978-3-319-91333-9.
48. Signorile, J.F.; Avedesian, J.M.; Babamoto, B.N.; Yan, Z.; Magyari, P.M. Electromyographic analysis of hip adduction exercises in collegiate female soccer players. *J. Strength Cond. Res.* **2019**, *33*, 1229–1235. [CrossRef]
49. Dello Iacono, A.; Padulo, J.; Seitz, L.D.; Ardigo, L.P. Lower-limb electromyographic analysis during an incremental cycling exercise until exhaustion. *J. Electromyogr. Kinesiol.* **2018**, *38*, 126–132. [CrossRef]
50. Kumar, S. (Ed.) *Electromyography in Ergonomics*, 1st ed.; Routledge: London, UK, 1996. [CrossRef]
51. Bęczkowska, S.; Celiński, D.; Grabarek, I.; Grzybowska, K.; Zysk, Z. (Nie)ergonomiczne warunki pracy ratownika w ambulansie medycznym. *Med. Pr. Work. Health Saf.* **2024**, *75*, 31–44. [CrossRef]
52. Marras, W.S. Overview of Electromyography in Ergonomics. *Proc. Hum. Factors Ergon. Soc. Annu. Meet.* **2000**, *44*, 5-534–5-536. Available online: https://journals.sagepub.com/doi/abs/10.1177/154193120004403037?journalCode=proe (accessed on 20 April 2024). [CrossRef]
53. Available online: https://www.researchgate.net/publication/352015010_A_Review_of_Electromyography_Signal_Analysis_of_Fatigue_Muscle_for_Manual_Lifting (accessed on 20 April 2024).
54. Kupa, E.J.; Roy, S.H.; Kandarian, S.C.; De Luca, C.J. Effects of muscle fiber type and size on EMG median frequency and conduction velocity. *J. Appl. Physiol.* **1995**, *79*, 23–32. [CrossRef] [PubMed]
55. Viitasalo, J.T.; Komi, P.V.; Hämäläinen, I. Changes in EMG frequency spectrum during fatigue. *Eur. J. Appl. Physiol. Occup. Physiol.* **1981**, *46*, 347–356. [CrossRef]

sensors

MDPI

Article

Asymmetries of Force and Power During Single-Leg Counter Movement Jump in Young Adult Females and Males

Jarosław Kabaciński *, Joanna Gorwa, Waldemar Krakowiak and Michał Murawa

Department of Biomechanics, Poznan University of Physical Education, 61-871 Poznan, Poland
* Correspondence: kabacinski@awf.poznan.pl; Tel./Fax: +48-61-835-53-92

Abstract: Background/Objectives: Inter-limb asymmetry of a given variable for vertical jumps is commonly assessed in both healthy individuals and those undergoing rehabilitation post-injury. The aim of this study was to compare the asymmetry index between the take-off and landing of a single-leg counter movement jump (CMJ), as well as between females and males. Methods: Twenty-three healthy females (age: 21.5 ± 1.6 years) and twenty-three healthy males (age: 21.1 ± 1.8 years) participated in this study. The assessment of two asymmetry indices (AI1 and AI2) was conducted for the peak vertical ground reaction force (PVGRF) and maximum power (MP) during single-leg CMJ take-offs and landings performed on the force platform. Results: The analysis showed significant main effects ($p < 0.001$) for the phase factor (only AI2) and for the gender factor (only AI1). Moreover, there was a non-significant interaction effect between the phase factor and gender factor ($p = 0.476$). Pairwise comparisons revealed significant differences in the values of (1) AI2 between the take-off and landing ($p < 0.001$) and (2) AI1 between females and males ($p < 0.001$). Conclusions: Findings showed significant effects of the phase factor (only for AI2) and gender factor (only for AI1) on the magnitude of inter-limb asymmetry during single-leg CMJs. Furthermore, this study reported the significantly higher asymmetry of the PVGRF and MP for landing than take-off, which may result from difficulties in controlling the jumper's landing technique on one foot at higher velocity. In addition, the assessment of asymmetry for single-leg CMJs using AI1 should be performed separately for females and males, as opposed to AI2. Participants of both genders generally demonstrated a higher AI level for the power than for the force.

Keywords: asymmetry; force; power; single-leg counter movement jump; gender

1. Introduction

Many biomechanical tests often involve comparing the function of one limb with the contralateral limb to determine the magnitude of asymmetry. The percentage difference of a given variable between limbs is provided by the so-called asymmetry index (AI), defined using various formulas. Among the various indices, the calculations provide the standard ratio index [1,2], the symmetry index [3–7], the strength asymmetry index [8,9], the Vagenas and Hoshizaki formula [10], and the formula containing the natural logarithm [11].

The AI value above 10% or 15% indicates a significant inter-limb asymmetry that may contribute to reduced performance of the weaker limb and increased risk of injury [2,12–14]. Researchers linked an increased asymmetry to factors such as overuse of the dominant limb in specific sports [15,16], previous injuries to one limb [17–19], the intensity of plyometric exercise involving jumps [20,21], and gender [22–24]. In some sports (e.g., football), above-threshold asymmetry of strength or power may impair exercise performance and negatively affect athletic outcomes [16,25–28]. In turn, in the athlete after anterior cruciate ligament (ACL) reconstruction, excessive asymmetry may hinder a timely return to training and increase the risk of re-injury [13,18,19,29].

Vertical jumps such as the counter movement jump (CMJ), squat jump (SJ), and drop jump (DJ) are commonly performed using a double-leg technique. However, the level of force and power can also be assessed during single-leg take-offs and landings of CMJs, SJs, or DJs. The evaluation of both variables for each lower extremity separately in these jumps is crucial, as many sport-specific movement patterns are unilateral in nature [30]. Therefore, single-leg vertical jumps have gained wide utility for examining inter-limb asymmetry in both healthy athletes and athletes rehabilitated after ACL reconstruction [13,30–32].

Previous studies have focused on assessing the asymmetry of selected variables during vertical jumps performed on a force platform in healthy individuals [13,21,22,25,26,30,33–36] and athletes with ACL injury [17,19,31,37,38]. Considering the take-off and landing, Paterno et al. [31] investigated the asymmetry of the peak vertical ground reaction force (PVGRF) during DJs in female athletes after ACL reconstruction. Furthermore, Cone et al. [21] determined the differences in the asymmetry index for PVGRF between the take-off and landing phases of the double-leg CMJs and double-leg DJs in men. However, the analysis of the available papers indicates incomplete data on the influence of concentric contraction (take-off) or eccentric contraction (landing) and gender on the magnitude of inter-limb asymmetry of a given variable in single-leg CMJs. Therefore, the aim of the study was to compare the asymmetry index between the take-off and landing, as well as between females and males, for the force and power developed during the single-leg CMJ.

2. Materials and Methods

2.1. Participants

A total of forty-six students from Poznan University of Physical Education participated in this study. This group included twenty-three females (age: 21.5 ± 1.6 years, body mass: 59.0 ± 5.0 kg, and body height: 1.66 ± 0.05 m) and twenty-three males (age: 21.1 ± 1.8 years, body mass: 72.5 ± 9.2 kg, and body height: 1.79 ± 0.07 m). The sample size was calculated using G*Power software (version 3.1.9.7). For an effect size of 0.5, a power of 0.80, and an alpha level of 0.05, a total sample size of 34 was obtained.

All participants were healthy and recreationally active. The International Physical Activity Questionnaire (IPAQ) was used to determine the physical activity of the participants [39]. The IPAQ results indicated that the activity level was high for all participants and sufficient in 6 participants. In addition, each student declared the right lower extremity (LE) as the functionally dominant during various movements (e.g., jumping, kicking). This dominance was confirmed in all participants by a ball-kicking test performed in the laboratory. Hence, the dominant LE (D) and the non-dominant LE (ND) were adopted. The inclusion criteria included (1) age between 18 and 24 years, (2) non-professional sports practice, (3) no history of ankle, knee, hip, or back injuries (one year before testing), (4) lack of potential medical problems, and (5) at least a sufficient level of physical activity based on the IPAQ. All participants were familiarized with the experimental procedures and provided informed consent to participate in this study. The study was conducted in accordance with the Declaration of Helsinki, and the protocol was approved by the Ethics Committee of the Poznan University of Medical Sciences (number 546/16, 10 June 2022).

2.2. Data Collection

The stationary force platform 800 Hz (BP400600, AMTI, Watertown, MA, USA) was used. The ground reaction forces were collected using the BTS Smart Capture software (version Smart-D, BTS Bioengineering, Milan, Italy). The single-leg counter movement jump (CMJ) was used to compare the peak vertical ground reaction force (PVGRF) and maximum power (MP) between the dominant LE (D) and non-dominant LE (ND) for both the take-off and landing. These tests were conducted over four days from 10 a.m. to 2 p.m. (June 2023). Measurements were preceded by a 10 min warm-up involving treadmill running as well as static and dynamic stretching exercises. Each student was instructed to keep their hands on their hips, jump as high as possible, take off from one foot, and land on the same foot during the CMJ. After a few trials, the jumper performed six successful single-leg CMJs, i.e., three for D and three for ND, alternately (first one LE and then the opposite LE) and randomly (first D or ND). The participant started the jump from an upright position (standing phase) and flexed their knee joint to an angle of approximately 90° (braking phase). Half-minute rest periods between these jumps and approximately one-minute rest periods between the CMJ trials and successful CMJs were assumed.

2.3. Data Analysis

The VGRF data vs. time for the 276 trials were exported as files with the .xls extension. Then, in Microsoft Excel 2019, the velocity values were calculated based on numerical integration according to Simpson's method. The following formulas were used:

$$\mathrm{a_Z} = \frac{\mathrm{R_Z}}{\mathrm{m}} - \mathrm{g} \tag{1}$$

where m represents body mass, $\mathrm{R_Z}$ is the vertical ground reaction force, and g is the gravity acceleration (9.80665 $\mathrm{m{\cdot}s^{-2}}$),

$$\mathrm{v_Z(t)} = \mathrm{v_{oz}} + \int \mathrm{a_Z(t)dt} \tag{2}$$

where $\mathrm{v_Z(t)}$ represents vertical velocity vs. time, $\mathrm{v_{oz}}$ is the initial vertical velocity, and $\mathrm{a_Z(t)}$ is vertical acceleration vs. time,

$$\mathrm{P_Z(t)} = \mathrm{R_Z(t){\cdot}v_Z(t)} \tag{3}$$

where $\mathrm{P_Z(t)}$ represents vertical mechanical power vs. time.

In this study, the asymmetry index (AI) values were calculated using Formula (4) [17,40] and Formula (5) [8–10].

$$\mathrm{AI1} = \frac{\mathrm{X_D - X_{ND}}}{\max(\mathrm{X_D, X_{ND}})}\cdot 100\% \tag{4}$$

$$\mathrm{AI2} = \frac{|\mathrm{X_D - X_{ND}}|}{\max(\mathrm{X_D, X_{ND}})}\cdot 100\% \tag{5}$$

where $\mathrm{X_D}$ and $\mathrm{X_{ND}}$ are the values of a given variable for the D and ND, respectively, related to a single trial.

2.4. Statistical Analysis

Statistical analysis was conducted using the IBM SPSS Statistics software for Windows, version 30.0 (Armonk, NY, USA: IBM Corp). The Shapiro–Wilk test was used to verify the distribution of variables. The paired samples *t*-test for the comparisons between the LEs was used. The mixed-factorial ANOVA with two factors (phase [take-off or landing] × gender [female or male]) for the PVGRF and MP was performed. Sphericity was examined using the Mauchly test. A Bonferroni correction for multiple pairwise comparisons was used. The effect size for the ANOVA test was determined using the partial eta-squared (η^2). According to the Cohen guidelines, values of η^2 were small for 0.01, medium for 0.06, and large for 0.14 [41]. Significance level alpha was set at $p < 0.05$.

3. Results

The means and standard deviations of the variables in females and males are presented in Table 1.

Table 1. The means and standard deviations of PVGRF and MP during the take-off and landing phases.

Variable	Phase	Females		Males	
		Non-Dominant	Dominant	Non-Dominant	Dominant
PVGRF (N)	Take-off	1163.9 ± 129.8	1217.8 ± 134.9	1572.4 ± 161.6	1597.0 ± 112.8
	Landing	2033.7 ± 432.1	2149.5 ± 367.8	2737.4 ± 463.1	2705.7 ± 401.8
MP (W)	Take-off	1733.0 ± 223.2	1853.1 ± 236.6	2580.3 ± 290.6	2548.7 ± 290.3
	Landing	2948.0 ± 514.0	3206.3 ± 502.3	4311.3 ± 711.6	4053.8 ± 1016.6

Notes: PVGRF—the peak vertical ground reaction force, MP—the maximum power.

Comparisons between LEs revealed significant differences in the values of PVGRF ($p = 0.001$) and MP ($p = 0.01$) for take-off in females and non-significant differences in the values of (1) PVGRF and MP for landing in females ($p > 0.05$) and (2) PVGRF and MP for take-off and landing in males ($p > 0.05$).

Effect sizes and p-values of the mixed-factorial ANOVA for the three factors and interactions are presented in Tables 2 and 3.

Table 2. Effect sizes of the mixed-factorial ANOVA for the AI1.

Factor	PVGRF		MP	
	η^2	p	η^2	p
Phase	0.003	0.717	0.018	0.379
Gender	0.058	0.108	0.175	0.004 *
Phase × Gender	0.012	0.467	0.041	0.178

Notes: PVGRF—the peak vertical ground reaction force, MP—the maximum power, AI1—the first asymmetry index, η^2—the partial eta-squared, *—significant difference.

Table 3. Effect sizes of the mixed-factorial ANOVA for the AI2.

Factor	PVGRF		MP	
	η^2	p	η^2	p
Phase	0.336	<0.001 *	0.367	<0.001 *
Gender	0.008	0.547	0.002	0.743
Phase × Gender	0.005	0.656	0.032	0.236

Notes: PVGRF—the peak vertical ground reaction force, MP—the maximum power, AI2—the second asymmetry index, η^2—the partial eta-squared, *—significant difference.

Considering the analyzed variables, the sphericity ($W = 1.0$; $p = 1.000$) of all factors and all interactions was fulfilled.

Analysis showed the non-significant main within-subject effect ($p > 0.05$) for the AI1 and the significant main within-subject effect ($p < 0.05$) for the AI2 at $F_{1,44} = 22.3$ (PVGRF) and $F_{1,44} = 25.5$ (MP). The significant between-subject main effect ($p < 0.05$) at $F_{1,44} = 9.3$ for the AI1 (MP) only was observed. A non-significant interaction effect ($p > 0.05$) for both variables was found.

Results of the η^2 indicated a (1) large effect size for phase factor (AI1 for MP and AI2 for PVGRF and MP), gender factor (AI1 for PVGRF and MP), and interaction factor (AI1 and AI2 for MP); (2) medium effect size for gender factor (AI2 for PVGRF) and interaction factor (AI1 for PVGRF); and (3) small effect size for phase factor (AI1 for PVGRF), gender factor (AI2 for MP), and interaction factor (AI2 for PVGRF).

The means and standard deviations of the AI1 and AI2 in females and males are presented in Figures 1 and 2. The analysis revealed significantly higher values of (1) AI1 in females than males for the take-off phase by 7.4% (MP) as well as the landing phase by 5.9% (PVGRF) and by 14.1% (MP) and (2) AI2 for the landing phase than the take-off phase by 8.1% (PVGRF) and by 6.2% (MP) in females as well as by 6.7% (PVGRF) and by 10.1% (MP) in males.

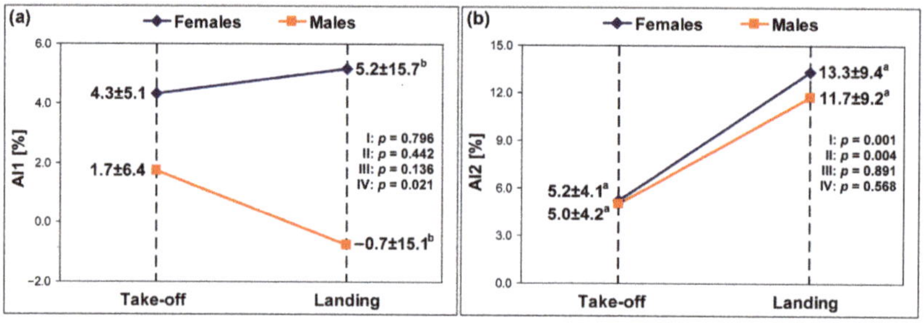

Figure 1. The means and standard deviations of (**a**) the AI1 and (**b**) the AI2 for the PVGRF. AI1—the first asymmetry index, AI2—the second asymmetry index, PVGRF—the peak vertical ground reaction force, I—take-off vs. landing for females, II—take-off vs. landing for males, III—females vs. males for take-off, IV—females vs. males for landing, a—significance for comparisons between take-off and landing, b—significance for comparisons between females and males.

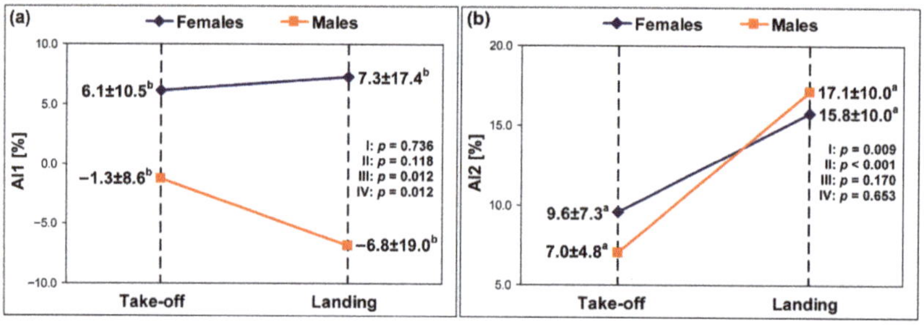

Figure 2. The means and standard deviations of (**a**) the AI1 and (**b**) the AI2 for the MP. AI1—the first asymmetry index, AI2—the second asymmetry index, MP—the maximum power, I—take-off vs. landing for females, II—take-off vs. landing for males, III—females vs. males for take-off, IV—females vs. males for landing, a—significance for comparisons between take-off and landing, b—significance for comparisons between females and males.

The pairwise comparisons also showed non-significant differences in the AI1 values: (1) between the take-off and landing phases in females and males for both variables ($p > 0.05$) and (2) between females and males during the take-off phase for PVGRF only ($p > 0.05$). Considering the AI2 values, non-significant differences between females and males for both variables were found ($p > 0.05$).

4. Discussion

This study compared two asymmetry indices for force (PVGRF) and power (MP) between the take-off and landing phases in single-leg CMJs, as well as between female and male students. The asymmetry index AI1—calculated according to Formula (4) [17,40], i.e., the ratio of D-ND and the greater value of D and ND—and the asymmetry index AI2—calculated according to Formula (5) [8–10], i.e., the ratio of |D-ND| and the greater value of D and ND—were used for the analysis.

The analysis showed generally non-significant differences in the mean results of both variables between D and ND, indicating similar force and power of one LE to the contralateral LE. In particular, the AI1 results indicated a non-significant asymmetry for PVGRF and MP (below the normative threshold of 10%) in participants, both for the take-off phase (mean AI1 in range: −1.3–6.1%) and landing phase (mean AI1 in range: −6.8–7.3%). Thus, expected AI values were obtained because the evaluation included healthy, recreationally active women and men. Most female students demonstrated slightly greater force and power during take-offs and landings for D than for ND (except for PVGRF for take-offs). In turn, the majority of male students performed non-significantly stronger and more powerful take-offs from ND and landings on ND compared to D, which resulted in a negative mean AI1 value. In contrast, the AI2 only provides positive results due to the absolute value in the numerator of Formula (5). Therefore, averaging negative and positive AI1 values led to a greater data dispersion (larger standard deviation) compared to AI2.

The findings revealed a significant main effect for the factor phase and thus its influence on the level of AI in both groups. However, only AI2 results indicated significantly greater PVGRF and MP asymmetry for landings than for take-offs in both females and males. This trend was not observed for AI1, as the mean values of this index for landings were considerably lower than those of AI2. In contrast to AI1, the AI2 formula contains an absolute value in the numerator; hence, it always provides a result greater than zero. Undoubtedly, the use of different AIs influenced the divergence of their results for comparisons between the take-off and landing phases.

The increased asymmetry in force and power observed for the landing phase of the single-leg CMJ can be attributed, among others, to poorer stability of the ND joints during the high eccentric loads. Greater dynamic loads imposed on the LE in the landing phase result from large VGRF and increased movement velocity. Additionally, a valgus knee alignment of the jumper in the frontal plane often occurs [42]. These factors contribute to greater instability of the knee joint, which leads to difficulties in controlling landing mechanics. Therefore, this study also assessed AI for power, i.e., a variable defined as the product of VGRF and velocity. In both females and males, higher AI values were found for power than for force due to the influence of movement velocity.

Some authors have identified knee instability during landings as a risk factor for non-contact ACL injuries, particularly in female athletes [21,24,43,44]. The ACL in women absorbs greater external loads due to the more extended knee position during the ground contact [45]. Therefore, a crucial strategy for preventing ACL injuries is the correct landing technique, minimizing unfavorable loads on the knee joint structures [43,46–48]. Furthermore, athletes should also perform soft and stable landings during eccentric exercises, such as CMJs and DJs, with both legs and one leg. In addition, such plyometric training, used to improve muscle capacity, knee stability, and neuromuscular control during the landing, is considered an important part of the rehabilitation program of athletes after ACL reconstruction [20,21,29,49].

Previous studies have assessed inter-limb force asymmetry during take-off and landing in vertical jumps on the force platform [21,26,31]. Furthermore, Cone et al. [21] compared AI between take-off and landing phases, and similarly to the present study, they reported significantly greater AI values for PVGRF in the landing phase than in the take-off phase of the CMJ. Surprisingly, Cone et al. [21] obtained such results using AI1 during bilateral jumps performed only by men on two force platforms. However, athletes such as volleyball, basketball, and soccer players frequently take off from one LE and land on one LE during games. There are also situations when a jumping athlete asymmetrically loads the LE, coming into contact with the ground with one foot before the other foot [21,31].

The importance of using AI2 is emphasized by the divergent results between both indices for comparisons between female students and male students. The analysis showed the influence of gender on the results of AI1 and the lack of such a tendency for AI2. In females, a non-significantly higher mean value of AI1 was observed than in males for both take-offs and landings. This difference may be attributed to the different movement biomechanics of women during the CMJ, determined by their different body structure in comparison with men. Considering volleyball jumps, Salci et al. [46] observed gender differences in the values of dynamic, kinetic, and kinematic variables for the knee, hip, and ankle during landings. However, AI2 results indicated non-significant differences in values of this index between both groups. Thus, the selection of the type of AI plays a role in determining the level of asymmetry in participants differentiated by gender. When using AI1, researchers should assess force and power asymmetries in vertical jumps separately for women and men. In addition, comparisons revealed a non-significant interaction effect between the gender factor and phase factor for AI1 and AI2; thus, the difference in AI values between the landing and take-off is not dependent on gender. In both females and males, greater asymmetries in force and power were generally observed for the landing phase than for the take-off phase.

This study had limitations. First, the refusals of some participants due to injuries, illness, and travel prevented the tests from being conducted in the second session with the same group size as in the first session. Second, the study included only recreationally active students, thus excluding athletes. Therefore, these findings are difficult to relate to the data obtained by the athletes.

5. Conclusions

A review of available papers suggests that this study is the first to compare different asymmetry indices of the force and power between the take-off and landing phases, as well as between females and males during the single-leg CMJ. For both groups, the findings revealed a significantly greater asymmetry of the PVGRF and MP for the landing than for the take-off, only in the case of AI2, consistent with the Vagenas and Hoshizaki formula [10]. It was explained that this trend, among others, may result from difficulties in controlling the jumper's landing technique on one foot at higher velocity compared to the take-off. Furthermore, a higher level of power asymmetry than force asymmetry was observed both in females and males due to the influence of velocity. In addition, it was proposed that the assessment of inter-limb asymmetry using the AI1 for the single-leg CMJ should be conducted separately in women and men, as opposed to AI2. Further tests involving populations of healthy individuals and athletes after ACL reconstruction, performing various vertical jumps on a force platform, are needed.

Author Contributions: Conceptualization, J.K. and M.M.; methodology, J.K., J.G., W.K. and M.M.; software, J.K., W.K. and M.M.; validation, J.K. and M.M.; formal analysis, J.K. and M.M.; investigation, J.K., W.K. and M.M.; resources, J.K., W.K. and M.M.; data curation, J.K. and M.M.; writing—original draft preparation, J.K., J.G. and M.M.; writing—review and editing, J.K., J.G. and M.M.; visualization, J.K.; supervision, J.K. and M.M.; funding acquisition, J.K., J.G. and M.M. All authors have read and agreed to the published version of the manuscript.

Funding: This research received no external funding.

Institutional Review Board Statement: The study was conducted in accordance with the Declaration of Helsinki and was approved by Poznan University of Medical Sciences (number 546/16).

Informed Consent Statement: Informed consent was obtained from all subjects involved in this study.

Data Availability Statement: The data are available upon request from the corresponding author.

Acknowledgments: The authors would like to thank all participating students.

Conflicts of Interest: The authors declare no conflicts of interest.

References

1. Ganguli, S.; Mukherji, P.; Bose, K.S. Gait evaluation of unilateral below-knee amputees fitted with patellar-tendon-bearing prostheses. *J. Indian Med. Assoc.* **1974**, *63*, 256–259.
2. Schiltz, M.; Lehance, C.; Maquet, D.; Bury, T.; Crielaard, J.M.; Croisier, J.L. Explosive strength imbalances in professional basketball players. *J. Athl. Train.* **2009**, *44*, 39–47. [CrossRef]
3. Robinson, R.O.; Herzog, W.; Nigg, B.M. Use of force platform variables to quantify the effects of chiropractic manipulation on gait symmetry. *J. Manip. Physiol. Ther.* **1987**, *10*, 172–176.
4. Wong, P.L.; Chamari, K.; Chaouachi, A.; Mao, D.W.; Wisløff, U.; Hong, Y. Difference in plantar pressure between the preferred and non-preferred feet in four soccer-related movements. *Br. J. Sports Med.* **2007**, *41*, 84–92. [CrossRef] [PubMed]
5. Bell, D.R.; Sanfilippo, J.L.; Binkley, N.; Heiderscheit, B.C. Lean mass asymmetry influences force and power asymmetry during jumping in collegiate athletes. *J. Strength Cond. Res.* **2014**, *28*, 884–891. [CrossRef]
6. Sugiyama, T.; Kameda, M.; Kageyama, M.; Kiba, K.; Kanehisa, H.; Maeda, A. Asymmetry between the dominant and non-dominant legs in the kinematics of the lower extremities during a running single leg jump in collegiate basketball players. *J. Sports Sci. Med.* **2014**, *13*, 951–957. [PubMed]
7. Marshall, B.; Franklyn-Miller, A.; Moran, K.; King, E.; Richter, C.; Gore, S.; Strike, S.; Falvey, É. Biomechanical symmetry in elite rugby union players during dynamic tasks: An investigation using discrete and continuous data analysis techniques. *BMC Sports Sci. Med. Rehabil.* **2015**, *7*, 13. [CrossRef] [PubMed]
8. Bishop, C.; Read, P.; Lake, J.; Chavda, S.; Turner, A. Interlimb asymmetries: Understanding how to calculate differences from bilateral and unilateral tests. *Strength Cond. J.* **2018**, *40*, 1–6. [CrossRef]
9. Impellizzeri, F.M.; Rampinini, E.; Maffiuletti, N.; Marcora, S.M. A vertical jump force test for assessing bilateral strength asymmetry in athletes. *Med. Sci. Sports Exerc.* **2007**, *39*, 2044–2050. [CrossRef]
10. Vagenas, G.; Hoshizaki, B. A multivariable analysis of lower-extremity kinematic asymmetry in running. *Int. J. Sport Biomech.* **1992**, *8*, 11–29. [CrossRef]
11. Plotnik, M.; Giladi, N.; Balash, Y.; Peretz, C.; Hausdorff, J.M. Is freezing of gait in Parkinson's disease related to asymmetric motor function? *Ann. Neurol.* **2005**, *57*, 656–663. [CrossRef]
12. Brumitt, J.; Heiderscheit, B.C.; Manske, R.C.; Niemuth, P.E.; Rauh, M.J. Lower extremity functional tests and risk of injury in division III collegiate athletes. *Int. J. Sports Phys. Ther.* **2013**, *8*, 216–227.
13. Vaisman, A.; Guiloff, R.; Rojas, J.; Delgado, I.; Figueroa, D.; Calvo, R. Lower limb symmetry: Comparison of muscular power between dominant and nondominant legs in healthy young adults associated with single-leg-dominant sports. *Orthop. J. Sports Med.* **2017**, *5*, 2325967117744240. [CrossRef]
14. Helme, M.; Tee, J.; Emmonds, S.; Low, C. Does lower-limb asymmetry increase injury risk in sport? A systematic review. *Phys. Ther. Sport.* **2021**, *49*, 204–213. [CrossRef] [PubMed]
15. Markou, S.; Vagenas, G. Multivariate isokinetic asymmetry of the knee and shoulder in elite volleyball players. *Eur. J. Sport Sci.* **2006**, *6*, 71–80. [CrossRef]
16. Michailidis, Y.; Stafylidis, A.; Mandroukas, A.; Kyranoudis, A.E.; Antoniou, G.; Kollias, R.; Kanaras, V.; Bamplekis, C.; Vardakis, L.; Semaltianou, E.; et al. Correlation of the asymmetry index from the single-leg countermovement jump with the asymmetry index from isokinetic strength in elite youth football players. *Appl. Sci.* **2025**, *15*, 2779. [CrossRef]
17. Jordan, M.J.; Aagaard, P.; Herzog, W. Lower limb asymmetry in mechanical muscle function: A comparison between ski racers with and without ACL reconstruction. *Scand. J. Med. Sci. Sports.* **2015**, *25*, e301–e309. [CrossRef]
18. Wiggins, A.J.; Grandhi, R.K.; Schneider, D.K.; Stanfield, D.; Webster, K.E.; Myer, G.D. Risk of secondary injury in younger athletes after anterior cruciate ligament reconstruction: A systematic review and meta-analysis. *Am. J. Sports Med.* **2016**, *44*, 1861–1876. [CrossRef] [PubMed]
19. Chen, P.; Wang, L.; Dong, S.; Ding, Y.; Jia, S.; Zheng, C. Can symmetry of single-leg vertical jump height represent normal lower limb biomechanics of athletes after anterior cruciate ligament reconstruction? *Sports Health* **2024**, *16*, 596–605. [CrossRef]
20. Chmielewski, T.L.; George, S.Z.; Tillman, S.M.; Moser, M.W.; Lentz, T.A.; Indelicato, P.A.; Trumble, T.N.; Shuster, J.J.; Cicuttini, F.M.; Leeuwenburgh, C. Low- versus high-intensity plyometric exercise during rehabilitation after anterior cruciate ligament reconstruction. *Am. J. Sports Med.* **2016**, *44*, 609–617. [CrossRef]
21. Cone, S.M.; Lee, S. Lower limb force asymmetries during landing and jumping exercises: A pilot study. *Int. J. Exerc. Sci.* **2021**, *14*, 544–551. [CrossRef] [PubMed]
22. Stephens, T.M.; Lawson, B.R.; Reiser, R.F. Bilateral asymmetries in max effort single-leg vertical jumps. *Biomed. Sci. Instrum.* **2005**, *41*, 317–322.

23. Stephens, T.M.; Lawson, B.R.; DeVoe, D.E.; Reiser, R.F. Gender and bilateral differences in single-leg countermovement jump performance with comparison to a double-leg jump. *J. Appl. Biomech.* **2007**, *23*, 190–202. [CrossRef]
24. Hewett, T.E.; Ford, K.R.; Hoogenboom, B.J.; Myer, G.D. Understanding and preventing acl injuries: Current biomechanical and epidemiologic considerations—Update 2010. *N. Am. J. Sports Phys. Ther.* **2010**, *5*, 234–251.
25. Bishop, C.; Coratella, G.; Beato, M. Intra- and inter-limb strength asymmetry in soccer: A comparison of professional and under-18 players. *Sports* **2021**, *9*, 129. [CrossRef] [PubMed]
26. Bishop, C.; Read, P.; McCubbine, J.; Turner, A. Vertical and horizontal asymmetries are related to slower sprinting and jump performance in elite youth female soccer players. *J. Strength Cond. Res.* **2021**, *35*, 56–63. [CrossRef]
27. Lin, J.; Shen, J.; Zhou, A.; Badicu, G.; Grosz, W.R. The effects of inter-limb asymmetry on change of direction performance: A systematic review. *Symmetry* **2022**, *14*, 2177. [CrossRef]
28. Michailidis, Y. Relation of jump and change of direction inter-limb asymmetries with fitness in youth male soccer players. *Medicina* **2023**, *59*, 1749. [CrossRef]
29. Buckthorpe, M.; Della Villa, F. Recommendations for plyometric training after ACL reconstruction—A clinical commentary. *Int. J. Sports Phys. Ther.* **2021**, *16*, 879–895. [CrossRef]
30. Hewit, J.K.; Cronin, J.B.; Hume, P.A. Asymmetry in multi-directional jumping tasks. *Phys. Ther. Sport.* **2012**, *13*, 238–242. [CrossRef] [PubMed]
31. Paterno, M.V.; Ford, K.R.; Myer, G.D.; Heyl, R.; Hewett, T.E. Limb asymmetries in landing and jumping 2 years following anterior cruciate ligament reconstruction. *Clin. J. Sport Med.* **2007**, *17*, 258–262. [CrossRef]
32. Ebben, W.P.; Flanagan, E.; Jensen, R.L. Bilateral facilitation and laterality during the countermovement jump. *Percept. Mot. Skills* **2009**, *108*, 251–258. [CrossRef]
33. McElveen, M.T.; Riemann, B.L.; Davies, G.J. Bilateral comparison of propulsion mechanics during single-leg vertical jumping. *J. Strength Cond. Res.* **2010**, *24*, 375–381. [CrossRef]
34. Kobayashi, Y.; Kubo, J.; Matsubayashi, T.; Matsuo, A.; Kobayashi, K.; Ishii, N. Relationship between bilateral differences in single-leg jumps and asymmetry in isokinetic knee strength. *J. Appl. Biomech.* **2013**, *29*, 61–67. [CrossRef]
35. Bishop, C.; de Keijzer, K.L.; Turner, A.N.; Beato, M. Measuring interlimb asymmetry for strength and power: A brief review of assessment methods, data analysis, current evidence, and practical recommendations. *J. Strength Cond. Res.* **2023**, *37*, 745–750. [CrossRef] [PubMed]
36. Wang, P.; Qin, Z.; Zhang, M. Association between pre-season lower limb interlimb asymmetry and non-contact lower limb injuries in elite male volleyball players. *Sci. Rep.* **2025**, *15*, 14481. [CrossRef]
37. Taylor, J.B.; Westbrook, A.E.; Head, P.L.; Glover, K.M.; Paquette, M.R.; Ford, K.R. The single-leg vertical hop provides unique asymmetry information in individuals after anterior cruciate ligament reconstruction. *Clin. Biomech.* **2020**, *80*, 105107. [CrossRef] [PubMed]
38. Ciccodicola, E.M.; Hanson, A.M.; Roberts, S.E.; Katzel, M.J.; Wren, T.A.L. Biomechanics and performance of single-leg vertical and horizontal hop in adolescents post-anterior cruciate ligament reconstruction. *Biomechanics* **2025**, *5*, 5. [CrossRef]
39. Craig, C.L.; Marshall, A.L.; Sjöström, M.; Bauman, A.E.; Booth, M.L.; Ainsworth, B.E.; Pratt, M.; Ekelund, U.; Yngve, A.; Sallis, J.F.; et al. International physical activity questionnaire: 12-country reliability and validity. *Med. Sci. Sports Exerc.* **2003**, *35*, 1381–1395. [CrossRef] [PubMed]
40. Cheung, R.T.; Smith, A.W.; Wong, D.P. H:Q ratios and bilateral leg strength in college field and court sports players. *J. Hum. Kinet.* **2012**, *33*, 63–71. [CrossRef]
41. Cohen, J. *Statistical Power Analysis for the Behavioral Sciences*, 2nd ed.; Lawrence Erlbaum Associates: Mahwah, NJ, USA, 1988.
42. Paterno, M.V.; Schmitt, L.C.; Ford, K.R.; Rauh, M.J.; Myer, G.D.; Huang, B.; Hewett, T.E. Biomechanical measures during landing and postural stability predict second anterior cruciate ligament injury after anterior cruciate ligament reconstruction and return to sport. *Am. J. Sport Med.* **2010**, *38*, 1968–1978. [CrossRef] [PubMed]
43. Griffin, L.Y.; Agel, J.; Albohm, M.J.; Arendt, E.A.; Dick, R.W.; Garrett, W.E.; Garrick, J.G.; Hewett, T.E.; Huston, L.; Ireland, M.L.; et al. Noncontact anterior cruciate ligament injuries: Risk factors and prevention strategies. *J. Am. Acad. Orthop. Surg.* **2000**, *8*, 141–150. [CrossRef]
44. Myer, G.D.; Brent, J.L.; Ford, K.R.; Hewett, T.E. Real-time assessment and neuromuscular training feedback techniques to prevent ACL injury in female athletes. *Strength Cond. J.* **2011**, *33*, 21–35. [CrossRef]
45. Colby, S.; Francisco, A.; Yu, B.; Kirkendall, D.; Finch, M.; Garrett, W., Jr. Electromyographic and kinematic analysis of cutting maneuvers. Implications for anterior cruciate ligament injury. *Am. J. Sports Med.* **2000**, *28*, 234–240. [CrossRef]
46. Salci, Y.; Kentel, B.B.; Heycan, C.; Akin, S.; Korkusuz, F. Comparison of landing maneuvers between male and female college volleyball players. *Clin. Biomech.* **2004**, *19*, 622–628. [CrossRef]
47. Reeser, J.C.; Verhagen, E.; Briner, W.W.; Askeland, T.I.; Bahr, R. Strategies for the prevention of volleyball related injuries. *Br. J. Sports Med.* **2006**, *40*, 594–600. [CrossRef] [PubMed]

48. Blackburn, J.T.; Padua, D.A. Sagittal-plane trunk position, landing forces, and quadriceps electromyographic activity. *J. Athl. Train.* **2009**, *44*, 174–179. [CrossRef] [PubMed]
49. Kasmi, S.; Zouhal, H.; Hammami, R.; Clark, C.C.T.; Hackney, A.C.; Hammami, A.; Chtara, M.; Chortane, S.G.; Salah, F.Z.B.; Granacher, U.; et al. The effects of eccentric and plyometric training programs and their combination on stability and the functional performance in the post-ACL-surgical rehabilitation eriod of elite female athletes. *Front. Physiol.* **2021**, *12*, 688385. [CrossRef]

sensors

MDPI

Article

Mechanosensitivity and Adipose Thickness as Determinants of Pressure to Reach Deep Fasciae in Cervical and Thoracolumbar Regions

Sílvia Pires [1,2,*], Marta Freitas [1,2,3], Francisco Pinho [1,2] and Sofia Brandão [1,2,*]

[1] Escola Superior de Saúde do Vale do Ave, Cooperativa de Ensino Superior Politécnico e Universitário, Rua José António Vidal, 81, 4760-409 Vila Nova de Famalicão, Portugal; marta.goncalves@ipsn.cespu.pt (M.F.); francisco.pinho@ipsn.cespu.pt (F.P.)

[2] H2M—Health and Human Movement Unit, Polytechnic University of Health, Cooperativa de Ensino Superior Politécnico e Universitário, Cooperativa de Responsabilidade Limitada, 4760-409 Vila Nova de Famalicão, Portugal

[3] Centre of Research Rehabilitation (CIR), Escola Superior de Saúde, Rua Dr. António Bernardino de Almeida 400, 4200-072 Porto, Portugal

* Correspondence: silvia.pires@ipsn.cespu.pt (S.P.); fernanda.brandao@ipsn.cespu.pt (S.B.)

Abstract: Objective: We aimed to quantify the mechanical pressure required to reach the deep cervical and thoracolumbar fasciae, to examine its association with pressure pain threshold (PPT) and adipose tissue thickness, and to determine whether PPT and adipose tissue thickness can predict the mechanical pressure needed to reach the fascia. Methods: Forty-three subjects' PPT, mechanical pressure and skinfold in the trapezius and lumbar regions were evaluated using an algometer, an ultrasound scanner, and an adipometer. The Wilcoxon test, Student's *t*-test, and Pearson and Spearman's correlation tests were used ($p < 0.05$). Results: The values of mechanical pressure in the cervical and lumbar regions were 6.06 ± 0.186 N/cm^2 and 5.85 ± 5.280, 7.287 N/cm^2, respectively. PPT values were 18.88 ± 0.917 N/cm^2, and 46.46 ± 2.408 N/cm^2, respectively ($p < 0.001$), and the adipose tissue thickness values in the cervical and lumbar regions were 0.88 ± 0.675 cm, 1.08 and 1.48 ± 0.069 cm ($p < 0.001$). There was no correlation between the variables in either region under study. Conclusions: The mechanical pressure required to reach the deep cervical and thoracolumbar fasciae was similar with an average value of approximately 6 N/cm^2, suggesting a consistent mechanical response across these anatomical regions. Mechanosensitivity and subcutaneous adipose tissue thickness did not influence the mechanical pressure needed to access the deep fascial tissue.

Keywords: deep fasciae; pressure pain threshold; mechanical pressure; adipose tissue thickness

1. Introduction

Fascia is a highly viscoelastic, uninterrupted connective tissue, forming a dense three-dimensional network of collagen, which plays a crucial role in the organisation, support, protection and movement of different systems [1–3]. In addition to its mechanical and structural functions, fascia is richly vascularised and innervated, containing blood vessels and sensory nerve endings - including mechanoreceptors and nociceptors—that contribute to its role in proprioception and pain modulation [4].

Several authors argue that, in addition to its structural role, the fascia also functions as an active sensory organ. This is due to the presence of mechanoreceptors, proprioceptors, nociceptors and interoceptors, which have a key role in pain perception, neuromuscular modulation and body awareness [2,5–7]. Recent evidence proposes a view of fascia as a body-wide layered system of connective tissues that enables tensional transmission, shearing mobility, and interstitial fluid flow across multiple scales [8]. This systemic perspective includes superficial, deep, visceral and neural components, as well as the fascial *interstitium*, hyaluronic acid-rich matrix involved in hydration, mechanotransduction and tissue communication [8].

The deep cervical and thoracolumbar fasciae are especially important due to their biomechanical role in spinal stability and movement. The deep cervical fascia provides structural support and facilitates cervical mobility, while the thoracolumbar fascia plays a crucial role in transmitting and distributing mechanical forces between the trunk and the lower limbs [6,9,10]. Nociceptive input does not arise exclusively from the fascia but from multiple tissue layers, including the epidermis, dermis, subcutaneous tissue and deeper structures. These layers differ in embryological origin and innervation: the epidermis, derived from the ectoderm (like the central nervous system), is innervated by autonomic $A\delta$ and C fibres responsible for nociception and thermal stimuli. In contrast, the dermis and subcutaneous tissues, of mesodermal origin, are innervated by somatic $A\beta$ fibres that respond to mechanical stimuli. This layered neuroanatomical arrangement explains the varied sensory responses elicited by manual pressure and highlights that any attempt to reach the deep fascia inevitably stimulates multiple nociceptive sources. As such, isolating fascial contribution in vivo remains methodologically challenging [11,12].

According to the literature, any restriction of the cervical and thoracolumbar fasciae, such as adhesions, stiffness or inflammation, can lead to mechanical hypersensitivity, which is a determining factor for the presence of pain, increased muscle tension, decreased joint mobility, flexibility deficits and altered nociception [5,13–15].

Among the various therapeutic modalities for myofascial treatment, application of manual pressure to the fascia is widely used in myofascial release techniques, with the aim of altering the density, viscosity, sensitivity and mobility of the tissue, as well as modulating the perception of pain [16,17]. However, it is important to note that any manual pressure applied to reach the fascia must first pass through the overlying skin layers: the epidermis, dermis, and subcutaneous tissue. These structures are not merely passive barriers but actively contribute to the autonomic response—initially via the epidermis and subsequently through mechanosensory input from the dermis. During myofascial therapy, the practitioner's hand is in direct contact with the epidermis. While deeper structures such as the dermis, subcutaneous tissue, and fascia are the intended therapeutic targets, they are indirectly affected by the mechanical transmission of pressure [12].

The presence of subcutaneous fat above the superficial fascia also seems to play a significant role in mechanosensitivity [18]. Studies suggest that changes in the amount and distribution of subcutaneous fat can alter the tension on the fascia and may interfere with mechanosensitivity and restrict fascial mobility, thereby reducing the ability to adapt to movement [19,20].

Although the role of fascia in pain modulation, particularly its mechanosensitivity and relationship with adiposity, has been increasingly explored in the literature, to our knowledge, few studies have directly quantified the mechanical pressure required to access the cervical and thoracolumbar deep fasciae. Existing research shows that fascial manipulation can reduce pain and modify fascial stiffness and thickness, particularly in individuals with chronic neck or low back pain [1,15]. However, studies are lacking that isolate the central autonomic effects of the epidermis on pain and mobility [21], and subsequently correlate the mechanical pressure required to reach deeper fascial layers with tissue thickness and subjective pain perception. This knowledge could facilitate the development of evidence-based guidelines for more effective manual therapy interventions for neck and low back pain [8,22,23].

Therefore, this study aimed to quantify the mechanical pressure required to reach the deep thoracolumbar and cervical fasciae, to examine its association with mechanosensitivity and adipose tissue thickness, and to determine whether mechanosensitivity and adipose tissue thickness can predict the mechanical pressure needed to reach the fascia, using linear regression analysis.

2. Materials and Methods

2.1. Study Design and Ethics

This cross-sectional observational study was conducted at the Escola Superior de Saúde do Vale do Ave (ESSVA), part of the Polytechnic Institute of Health of the North (IPSN), Portugal. Data were collected between October and December 2023. Forty-three participants were assessed in a single experimental session, all of which were conducted at approximately the same time of day (morning) to minimise potential circadian effects on fascial tone [24]. The study was designed and reported in accordance with the Strengthening the Reporting of Observational Studies in Epidemiology (STROBE) guidelines (BIBLO).

The study was approved by the Ethics Committee of the IPSN (references: 41 and 48/CE-IPSN/2023). All participants provided written informed consent prior to participation, in accordance with the Declaration of Helsinki.

2.2. Participants

Participants were volunteers recruited through convenience sampling by direct invitation, using academic contacts. A total of forty-three university students of both sexes were available to participate. Inclusion criteria were being a healthy adult aged between 18 and 30 years. Exclusion criteria included the presence of neurological disorders, neck, shoulder or lumbar pain at the time of assessment, torticollis, inflammatory rheumatic conditions, history of spinal surgery, and fibromyalgia [25]. No formal sample size calculation was performed, as this was an exploratory observational study. The sample size was determined pragmatically, based on the feasibility and accessibility of the population. This approach is considered appropriate in early-phase exploratory research, where the aim is to generate preliminary insights and guide future hypothesis-driven studies. Moreover, the use of healthy university students ensured homogeneity in terms of age and activity levels, reducing potential confounding variability.

2.3. Instruments

Sample Selection and Characterisation

Sample characterisation was carried out through a structured questionnaire that included sociodemographic and anthropometric data, smoking habits, lifestyle, general health status, and exclusion criteria. This non-validated instrument was used solely for descriptive purposes to characterise the sample and ensure eligibility. No inferential analyses were conducted based on these data.

To assess the main outcome variables, we used a digital algometer, an ultrasound scanner, and a skinfold calliper (adipometer).

To access the pressure pain threshold (PPT), the digital algometer was a Wagner FORCE ONE FDIX (Wagner Instruments, Greenwich, CT, USA) equipped with a round rubber tip of 1 cm^2.

In the second stage, ultrasound imaging was performed using a General Electric VIVID E scanner (GE HealthCare, Chicago, IL, USA) with a linear probe (5 cm^2). The probe was adapted to support the algometer, allowing simultaneous monitoring of fascial deformation and quantification of the mechanical applied pressure (Figure 1). To accurately quantify the pressure applied to the fasciae, the force displayed by the algometer (in kgf) was divided by the fixed contact area of the ultrasound transducer (5 cm^2), yielding pressure in N/cm^2. This setup enabled synchronised measurement of both force and fascial deformation in real time. The system was pre-tested to ensure mechanical stability and reproducibility, and the adaptation ensured that the pressure was applied perpendicularly to the tissue without compromising image quality or measurement reliability.

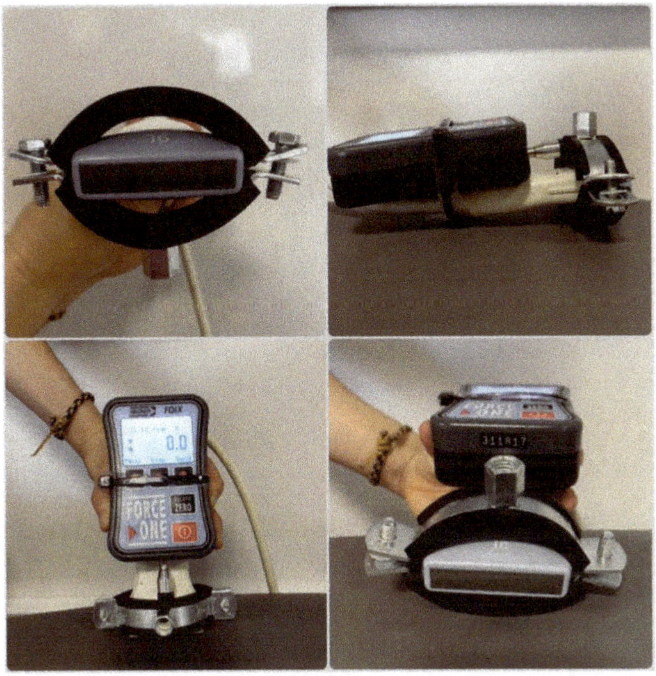

Figure 1. Custom-designed device used to couple the ultrasound probe with the algometer, allowing simultaneous measurement of applied mechanical pressure and real-time visualisation of fascial deformation.

A gradual increase in pressure was applied perpendicularly until fascial contact was confirmed sonographically, defined by loss of fascial sliding or visible deformation of the fascial plane. This criterion was standardised during a pilot phase and applied consistently by a single experienced radiologist. Pressure was applied at a constant rate of approximately 1 kgf/s. According to the manufacturer, the algometer has a margin of error of ±0.1 kg.

To ensure consistency in anatomical site selection, the cervical region was assessed with participants seated, at the midpoint between the spinous process of C7 and the lateral edge of the acromion. The thoracolumbar region was assessed in a prone position, at a point located 5 cm lateral to the spinous process of L1, over the erector spinae muscle. All measurements were performed on the same side, arbitrarily chosen, and repeated three times, with 30 s rest intervals between trials.

Subcutaneous adipose tissue thickness was measured in millimetres using a Baseline® skinfold calliper (Fabrication Enterprises, White Plains, NY, USA), at the same anatomical sites (upper trapezius and lumbar region), following standardised procedures [26].

2.4. Procedures

Data collection took place in a controlled environment within the facilities of the research laboratory. Ambient conditions were kept stable, with temperature maintained between 22 and 24 °C and relative humidity between 40 and 60%, as monitored by a digital thermohygrometer. Noise and visual distractions were minimised, and all sessions were conducted under consistent artificial lighting. Participants were instructed to remain seated and relaxed for at least 10 min prior to assessment to allow for physiological acclimatisation. All procedures were carried out by the same researcher to minimise inter-rater variability [27].

Before starting the main assessments, anthropometric data, including body mass and height, were recorded for each participant. These values were used to calculate the Body Mass Index (BMI), expressed in kg/m^2, using the standard formula BMI = weight (kg)/[height (m)]^2 [28].

To ensure consistency and accuracy in the use of instruments and methodological procedures, a pilot study was conducted with six healthy volunteers. This preliminary phase enabled the standardisation of all procedures, including the use of the algometer (pressure application rate, positioning), the skinfold calliper (grasping technique, timing, and application angle), the ultrasound scanner (probe adaptation and imaging parameters), and the structured questionnaire used to assess sociodemographic data, general health status, and lifestyle habits. Although this questionnaire was not a validated instrument, it was developed by the research team and tested in the pilot phase to ensure clarity, feasibility, and relevance to the target population.

Intra-observer reliability was assessed through repeated measurements of pressure pain threshold and skinfold thickness, taken three days apart by the same examiner. The results showed excellent reliability, with ICC values of 0.96 and 0.98, respectively.

Data collection began with the assessment of PPT, mechanical pressure, and adipose tissue thickness, conducted in a randomised order to minimise measurement bias. All measurements were performed by a single trained examiner using a consistent protocol and imaging orientation, ensuring high methodological reproducibility.

Mechanosensitivity was assessed by evaluating PPT at two anatomical locations: the upper trapezius and the lumbar paraspinal region, bilaterally [29]. Pressure was applied perpendicularly to the skin at a constant rate of approximately 1 kgf/s until the participant reported the first sensation of pain. The mean of three consecutive measurements at each site was recorded, with a 30 s rest interval between repetitions [30]. To ensure standardisation across participants, specific anatomical landmarks and participant positions were used for each measurement:

- Cervical region: Participants were seated on a chair, with their feet flat on the floor and hands resting on their thighs [30]. Given that the deep fascia of the cervical region involves the upper trapezius muscle [31], the measurement site was defined as the midpoint between the spinous process of the C7 vertebra and the lateral edge of the acromion [30].
- Thoracolumbar region: Participants were placed in a relaxed prone position. The measurement site corresponded to the erector spinae muscle, 5 cm lateral to the spinous process of the L1 vertebra [32].

While ideally both regions would be assessed in the same position, this was not feasible due to anatomical constraints and differences in muscular orientation and accessibility between the cervical and lumbar regions. Supine positioning does not provide reliable acoustic windows or palpation access for either of the targeted fascia. Therefore, the seated and prone positions were selected based on established protocols in the literature and were validated during our pilot study in terms of reproducibility and image quality.

The order of assessments (cervical or lumbar first) was randomised across participants to minimise potential order effects or fatigue.

Regarding side selection, ultrasound-assisted fascial compression was performed unilaterally, with the side randomised for each participant. This decision was based on prior literature reporting no significant differences in fascial thickness or mechanosensitivity between dominant and non-dominant sides in healthy individuals [33]. Additionally, the technical complexity and time constraints of simultaneous ultrasound and algometry limited the feasibility of bilateral assessment.

The algometer was then combined with the ultrasound probe to evaluate the mechanical pressure required to reach the deep cervical and thoracolumbar fasciae. These non-diagnostic procedures were performed by a radiologist with 25 years of experience.

The power and overall gain of the ultrasound machine were adjusted to optimise the visualisation of the fascia and muscles and to obtain the best possible visualisation. The probe was placed on the skin to avoid tissue compression but also stable enough to maintain adequate contact between the probe and skin for consistent images. Pressure was applied perpendicularly and progressively increased until fascial contact was confirmed through real-time ultrasound imaging in the longitudinal plane (Figures 2 and 3). The value displayed at that precise moment was recorded. These measurements were repeated three times, with 30 s intervals between each.

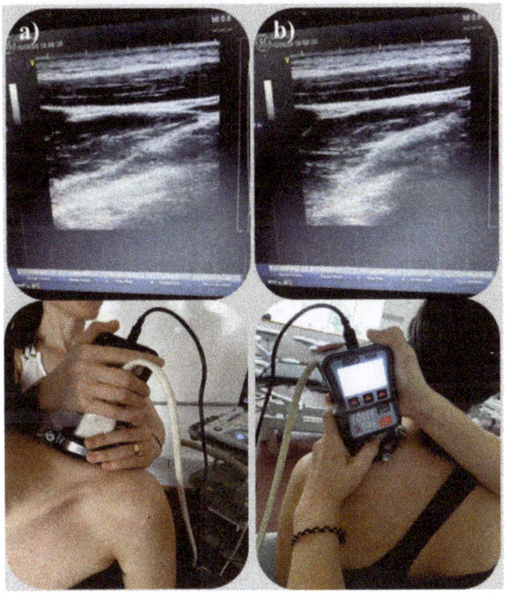

Figure 2. Ultrasound image and probe coupled with the algometer in the cervical region: (**a**) before pressure application and (**b**) after the application of pressure resulting in deformation of the deep cervical fascia. These images illustrate the methodological procedure used to identify fascial deformation in real time, validating the point at which the recorded mechanical pressure corresponds to fascial engagement.

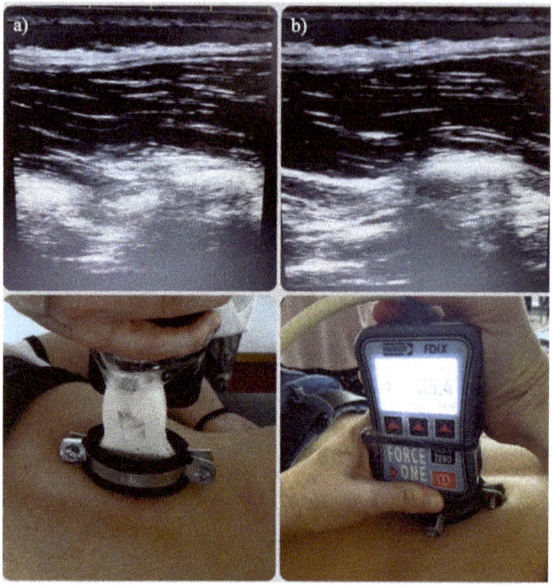

Figure 3. Ultrasound image and probe coupled with the algometer in the thoracolumbar region: (**a**) before pressure application and (**b**) after the application of pressure resulting in deformation of the deep thoracolumbar fascia. These images demonstrate the consistency of the procedure across different anatomical regions, supporting the comparison of fascial accessibility in areas with distinct structural characteristics.

Adipose tissue thickness was measured by manually grasping a skinfold using the thumb and index finger of the left hand, while applying the adipometer perpendicularly with the right hand to the axis of the fold. The fold was maintained for approximately two seconds, after which the value shown on the adipometer was recorded.

Three consecutive measures were taken, with a 15 s interval between them to allow the skin and underlying tissues to return to their baseline state and minimise measurement bias due to tissue compression. This interval is consistent with procedures used in similar anthropometric studies. The order of skinfold assessments was randomised across anatomical sites to prevent systematic bias or tissue fatigue effects. The mean of the three measurements was used in subsequent analyses of both pressure pain threshold and adipose tissue thickness [34].

2.5. Statistical Analysis

For each outcome variable—PPT, adipose tissue thickness, and mechanical pressure required to reach the deep fasciae—the mean value of three consecutive measurements was calculated. Before proceeding with statistical analysis, the dataset was checked for completeness, input errors, and distribution characteristics. Regarding the mechanical pressure variable, considering that the ultrasound transducer had a surface area of 5 cm^2 and the algometer used to assess PPT had a surface area of 1 cm^2, the mechanical pressure values were normalised by area. Accordingly, the mechanical pressure values were divided by 5, resulting in the study variable 'mechanical pressure'.

Data analysis was performed using IBM SPSS Statistics version 30.0 (IBM Corporation, Armonk, NY, USA), with the significance level set at 0.05. The normality of continuous variables was assessed using the Shapiro–Wilk test. Descriptive statistics were used to summarise the data. Means and standard deviations were reported for normally distributed variables, while medians and interquartile ranges (25th and 75th percentiles) were calculated when the assumption of normality was not met.

To compare the mechanical pressure required to reach the deep fascia between the cervical and lumbar regions, either a paired-samples *t*-test or the Wilcoxon signed-rank test was applied, depending on the distribution of the data.

To examine associations between PPT, mechanical pressure and adipose tissue thickness, correlation analyses were conducted using Pearson's or Spearman's correlation coefficients, according to data normality. These analyses were performed separately for the cervical and lumbar regions.

Additionally, simple linear regression analyses were performed to evaluate whether PPT or adipose tissue thickness individually predicted the mechanical pressure required to reach the deep fascia.

3. Results

The sample consisted of 43 participants, 23 females and 20 males, whose characteristics are summarised in Table 1.

Table 1. Participants' characteristics: mean and standard deviation values for height, weight and IMC, and median and 25th and 75th percentiles for age.

Variable	Mean (SD)	Med (P25; P75)
Age (years)		21 (19; 24)
Weight (Kg)	64.77 (12.793)	
Height (m)	1.70 (0.095)	
BMI (Kg/m^2)	22.38 (3.565)	

Med—median; P25—25th percentile; P75—75th percentile; Kg—kilogram; m—metre; Kg/m^2—kilogram per square metre.

The results of descriptive analysis of the mechanosensitivity (PPT), mechanical pressure, and adipose tissue thickness in both cervical and thoracolumbar fasciae are shown in Table 2.

Table 2. Mean and standard deviation values, and median and 25th and 75th percentiles of mechanical pressure, pressure pain threshold and adipose tissue thickness in both cervical and thoracolumbar fasciae.

Variable	Mean (SD)		Med (P25; P75)		*p*-Value
	Cervical	Thoracolumbar	Cervical	Thoracolumbar	0.80 *
Mechanical pressure (N/cm^2)	6.06 (0.186)			5.85 (5.280; 7.287)	<0.001 #
Pressure pain threshold (N/cm^2)	18.88 (0.917)	46.46 (2.408)			
Adipose tissue thickness (cm)		1.48 (0.069)	0.88 (0.675;1.08)		<0.001 *

Med—median; P25—25th percentile; P75—75th percentile; N/cm^2—Newton per square centimetre; cm—centimetre; * Wilcoxon test; # Student *t*-test.

Paired-samples analyses were conducted to compare values between the cervical and lumbar regions. While the measurements were performed under different postural conditions (seated for cervical; prone for lumbar), this comparison was maintained for descriptive purposes only and should be interpreted with caution. The values of mechanosensitivity were significantly higher in the cervical region ($p < 0.001$), and lumbar adipose tissue thickness was significantly greater than cervical thickness ($p < 0.001$; Wilcoxon signed-rank test).

Pearson's correlation between the mechanical pressure required to reach the deep cervical fascia and the mechanosensitivity showed a weak, non-significant positive correlation ($r = 0.262$, $p = 0.089$) (Table 3). This finding was consistent with the untransformed data, suggesting a possible trend but no statistically significant association.

Table 3. Pearson and Spearman's correlation analysis of mechanical pressure and pressure pain threshold, and mechanical pressure and adipose tissue thickness for cervical and thoracolumbar regions.

Region		r/ρ; *p*
Cervical	Mechanical Pressure vs. PPT	0.262 *; 0.089
	Mechanical Pressure vs. Adipose Tissue Thickness	0.134 #; 0.392
Thoracolumbar	Mechanical Pressure vs. PPT	0.139 #; 0.375
	Mechanical Pressure vs. Adipose Tissue Thickness	−0.214 #; 0.169

* r value for the Pearson correlation coefficient; # ρ value for Spearman's correlation coefficient. PPT—pressure pain threshold.

In the cervical region, Spearman's rank correlation showed a very weak, non-significant association between adipose tissue thickness and the mechanical pressure ($\rho = 0.134$, $p = 0.392$). This suggests that subcutaneous fat in the cervical region may have little to no influence on mechanical pressure in this sample.

In the thoracolumbar region, Spearman's rank correlation revealed a very weak and non-significant association between the mechanosensitivity and the pressure required to reach the deep fascia ($\rho = 0.139$, $p = 0.375$). This suggests that in this sample, mechanosensitivity was not meaningfully associated with the applied pressure to access the lumbar fascia.

Spearman's correlation revealed a weak, non-significant negative association between lumbar adipose tissue thickness and mechanical pressure ($\rho = -0.214$, $p = 0.169$), suggesting that subcutaneous fat did not meaningfully influence the pressure to access the thoracolumbar fascia.

A simple linear regression was conducted to evaluate whether mechanosensitivity and adipose tissue thickness predict the mechanical pressure required to reach the deep cervical and thoracolumbar fasciae. Figures 4 and 5 show the simple linear regression for the cervical and thoracolumbar regions, respectively.

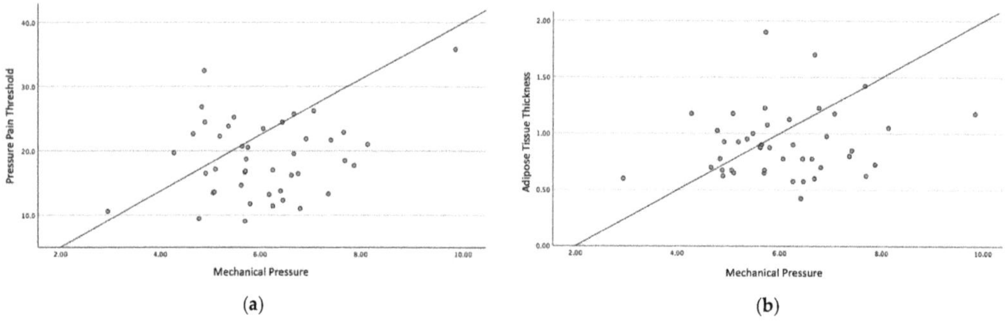

Figure 4. (**a**) Simple linear regression analysis between PPT and mechanical pressure for the cervical region; (**b**) simple linear regression analysis between adipose tissue thickness and mechanical pressure for the cervical region.

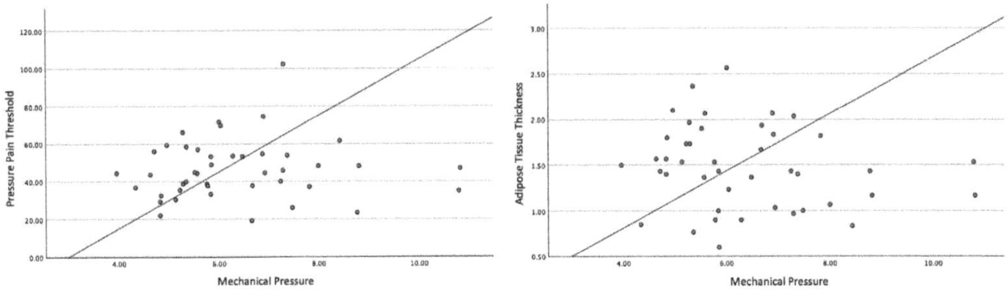

(**a**) (**b**)

Figure 5. (**a**) Simple linear regression analysis between PPT and mechanical pressure for the thoracolumbar region; (**b**) simple linear regression analysis between adipose tissue thickness and mechanical pressure for the thoracolumbar region.

Regarding mechanosensitivity in the cervical region, the model showed a non-significant trend toward a positive association (p = 0.089), explaining 6.9% of the variance (adjusted R^2 = 0.046). Mechanosensitivity was not a statistically significant predictor (B = 0.053, p = 0.089).

Also, the model for the adipose tissue thickness was not statistically significant (p = 0.289) and explained only 2.7% of the variance (adjusted R^2 = 0.004). Adipose tissue thickness did not significantly predict fascial pressure (B = 0.671, p = 0.289).

In the lumbar region, for the mechanosensitivity, the model was not statistically significant (p = 0.785) and explained only 0.2% of the variance (adjusted R^2 = −0.023). Mechanosensitivity was not a significant predictor (B = 0.004, p = 0.785).

To examine whether lumbar adipose tissue thickness predicts the pressure required to reach the deep fascia, the model was not statistically significant (p = 0.257), explaining only 3.1% of the variance (adjusted R^2 = 0.008).

Adipose tissue thickness did not significantly predict fascial pressure (B = −0.604, p = 0.257).

4. Discussion

This study investigated the mechanical pressure required to reach the deep cervical and thoracolumbar fasciae, examined its association with mechanosensitivity and adipose tissue thickness, and determined whether mechanosensitivity and adipose tissue thickness can predict the mechanical pressure needed to reach the fascia, using linear regression analysis.

4.1. Regional Patterns and Tissue Behaviour

While established anatomical principles suggest that both mechanosensitivity and superficial tissue thickness could influence fascial accessibility, our findings challenge these assumptions and offer new perspectives for clinical reasoning and future research.

Consistent with previous anatomical and imaging studies, the lumbar region demonstrated significantly higher adiposity and reduced mechanosensitivity than the cervical region [35]. Surprisingly, these regional differences did not yield corresponding variation in the pressure required to reach deep fascia, suggesting that fascial accessibility may depend less on superficial characteristics than one can assume. It is important to clarify that the cervical and lumbar fasciae were assessed under different postural conditions—seated and prone, respectively—which may have influenced local muscle tone and tissue behaviour. Therefore, direct comparisons between regions should be interpreted with caution. Nonetheless, we present these regional data side-by-side not as strict comparisons, but to illustrate that—despite differing superficial profiles—both regions required similar mechanical pressure to reach the deep fascia. This unexpected finding raises important questions about the assumed influence of overlying tissues and supports the need for further targeted investigation.

The results of our study demonstrated that the mechanical pressure required to reach the deep cervical and thoracolumbar fasciae was similar, approximately 6 N/cm^2. Notably, participants exhibited mechanosensitivity values higher than the pressure required to engage fascia, indicating that fascial engagement may occur before pain threshold is exceeded, which was also found in the present study, and is a valuable consideration in pain-sensitive populations. This evidence is particularly relevant considering that some myofascial induction techniques are based on the application of sustained mechanical pressure on the fascia [36]. As the mechanical pressure was substantially lower than the mechanosensitivity thresholds observed in the cervical (18.88 ± 0.917 N/cm^2) and lumbar (46.46 ± 2.408 N/cm^2) regions, the myofascial technique may represent an effective therapeutic approach, potentially capable of reaching the fascia without inducing symptomatology. However, it is important to note that the participants were healthy and asymptomatic, which may limit the generalisability of the results to populations with pain or associated pathologies. Furthermore, the role of epidermal cells was not directly assessed in this study. These cells, innervated by autonomic Aδ and C fibres, may contribute to pain modulation and functional recovery through their involvement in neuroimmune and neurosensory mechanisms [11,12]. Therefore, their potential influence during fascial compression should not be overlooked.

When we compared mechanosensitivity between the cervical and thoracolumbar fasciae, we observed that the cervical region showed significantly greater mechanosensitivity, which could possibly be explained by various anatomical, neurophysiological and functional factors. One such factor is the involvement of the epidermis, which contains dense networks of free nerve endings—particularly Aδ and C fibres—associated with nociceptive and autonomic signalling. Although the epidermis was not the primary focus of this study, its stimulation is unavoidable during manual pressure application. Recent studies, including those by Selva-Sarzo et al. [21] and Talagas et al. [12], suggest that epidermal stimulation can modulate pain perception and enhance functional outcomes, underscoring its relevance when interpreting regional differences in mechanosensitivity. The introduction of this concept at this stage aims to integrate superficial neuroanatomical contributions to our findings, thereby complementing earlier discussions on tissue innervation.

Marzvanyan & Alhawaj [37] state that the type and density of innervation, specifically receptors, can vary according to the different regions of the body, with the cervical region having a higher concentration of sensory receptors and free nerve endings, which can make it more sensitive to mechanical stimuli. In addition, from a biomechanical point of view, the cervical region is more mobile, while the lumbar region is more robust and adapted to withstand greater loads, which may influence tissue sensitivity, making the cervical region more susceptible to lower intensity mechanical stimuli. Also, the thickness of the fascia and the thickness of the tissue can facilitate the transmission of mechanical stimuli to nociceptors, which in a way seems to agree with the results of our study, as the thickness of adipose tissue was significantly lower in the cervical region when compared to the lumbar region. On the other hand, postural factors may also be at the core of these differences, because the cervical region is more prone to chronic postural tensions, particularly in populations that spend a lot of time sitting or using electronic devices, as is the case with the participants in our sample. In this context, repetitive and/or sustained posture and physical exercise can increase the thickening of the fascia and the release of chemical substances that can sensitise the receptors, which may explain the greater mechanosensitivity in the cervical region, an idea corroborated by Martinez-Merinero et al. [38] who found that individuals with cervical anteriorisation showed increased mechanosensitivity. Some physical and chemical properties of the hyaluronic acid found between the deep fascia and the muscle may also be the basis of the differences found between the regions studied, as they may contribute to changes in the viscoelasticity, mechanical plasticity and non-linear elasticity of the fascia's extracellular matrix. Thus, the biomechanical properties of connective tissue can change due to the presence of lactic acid resulting from exercise, as well as the decrease in pH, which can favour thickening and alter the sensitivity of receptors [39,40]. As for the thickness of the adipose tissue, the fact that the neck is not a typical region for fat accumulation may have justified significantly lower values when compared to the lumbar region, which is more likely to accumulate fat. However, the results showed no statistically significant association with mechanical pressure, which suggests that the pressure that is transmitted is not absorbed by the fat, allowing pressure to be transferred to deeper tissues.

4.2. Mechanosensitivity, Adipose Tissue Thickness and Predictive Value

No significant correlations were observed between mechanosensitivity or adipose tissue thickness and fascial pressure in either study. This contradicts the expectation that thicker adipose layers act as a mechanical buffer. As Chaudhry et al. [41] noted, pressure is not "absorbed" by fat tissue in a way that impedes fascial deformation; adipose tissue is highly deformable and allows transmission of pressure to deeper layers. Recent biomechanical models and experimental compression tests have demonstrated that subcutaneous adipose tissue exhibits low resistance and high deformability under vertical load, allowing for efficient force transmission into deeper structures such as fasciae. This supports the interpretation that adipose tissue does not impede fascial deformation and reinforces its minor role as a mechanical buffer [42].

Interestingly, the lack of significant correlations between mechanosensitivity, adipose tissue thickness, and the mechanical pressure required to access the fascia is a particularly relevant finding. It challenges the common clinical assumption that superficial adiposity predicts the force needed for effective manual intervention. Clinicians often adjust pressure based on palpated fat thickness or perceived tenderness, yet our results suggest that these variables may not reliably indicate fascial accessibility [43]. This discrepancy calls for a reassessment of such assumptions and highlights the need for more objective criteria to guide pressure modulation during manual therapies. Theoretical explanations for this lack of association may include the viscoelastic behaviour of connective tissues, inter-individual variability in fascial architecture, and the role of other less visible variables such as hydration, hyaluronic acid concentration, or even neural modulation [44]. Recognising these complexities can lead to more nuanced and evidence-informed manual therapy practices.

The absence of correlation with mechanosensibility may also reflect the influence of participant characteristics. A large proportion of the sample engaged in regular physical activity, which could have contributed to elevated pain tolerance and altered tissue sensitivity. The literature shows that individuals with greater muscle strength tend to exhibit higher pain thresholds, a factor that might explain the lack of association between PPT and fascial access pressure [45]. Additionally, the posture adopted during assessment may have influenced mechanosensitivity measurements. While the lumbar region was assessed in a relaxed prone position, the cervical region was evaluated in a seated posture, potentially involving greater muscle activation. This difference in physiological context may have attenuated the comparability between regions and could partly explain the lack of association between pressure pain threshold and fascial access pressure. Future studies may benefit from standardising participant positioning—such as using a supine posture—to minimise muscular interference and improve methodological consistency.

Additionally, muscle mass and physical activity levels can influence subcutaneous fat distribution. Participants with higher muscle tone may exhibit lower adiposity and increased fascia compliance [46], further hampering the ability to establish a relationship between superficial and deep tissues. These insights reinforce the idea that surface-level measures alone are insufficient to predict mechanical outcomes, especially in healthy or athletic populations such as the one in the present study.

4.3. Considerations and Future Directions

The findings of our study carry important clinical implications. The ability to reach deep fascia before triggering nociceptive responses suggests that fascial techniques can be applied effectively and safely. Moreover, the lack of a strong influence from superficial adiposity implies that manual therapy protocols may be broadly applicable without substantial individual adjustment, aligning with recent clinical guidance for standardised practice [47].

These insights expand upon the neurophysiological models of fascia, which recognise its role in proprioception, interoception, and nociception [48]. Given that fascia deformation occurs prior to discomfort, manual pressure may produce local and systemic effects without provoking pain, contributing to functional improvements in patients with back pain or myofascial dysfunction.

However, this study has some limitations. First, the influence of cutaneous structures—particularly the epidermis—was not directly assessed. Reflexes mediated by epidermal cells, which are innervated by Aδ and C fibres and known to modulate pain and mobility, may have contributed to the observed responses. Second, although care was taken to standardise procedures, slight variations in probe positioning are inevitable during manual application. These small angular deviations or shifts may compromise the reproducibility of pressure readings. Finally, the lack of direct control over the stimuli applied to superficial tissues further limits the interpretation of the mechanosensory response as being fascia-specific.

Moreover, the relatively small sample size and the inclusion of only healthy young adults restrict the generalisability of our findings. The inclusion of symptomatic individuals—particularly those with chronic musculoskeletal conditions—could offer greater insight into the clinical relevance of fascial mechanosensitivity. Future research should explore these mechanisms in clinical populations and assess potential interactions between fascial architecture and neuromuscular factors.

Although this study examined the cervical and thoracolumbar regions, it is important to acknowledge that a direct comparison between them is not methodologically valid due to differences in participant positioning and muscular activation during assessment. Nonetheless, both regions were included to characterise regional variability in fascial accessibility and to provide foundational data for future research. The inclusion of dynamic assessments and shear-wave ultrasound elastography could offer more refined insights into fascial behaviour under varying mechanical loads. Future investigations should also explore additional anatomical regions to determine whether the observed patterns are consistent across different body areas, thereby providing a more comprehensive understanding of fascial engagement in clinical and non-clinical populations. Moreover, given the cross-sectional nature of this study, longitudinal designs are warranted to examine how mechanosensitivity, adiposity, and fascial behaviour evolve over time, particularly in response to pain or rehabilitation interventions. This would enhance our understanding of the temporal dynamics underlying fascia-related dysfunction and recovery.

Due to laboratory constraints and time limitations during data collection, it was not feasible to record additional participant characteristics such as handedness, limb dominance, or physical activity habits (e.g., frequency, intensity, or whether the activity was predominantly unilateral or bilateral). Although the side of assessment was randomised or arbitrarily chosen depending on the procedure, these individual characteristics may influence baseline muscle tone and fascial properties, particularly in regions subjected to habitual loading or asymmetrical use. The absence of this information limits the ability to fully control for or interpret potential sources of variability. Future studies should consider including these variables to enhance the understanding of individual differences in mechanosensitivity and tissue thickness.

In clinical terms, the present findings encourage a more standardised and evidence-based application of fascial techniques, especially in settings where manual pressure is used therapeutically. The fact that deep fascia can be engaged before pain thresholds are exceeded reinforces the safety of these techniques, even in patients with heightened pain sensitivity. Moreover, the absence of a significant role of adipose thickness or mechanosensitivity in predicting fascial access pressure suggests that clinicians should be cautious about relying on superficial palpation or visual estimates when modulating force. Instead, integrating objective tools or structured protocols may enhance treatment efficacy and reduce variability between practitioners. These insights are particularly relevant for manual therapists, physiotherapists, and osteopaths aiming to optimise outcomes while minimising discomfort and tissue overload.

5. Conclusions

This study sets out the mechanical pressure required to reach the deep cervical and thoracolumbar fasciae and to evaluate whether subcutaneous adipose tissue thickness and pressure pain threshold could predict this pressure.

The mechanical pressure required to reach the deep cervical and thoracolumbar fasciae was similar, with an average value of approximately 6 N/cm^2, suggesting a consistent mechanical response across these anatomical regions. Mechanosensitivity was higher in the deep cervical fascia, whereas subcutaneous adipose tissue thickness was greater in the thoracolumbar region; however, these differences do not significantly influence fascial accessibility.

This study supports a more inclusive and standardised application of manual therapies, reducing reliance on body composition as a guide for treatment decisions.

Ultimately, by demonstrating that commonly assumed predictors such as adipose thickness and pressure pain threshold do not significantly influence fascial access, this research invites a re-evaluation of clinical reasoning surrounding soft tissue therapy. More importantly, this study positions fascia not merely as a passive structural element, but as a dynamic, context-sensitive interface. Its behaviour may be modulated by superficial layers, such as the epidermis, through reflexive and autonomic pathways. These mechanisms can influence mechanosensitivity, contribute to mobility limitations, and intensify pain perception. Therefore, integrated assessments that consider both structural and neurophysiological dimensions are warranted to better inform rehabilitation strategies.

Author Contributions: Conceptualisation, S.P.; methodology, S.P., F.P. and S.B.; validation, S.P. and S.B.; data analysis, S.P. and M.F.; writing—original draft preparation, S.P. and S.B.; writing—review and editing, S.P. and S.B. All authors have read and agreed to the published version of the manuscript.

Funding: This research received no external funding.

Institutional Review Board Statement: The study was conducted in accordance with the Declaration of Helsinki and approved by the Ethics Committee of the Vale do Ave School of Health (ESSVA), Polytechnic and University Higher Education Cooperative (IPSN), CESPU (protocol code 41 and 48/CE-IPSN/2023, 13 July 2023).

Informed Consent Statement: Informed consent was obtained from all subjects involved in the study.

Data Availability Statement: Data are unavailable due to privacy or ethical restrictions.

Conflicts of Interest: The authors declare no conflicts of interest.

Abbreviations

The following abbreviations are used in this manuscript:

cm	Centimetre
Kg	Kilogram
Kgf/s	Kilogram-force per second
m	Metre
Med	Median
N	Newton
PPT	Pressure pain threshold
SD	Standard deviation
SPSS	Statistical Package for the Social Sciences

References

1. Devantéry, K.; Morin, M.; Grimard, J.; Gaudreault, N. Effects of a Myofascial Technique on the Stiffness and Thickness of the Thoracolumbar Fascia and Lumbar Erector Spinae Muscles in Adults with Chronic Low Back Pain: A Randomized before-and-after Experimental Study. *Bioengineering* **2023**, *10*, 332. [CrossRef] [PubMed]
2. Weiss, K.; Kalichman, L. Deep fascia as a potential source of pain: A narrative review. *J. Bodyw. Mov. Ther.* **2021**, *28*, 82–86. [CrossRef] [PubMed]
3. Stecco, C.; Pirri, C.; Fede, C.; Fan, C.; Giordani, F.; Stecco, L.; Foti, C.; De Caro, R. Dermatome and fasciatome. *Clin. Anat.* **2019**, *32*, 896–902. [CrossRef]
4. Suarez-Rodriguez, V.; Fede, C.; Pirri, C.; Petrelli, L.; Loro-Ferrer, J.F.; Rodriguez-Ruiz, D.; De Caro, R.; Stecco, C. Fascial Innervation: A Systematic Review of the Literature. *Int. J. Mol. Sci.* **2022**, *23*, 5674. [CrossRef]
5. Stecco, A.; Giordani, F.; Fede, C.; Pirri, C.; De Caro, R.; Stecco, C. From Muscle to the Myofascial Unit: Current Evidence and Future Perspectives. *Int. J. Mol. Sci.* **2023**, *24*, 4527. [CrossRef]
6. Kodama, Y.; Masuda, S.; Ohmori, T.; Kanamaru, A.; Tanaka, M.; Sakaguchi, T.; Nakagawa, M. Response to Mechanical Properties and Physiological Challenges of Fascia: Diagnosis and Rehabilitative Therapeutic Intervention for Myofascial System Disorders. *Bioengineering* **2023**, *10*, 474. [CrossRef]
7. Schleip, R.; Hedley, G.; Yucesoy, C.A. Fascial nomenclature: Update on related consensus process. *Clin. Anat.* **2019**, *32*, 929–933. [CrossRef]
8. Stecco, C.; Pratt, R.; Nemetz, L.D.; Schleip, R.; Stecco, A.; Theise, N.D. Towards a comprehensive definition of the human fascial system. *Am. J. Anat.* **2025**, *246*, 1084–1098. [CrossRef]
9. Brandl, A.; Egner, C.; Schleip, R. Immediate Effects of Myofascial Release on the Thoracolumbar Fascia and Osteopathic Treatment for Acute Low Back Pain on Spine Shape Parameters: A Randomized, Placebo-Controlled Trial. *Life* **2021**, *11*, 845. [CrossRef]
10. Willard, F.H.; Vleeming, A.; Schuenke, M.D.; Danneels, L.; Schleip, R. The thoracolumbar fascia: Anatomy, function and clinical considerations. *Am. J. Anat.* **2012**, *221*, 507–536. [CrossRef] [PubMed]
11. Talagas, M.; Lebonvallet, N.; Leschiera, R.; Marcorelles, P.; Misery, L. What about physical contacts between epidermal keratinocytes and sensory neurons? *Exp. Dermatol.* **2017**, *27*, 9–13. [CrossRef]
12. Talagas, M. Anatomical contacts between sensory neurons and epidermal cells: An unrecognized anatomical network for neuro-immuno-cutaneous crosstalk. *Br. J. Dermatol.* **2022**, *188*, 176–185. [CrossRef]
13. Overmann, L.; Schleip, R.; Michalak, J. Exploring fascial properties in patients with depression and chronic neck pain: An observational study. *Acta Psychol.* **2024**, *244*, 104214. [CrossRef]
14. Pirri, C.; Pirri, N.; Guidolin, D.; Macchi, V.; Porzionato, A.; De Caro, R.; Stecco, C. Ultrasound Imaging of Thoracolumbar Fascia Thickness: Chronic Non-Specific Lower Back Pain versus Healthy Subjects; A Sign of a "Frozen Back"? *Diagnostics* **2023**, *13*, 1436. [CrossRef] [PubMed]
15. Raja G, P.; Bhat, S.; Gangavelli, R.; Prabhu, A.; Stecco, A.; Pirri, C.; Jaganathan, V.; Fernández-de-Las-Peñas, C. Effectiveness of Deep Cervical Fascial Manipulation® and Sequential Yoga Poses on Pain and Function in Individuals with Mechanical Neck Pain: A Randomised Controlled Trial. *Life* **2023**, *13*, 2173. [CrossRef]

16. Van Amstel, R.; Noten, K.; Malone, S.; Vaes, P. Fascia Tissue Manipulations in Chronic Low Back Pain: A Pragmatic Comparative Randomized Clinical Trial of the 4xT Method® and Exercise Therapy. *Life* **2023**, *14*, 7. [CrossRef]
17. Ożóg, P.; Weber-Rajek, M.; Radzimińska, A. Effects of Isolated Myofascial Release Therapy in Patients with Chronic Low Back Pain—A Systematic Review. *J. Clin. Med.* **2023**, *12*, 6143. [CrossRef] [PubMed]
18. Benjamin, M. The fascia of the limbs and back—A review. *Am. J. Anat.* **2008**, *214*, 1–18. [CrossRef]
19. Mandel, J.B.; Solorio, L.; Tepole, A.B. Geometry of adipocyte packing in subcutaneous tissue contributes to nonlinear tissue properties captured through a Gaussian process surrogate model. *Soft Matter* **2024**, *20*, 4197–4207. [CrossRef]
20. Chen, D.Z.; Ganapathy, A.; Nayak, Y.; Mejias, C.; Bishop, G.L.; Mellnick, V.M.; Ballard, D.H. Analysis of Superficial Subcutaneous Fat Camper's and Scarpa's Fascia in a United States Cohort. *J. Cardiovasc. Dev. Dis.* **2023**, *10*, 347. [CrossRef]
21. Selva-Sarzo, F.; Romero, E.A.S.; Cuenca-Zaldívar, J.N.; García-Haba, B.; Akiyama, C.; Sillevis, R.; Fernández-Carnero, S. Effects on perceived pain and somatosensory function after transcutaneous neuromodulation in patients with chronic low back pain: A quasi-experimental study with a crossover intervention. *Front. Pain Res.* **2025**, *6*, 1525964. [CrossRef] [PubMed]
22. Taljanovic, M.S.; Gimber, L.H.; Becker, G.W.; Latt, L.D.; Klauser, A.S.; Melville, D.M.; Gao, L.; Witte, R.S. Shear-Wave Elastography: Basic Physics and Musculoskeletal Applications. *RadioGraphics* **2017**, *37*, 855–870. [CrossRef]
23. Chaudhry, H.; Schleip, R.; Ji, Z.; Bukiet, B.; Maney, M.; Findley, T. Three-Dimensional Mathematical Model for Deformation of Human Fasciae in Manual Therapy. *J. Am. Osteopat. Assoc.* **2008**, *108*, 379–390. [CrossRef] [PubMed]
24. Vosseler, M.; El Shazly, A.; Parker, J.D.; Münzel, T.; Gori, T. Resting and recruitable endothelial function – Evidence of two distinct circadian patterns. *Clin. Hemorheol. Microcirc.* **2020**, *74*, 139–146. [CrossRef]
25. Ylinen, J.; Häkkinen, A.; Nykänen, M.; Kautiainen, H.; Takala, E.-P. Neck muscle training in the treatment of chronic neck pain: A three-year follow-up study. *Eur. Medicophysica* **2007**, *43*, 161–169.
26. Costa, S.G.; Simim, M.A.; Barbosa, L.F.; Lima, L.C.; Assumpção, C.O. Utilização de diferentes adipómetros e a experiência dos avaliadores não implicam em erros de estimativas da composição corporal. *Rev. Bras. Prescrição Fisiol. Exercício* **2021**, *14*, 566–572.
27. Zuo, C.; Luo, L.; Liu, W. Effects of increased humidity on physiological responses, thermal comfort, perceived air quality, and Sick Building Syndrome symptoms at elevated indoor temperatures for subjects in a hot-humid climate. *Indoor Air* **2020**, *31*, 524–540. [CrossRef]
28. Murguía-Romero, M.; Jiménez-Flores, R.; Méndez-Cruz, A.R.; Villalobos-Molina, R. Improving the Body Mass Index (BMI) Formula with Heuristic Search. In Proceedings of the 2012 11th Mexican International Conference on Artificial Intelligence, San Luis Potos, Mexico, 27 October–4 November 2012; pp. 100–104. [CrossRef]
29. Kim, Y.M.; Kim, K. Abdominal examination using pressure pain threshold algometer reflecting clinical characteristics of complementary and alternative medicine in Korea: A systematic review and a brief proposal. *Medicine* **2022**, *101*, e31417. [CrossRef]
30. Zamani, S.; Okhovatian, F.; Naimi, S.S.; Baghban, A.A. Intra- Examiner and Between-Day Reliability of Algometer for Pressure Pain Threshold and Pain Sensitivity in Upper Trapezius Muscle in Asymptomatic Young Adult Women. *J. Clin. Physiother. Res.* **2017**, *2*, 15–20.
31. Feigl, G.; Hammer, G.P.; Litz, R.; Kachlik, D. The intercarotid or alar fascia, other cervical fascias, and their adjacent spaces—A plea for clarification of cervical fascia and spaces terminology. *Am. J. Anat.* **2020**, *237*, 197–207. [CrossRef]
32. de Oliveira, R.F.; Liebano, R.E.; Costa, L.d.C.M.; Rissato, L.L.; Costa, L.O.P. Immediate Effects of Region-Specific and Non–Region-Specific Spinal Manipulative Therapy in Patients With Chronic Low Back Pain: A Randomized Controlled Trial. *Phys. Ther.* **2013**, *93*, 748–756. [CrossRef]
33. Fischer, A.A. Pressure algometry over normal muscles. Standard values, validity and reproducibility of pressure threshold. *Pain* **1987**, *30*, 115–126. [CrossRef] [PubMed]
34. American College of Sports Medicine. *ACSM's Guidelines for Exercise Testing and Prescription*, 8th ed.; Lippincott Williams & Wilkins: Philadelphia, PA, USA, 2009.
35. Finocchietti, S.M.; Mørch, C.D.; Arendt-Nielsen, L.P.; Graven-Nielsen, T.P. Effects of Adipose Thickness and Muscle Hardness on Pressure Pain Sensitivity. *Clin. J. Pain* **2011**, *27*, 735–745. [CrossRef] [PubMed]
36. Ajimsha, M.; Daniel, B.; Chithra, S. Effectiveness of Myofascial release in the management of chronic low back pain in nursing professionals. *J. Bodyw. Mov. Ther.* **2014**, *18*, 273–281. [CrossRef] [PubMed]
37. Marzvanyan, A.; Alhawaj, A.F. Physiology, Sensory Receptors. In *StatPearls*; StatPearls Publishing LLC: Tampa, FL, USA, 2023; p. 14.
38. Martinez-Merinero, P.; Nuñez-Nagy, S.; Achalandabaso-Ochoa, A.; Fernandez-Matias, R.; Pecos-Martin, D.; Gallego-Izquierdo, T. Relationship between Forward Head Posture and Tissue Mechanosensitivity: A Cross-Sectional Study. *J. Clin. Med.* **2020**, *9*, 634. [CrossRef]
39. Chaudhuri, O.; Cooper-White, J.; Janmey, P.A.; Mooney, D.J.; Shenoy, V.B. Effects of extracellular matrix viscoelasticity on cellular behaviour. *Nature* **2020**, *584*, 535–546. [CrossRef]

40. Cowman, M.K.; Lee, H.; Schwertfeger, K.L.; McCarthy, J.B.; Turley, E.A. The content and size of hyaluronan in biological fluids and tissues. *Front. Immunol.* **2015**, *2*, 261. [CrossRef]
41. Chaudhry, H.; Bukiet, B.; Ji, Z.; Stecco, A.; Findley, T.W. Deformations Experienced in the Human Skin, Adipose Tissue, and Fascia in Osteopathic Manipulative Medicine. *J. Am. Osteopath. Assoc.* **2014**, *144*, 780–787. [CrossRef]
42. Fischer, A.; Anwar, M.; Hertwig, A.; Hahn, R.; Pesta, M.; Timmermann, I.; Siebenrock, T.; Liebau, K.; Hiesmayr, M. Ultrasound method of the USVALID study to measure subcutaneous adipose tissue and muscle thickness on the thigh and upper arm: An illustrated step-by-step guide. *Clin. Nutr. Exp.* **2020**, *32*, 38–73. [CrossRef]
43. Bordoni, B.; Escher, A.R. Fascial Manual Medicine: The Concept of Fascial Continuum. *Cureus* **2025**, *17*, e82136. [CrossRef]
44. Branchini, M.; Lopopolo, F.; Andreoli, E.; Loreti, I.; Marchand, A.M.; Stecco, A. Fascial Manipulation® for chronic aspecific low back pain: A single blinded randomized controlled trial. *F1000Research* **2016**, *4*, 1208. [CrossRef] [PubMed]
45. Melo, B.L.; Silva, L.L.; Almeida, P.F. Relação da força muscular e limiar de tolerância à dor à pressão em pacientes com lombalgia crónica. *Acta Fisiátrica* **2019**, *26*, 134–138. [CrossRef]
46. Descarreaux, M.; Blouin, J.; Drolet, M.; Papadimitriou, S.; Teasdale, N. Efficacy of Preventive Spinal Manipulation for Chronic Low-Back Pain and Related Disabilities: A Preliminary Study. *J. Manip. Physiol. Ther.* **2004**, *27*, 509–514. [CrossRef]
47. Georgoudis, G.; Oldham, J.; Watson, P.J.; Grammatopolou, E. Reliability Measures of Subcutaneous Pressure Pain Threshold Measurements: A Proposed Method of Assessing Painful Musculoskeletal Disorders. *J. Nov. Physiother.* **2014**, *4*, 1000234. [CrossRef]
48. Stecco, C.; Schleip, R. A fascia and the fascial system. *J. Bodyw. Mov. Ther.* **2016**, *20*, 139–140. [CrossRef] [PubMed]

sensors

Article

Effect of Walking Speed on the Reliability of a Smartphone-Based Markerless Gait Analysis System

Edilson Fernando de Borba [1], Jorge L. Storniolo [2,*], Serena Cerfoglio [3,4], Paolo Capodaglio [4,5], Veronica Cimolin [3,4], Leonardo A. Peyré-Tartaruga [6], Marcus P. Tartaruga [1,7] and Paolo Cavallari [2,8]

1 Physical Education Department, Federal University of Paraná, Curitiba 81530-000, PR, Brazil; edilson.borba@ufpr.br (E.F.d.B.); mtartaruga@unicentro.br (M.P.T.)
2 Laboratorio Sperimentale di Fisiopatologia Neuromotoria, Istituto Auxologico Italiano, 20821 Meda, Italy; paolo.cavallari@unimi.it
3 Department of Electronics, Information and Bioengineering, Politecnico di Milano, 20133 Milan, Italy; serena.cerfoglio@polimi.it (S.C.); veronica.cimolin@polimi.it (V.C.)
4 Research Laboratory in Biomechanics, Rehabilitation and Ergonomics, Istituto Auxologico Italiano, 28824 Piancavallo, Verbania, Italy; p.capodaglio@auxologico.it
5 Department of Biomedical, Surgical and Dental Sciences, La Statale University, 20133 Milan, Italy
6 Human Locomotion Laboratory (LOCOLAB), Department of Public Health, Experimental and Forensic Medicine, University of Pavia, 27100 Pavia, Italy; leonardoalexandre.peyretartaruga@unipv.it
7 Physical Education Department, Midwestern Parana State University-UNICENTRO, Guarapuava 85040-080, PR, Brazil
8 Human Physiology Section of the Department of Pathophysiology and Transplantation, Università Degli Studi, 20133 Milan, Italy
* Correspondence: l.storniolo@auxologico.it

Highlights

This study tested OpenCap, a smartphone app that tracks movement without markers, by comparing it to a traditional setup at different walking speeds. OpenCap was really reliable for measuring movement timing and joint angles, with errors usually under 2°. However, it was less accurate for joint range of motion at higher speeds, especially at the hip and ankle. Overall, OpenCap is a convenient tool for gait analysis, but be cautious when looking at ROM at faster speeds.

What are the main findings?

- OpenCap showed excellent agreement with MoCap for spatiotemporal gait parameters and continuous joint kinematics across different walking speeds.
- Discrete joint range of motion (especially at the hip and ankle) exhibited lower and speed-dependent reliability, although systematic biases remained small and clinically acceptable.

What is the implication of the main finding?

- OpenCap can be reliably applied for gait assessment and monitoring of spatiotemporal and continuous kinematic variables across various walking speeds.
- Clinicians should interpret range of motion outcomes with caution at higher speeds, as their accuracy decreases compared with marker-based measurements.

Abstract: Quantitative gait analysis is essential for understanding motor function and guiding clinical decisions. While marker-based motion capture (MoCap) systems are accurate, they are costly and require specialized facilities. OpenCap, a markerless alternative, offers a more accessible approach; however, its reliability across different walking speeds remains uncertain. This study assessed the agreement between OpenCap and MoCap in measuring spatiotemporal parameters, joint kinematics, and center of mass (CoM) displacement during level walking at three speeds: slow, self-selected, and fast. Fifteen healthy adults performed multiple trials simultaneously, recorded by both systems. Agreement was analyzed using intraclass correlation coefficients (ICC), minimal detectable change (MDC), Bland–Altman analyses, root mean square error (RMSE), Statistical Parametric Mapping (SPM), and repeated-measures ANOVA. Results indicated excellent agreement for spatiotemporal variables (ICC $\geq$ 0.95) and high consistency for joint waveforms (RMSE < 2°) and CoM displacement (RMSE < 6 mm) across all speeds. However, the joint range of motion (ROM) showed lower reliability, especially at the hip and ankle, at higher speeds. ANOVA revealed no significant System $\times$ Speed interactions for most variables, though a significant effect of speed was noted, with OpenCap underestimating walking speed more at fast speeds. Overall, OpenCap is a valuable tool for gait assessment, very accurate for spatiotemporal data and CoM displacement. Still, caution should be taken when interpreting joint kinematics and speed at different walking speeds.

Keywords: gait analysis; OpenCap; MoCap; walking; biomechanics

1. Introduction

Overground walking in daily life can yield numerous biomechanical insights pertinent to neurological functions and orthopedic outcomes [1]. In this view, quantitative gait analysis plays a central role in clinical decision-making, particularly for initial evaluation and rehabilitation programs that require long-term treatment [2]. Specifically, assessing spatiotemporal parameters and 3D joint kinematics of the lower limbs can provide objective indicators of motor function, disease severity, and treatment response [3,4].

The current gold standard for measuring kinematic variables is 3D motion capture systems (MoCap), which utilize 6–8 high-resolution cameras to provide reliable data on joint angles and velocities. However, the high cost and setup time required, such as the technician's expertise to properly place the reflective markers, the calibration demands, and the data processing requirements, discourage the most targeted audience from using this procedure. Although new devices have been introduced to the market in recent years to address this issue, utilizing simple mechanisms such as accelerometers [5], they still require costly options for use in daily clinical settings.

These obstacles have spurred the development of markerless, computer vision-based options that estimate human pose directly from video. Recent progress in pose estimation and physics-based modeling shows that markerless systems can achieve the same accuracy as marker-based systems for many locomotor tasks [6]. Among the systems proposed, OpenCap is a markerless pipeline that reconstructs 3D kinematics from synchronized multi-view videos through pose estimation and musculoskeletal modeling [7]. Due to its accessible hardware and streamlined processing, OpenCap enables scalable gait assessment in both clinical and field settings, requiring only smartphones for measurements.

Nevertheless, performance levels assessed by OpenCap technology may vary depending on the population studied [8,9], the setup used for data collection [10], and the specific task demands [11–13]. As demonstrated by Martiš et al. [11], who compared walking away and towards the OpenCap system. Although spatiotemporal variables correlated well with the marker-based system during walking in both directions, some joint-angle parameters showed limited agreement when recording was done while walking away from the cameras, resulting in a roughly 12° root mean square error (RMSE). Similarly, Svetek et al. [12] found good agreement in spatiotemporal parameters but observed more errors in hip joint angle assessments during treadmill walking.

Despite these conflicting results, some recommendations regarding gait analysis, such as (i) maintaining an appropriate distance to ensure a good camera angle (30° from the interest area, 3 m away) [7]; (ii) directing gait towards the cameras [11]; and (iii) wearing minimal clothing [10], seem to help researchers reduce overall variability when using specifically OpenCap. Nonetheless, the reliability of measurements at various gait speeds remains a matter of debate. Although markerless systems have shown promising results across different walking and running speeds [14–16], their impact in the context of OpenCap has not been explored.

Since walking speed is a key clinical marker for patient evaluation and control during physical therapy [2,17–19], interpreting small changes in data can be challenging and lead to errors in speed measurement. To enrich the current findings in the literature related to gait analysis, which focused on fixed spontaneous walking speeds only [7,8,10–12,20], the present study aimed to evaluate the agreement between OpenCap and a marker-based system during walking at three different speeds: slow, self-selected (self), and fast. By establishing accuracy across various walking speeds, this work aims to support the practical application of OpenCap for gait assessment, focusing on spatiotemporal variables and lower-limb joint angles, in routine clinical practice.

2. Materials and Methods

2.1. Participants

Fifteen healthy participants (7 females and 8 males), all without musculoskeletal injuries, with an average age of 32.3 ± 8.3 years (mean ± SD), a height of 1.74 ± 0.1 m, and a weight of 71.1 ± 21.6 kg, were enrolled in this study. Participants were required to be adults who could ambulate independently, with no history of neurological, cardiovascular, or musculoskeletal disorders that could affect their gait, and no lower-limb surgeries or injuries. All demonstrated a regular gait pattern without significant functional deficits. The experimental procedure was carried out following the standards laid down in the Declaration of Helsinki and approved by the "Comitato Etico di Ateneo dell'Università degli Studi di Milano" (council 23/23).

2.2. Experimental Setup

The experimental session involved analyzing walking on the ground at three different speeds. Before beginning each trial, they completed a series of walks until they felt confident and comfortable with their self, faster, and slower speeds (respectively), each lasting between 2 and 3 min. The self-speed served as a baseline for the fast and slow speeds. The order of the tests was fixed for all participants. First, the self-selected speed, followed by the fast and slow speeds, respectively. This standardized sequence was selected so that each participant could use their own speed as a reference point for the other two conditions. The fast and slow conditions were therefore defined subjectively by each participant and visually verified by the duration of each trial. For the fast condition, participants were asked to walk slightly faster than their self-paced speed, and for the slow condition, they were asked to walk marginally slower than their self-paced speed. It did not impose a fixed percentage of variation, allowing participants to determine these speeds themselves to ensure a natural gait pattern.

For each speed, participants were instructed to walk as naturally as possible in an 8-m track after hearing a verbal prompt. Verbal feedback on their rhythm was provided at the end of each trial.

All participants wore minimal clothing, including shorts and sports shoes for walking, and a sports bra for females.

2.3. Recordings

Data were collected simultaneously using a MoCap and an OpenCap system (Figure 1). Participants walked along an 8-m walkway, but only the central 4 m were analyzed. This region was chosen because it corresponded to the adequate capture volume of the OpenCap system (4 × 4 m), spanning ± 2 m from the calibration point, and ensuring the most natural walking possible, which matched the optimal field of view of the two OpenCap cameras. The two systems were synchronized in time using a light signal emitted by a handheld flashlight, given before each walking trial began. This synchronization was used solely to pair corresponding strides across systems. Considering the frame rates of each auxiliary video (25 Hz for MoCap and 120 Hz for OpenCap), the maximum possible temporal mismatch after alignment was approximately ±0.04 s.

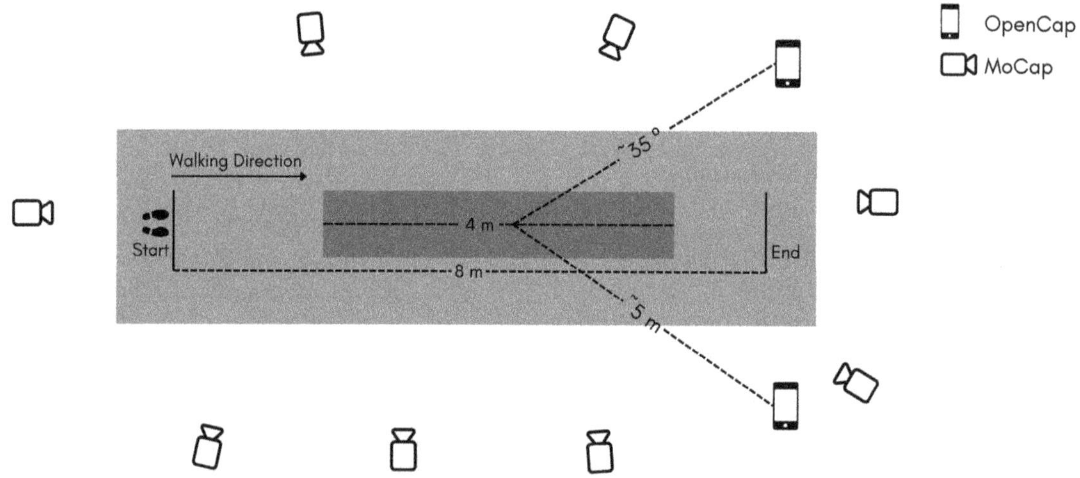

Figure 1. Laboratory setup for both systems, MoCap and OpenCap, during the test. The darker gray area represents the 4-m walkway in OpenCap's acquisition volume.

2.3.1. MoCap

An optoelectronic MoCap system with eight cameras (SMART DX 100, BTS Bioengineering SPA, Milan, Italy) was used, set to record data at a rate of 100 Hz. Twenty-two reflective markers were placed on anatomical landmarks following the model described by Davis et al. [21] (Figure 2a). The system was calibrated according to the manufacturer's recommendations, and a static calibration trial was performed with the participant in a standing position. Raw kinematic trajectories were reconstructed using the system's proprietary software (SMART-Clinic, BTSBioengineering SPA, Milan, Italy) and exported in *.trc* format for further processing and analysis.

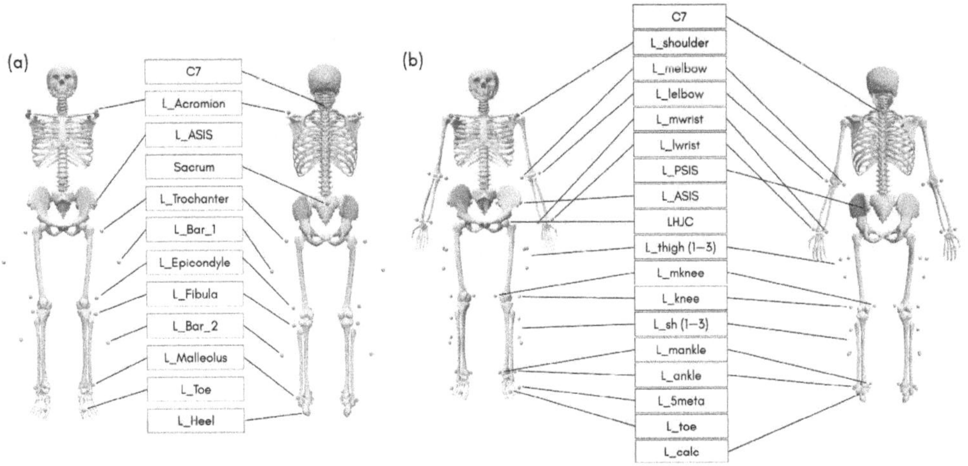

Figure 2. Representative models of MoCap (**a**) and OpenCap (**b**) systems in anterior and posterior views. The markers are listed for MoCap as the seventh cervical vertebra (C7), acromion (Acromion), anterior superior iliac spine (ASIS), sacrum (Sacrum), greater trochanter (Trochanter), upper lateral marker on the rigid bar attached to the thigh (Bar_1), lateral femoral epicondyle (Epicondyle), mid-lateral shank (Fibula), lower lateral marker on the rigid bar attached to the shank (Bar_2), lateral malleolus (Malleolus), head of the second metatarsal (Toe), and posterior calcaneus (Heel). The markers are listed for OpenCap as the seventh cervical vertebra (C7), acromion (shoulder), medial humeral epicondyle (melbow), lateral humeral epicondyle (lelbow), medial wrist styloid process (mwrist), lateral wrist styloid process (lwrist), posterior superior iliac spine (PSIS), anterior superior iliac spine (ASIS), hip joint center (HJC), three markers distributed along the lateral thigh (thigh 1–3), medial femoral epicondyle (mknee), lateral femoral epicondyle (knee), three markers distributed along the lateral shank (sh 1–3), medial malleolus (mankle), lateral malleolus (ankle), head of the fifth metatarsal (5meta), head of the second metatarsal (toe), and posterior calcaneus (calc).

2.3.2. OpenCap

Simultaneously, data for the OpenCap system were collected using two iOS smartphones (iPhone 13 and iPhone 13 Pro, Apple Valley, CA, USA), each mounted on a tripod. The cameras were positioned approximately 35° relative to the central axis of the walkway, with the lenses 1.2 m above the ground and perpendicular to the floor, about 5 m from the calibrator. A system calibration was performed following the developer's recommendations, and a static calibration trial was conducted with the participant in a standing position. Videos were recorded at 120 Hz and processed in the cloud using the HrNet pose estimation algorithm, with default settings recommended by OpenCap. The musculoskeletal model used was the default Full Body model, based on the models proposed by Lai et al. [22] and Rajagopal et al. [23], with modifications to the hip abductor muscle trajectories as described by Uhlrich et al. [7] (Figure 2b). The OpenCap version used was from July 2025, and all procedures adhered to the developer's recommendations and best-practice guidelines available at www.opencap.ai (accessed on 01 July 2025).

2.4. Raw Data Processing

The reconstructed marker trajectories from the MoCap system were used to perform inverse kinematics in OpenSim. For model scaling, the marker set from the adopted model was applied to the musculoskeletal model [23]. Scaling was carried out according to each participant's anthropometric proportions, and marker positions were adjusted based on data collected during a static trial (i.e., calibration). Before applying inverse kinematics, the 3D marker trajectories were low-pass filtered using an 8 Hz Butterworth filter, as implemented in OpenSim, to reduce measurement noise and prevent spurious peaks in the subsequent joint angle calculations. After completing the inverse kinematics, the motion data were exported and analyzed in OpenSim using the Analysis tool with the BodyKinematics module to determine the position of the center of mass (CoM).

OpenCap automatically performs inverse kinematics and, after download, provides three-dimensional marker position files (*.trc*), joint angle data (*.mot*), and the scaled model customized to the individual's anthropometrics. To determine the CoM position, these data were processed in OpenSim using the *BodyKinematics* tool. OpenSim version 4.5 for macOS was used.

The synchronization between systems was done manually using videos recorded by both MoCap and OpenCap. The videos were loaded into a media player, and the frame showing the flashlight flash was identified and used as the reference point to synchronize the events recorded by both systems in time.

With the *.trc*, *.mot*, and CoM position files saved, along with the identified synchronization times, the data were imported into a custom routine developed in Python 3.12. All signals were interpolated to 100 Hz and low-pass filtered using a second-order Butterworth filter with a cutoff frequency of 6 Hz. The native sampling frequencies were 100 Hz for MoCap and 120 Hz for OpenCap; the latter was resampled to 100 Hz using linear interpolation to enable direct comparison. We chose linear interpolation because it is a reliable and simple method commonly used in gait analysis when the temporal resolution is high, and the risk of aliasing is minimal. The 6 Hz cutoff was chosen following the consolidated practice in gait biomechanics and has been consistently adopted, providing an effective balance between noise reduction and signal preservation [24].

Marker positions were used to identify touchdown (TD) and take-off (TO) events following the protocol described by Zeni et al. [25]. Specifically, TD was defined as the frame in which the heel/calc (MoCap/OpenCap) marker reached its most forward position relative to the pelvis, while TO was defined as the frame in which the toe marker reached its most backward position relative to the pelvis. These events were used to segment strides and compute spatiotemporal parameters, along with joint angular data. Only events with corresponding detections in both systems were analyzed, and those without simultaneous matches were excluded.

There were no marker losses during MoCap recordings, and OpenCap successfully reconstructed all key joints without issues. Additionally, all automatically detected TD and TO events were visually inspected to confirm the correct sequence of strides.

All processed data were saved in an Excel file (.xlsx), organized into multiple sheets containing raw data, processed outputs, stride-averaged summaries by participant, and interpolated continuous curves for subsequent statistical analysis.

2.5. Experimental Variables

2.5.1. Spatiotemporal

The protocol by Zeni et al. [25] for identifying gait events, which relies on the forward and backward movement of heel and toe markers, served as the basis for our spatiotemporal analysis results.

A stride is the period between two successive TD events of the same foot. Stride Time measures the interval between these events, and Stride Length is derived from the heel marker's anterior–posterior displacement during that period. Double Support Time is the interval from the TD of one foot to the TO of the opposite foot, indicating when both feet contact the ground simultaneously. Cadence is calculated by dividing the total number of steps by the analysis duration, expressed in steps per minute. Walking speed was determined by dividing the total front–back displacement of the virtual mid-hip marker by the total recording time, which is the elapsed period between the first and last detected foot-contact events within each trial. The choice of mid-hip represents a standardized point available in both MoCap and OpenCap systems.

2.5.2. Joint Angles

Joint angle variables were derived from the joint kinematics files generated by OpenSim (*.mot*) for both the MoCap and OpenCap systems. Joint angle waveforms were segmented based on the previously defined stride events, considering complete cycles between two consecutive touchdowns of the same limb. Each cycle was interpolated to 101 points using linear interpolation, representing 0–100% of the gait cycle in normalized form. From these continuous curves, three discrete variables were calculated for each joint: the minimum value (Min), the maximum value (Max), and the range of motion (ROM), defined as the absolute difference between the maximum and minimum values observed within the cycle, averaged across all valid strides of each participant within each condition.

Analyses were performed separately for each joint (hip, knee, and ankle), with all the angular variables assessed in the sagittal plane. Since participants were healthy and did not present any clinically perceptible gait asymmetry, values from the left and right limbs were averaged to reduce redundancy and obtain a single representative measure per variable.

2.6. Statistics

Data normality was verified using the Shapiro–Wilk test, with no violations detected ($p > 0.05$). Accordingly, descriptive statistics were presented as means and standard deviations (SD), and parametric methods were used for comparisons [26]. Agreement between systems for the discrete variables (stride length (m), stride time (s), double support (s), cadence (Hz), walking speed (km.h^{-1}), hip ROM (°), knee ROM (°), and ankle ROM (°)) was evaluated using multiple complementary approaches.

We generated Bland–Altman plots with 95% limits of agreement (LoA) to assess systematic bias and the range of agreement. Reliability was measured using the intraclass correlation coefficient (ICC, model 2,1), while Pearson's correlation coefficient was used to analyze linear association. We included both metrics because they offer complementary insights: the ICC evaluates absolute agreement between systems, whereas Pearson's r measures the strength of the linear relationship regardless of constant differences. Although the ICC is generally more useful for agreement, Pearson's r was also included to facilitate comparison with previous validation studies, which often report correlations. Furthermore, the minimal detectable change (MDC) at the 95% confidence level was calculated to indicate the smallest difference that can be detected beyond measurement error. This MDC was calculated from the standard error of measurement (SEM), which we estimated from the standard deviation of the between-system differences.

For continuous joint angles data (i.e., hip, knee, and ankle) and CoM displacement, agreement was additionally examined by calculating the average magnitude of the differences between predicted and actual values using the root mean square error (RMSE) and performing Statistical Parametric Mapping (SPM) to identify regions of the gait cycle with statistically significant differences. SPM analyses were performed separately for each sagittal joint angle (hip, knee, and ankle) using paired *t*-tests ($\alpha = 0.05$), considering all strides from all participants. Significant intervals were highlighted in the plots, and for each of these regions, we also reported the local RMSE. The overall RMSE values were calculated by combining the data from all strides and participants. RMSE values below 5° for angular variables were considered indicative of good agreement, following previously established clinical thresholds [27,28].

To determine whether differences across walking speeds were consistent within each system and to evaluate a System × Speed interaction, we conducted a 2 × 3 repeated-measures ANOVA with within-subject factors system (MoCap, OpenCap) and speed (slow, self, fast). Sphericity was tested with Mauchly's test; if violated, Greenhouse–Geisser (G-G) corrections were applied. Significant effects were followed by Bonferroni-adjusted simple-effects comparisons: (i) speed differences within each system and (ii) system differences at each speed. We selected the Bonferroni correction due to its simplicity and strong control of type I error. In addition to F and p values, we also reported partial eta squared (ηp^2) as a measure of effect size for main effects and interactions.

We quantified the between-system error for each discrete variable as Δ = OpenCap − MoCap computed per trial. The Δ was regressed on MoCap walking speed (km.h^{-1}) using ordinary least squares with speed mean-centered for interpretability. We confirmed the adequacy of the linear model by testing a quadratic term, which was not significant across all variables ($p \geq 0.12$, Δ AIC < 2), and by conducting the Ramsey RESET test, which showed no evidence of model misspecification ($p \geq 0.19$). These results support the use of a linear model, for which regressions were conducted at the trial level. We report the slope (two-tailed $\alpha = 0.05$), Pearson's r, and R^2; a positive slope indicates an increasing overestimation of OpenCap with higher speed (proportional bias).

All statistical analyses were carried out using JASP (version 0.95) and Python (version 3.12). In Python, the following packages: NumPy (v1.26), pandas (v2.2), SciPy (v1.13), statsmodels (v0.14), pingouin (v0.5), and spm1d (v0.4) were used for descriptive statistics, repeated-measures ANOVA, post hoc tests, effect size estimation, and Statistical Parametric Mapping (SPM) analyses.

3. Results

In the overall dataset, each participant completed an average of 3.8 ± 1.1 walking trials (mean and ± SD), totaling 169 trials. The average number of detected strides was 6.7 ± 3.4 (mean and ± SD), with 297 strides analyzed in total. The overall average walking speed was 4.7 ± 1.1 km.h^{-1} (mean and ± SD). When divided by speed, the slow, self, and fast groups had, respectively, 3.6 ± 1.1, 3.9 ± 1.4, and 4.0 ± 1.0 trials per participant (mean and ± SD). The mean number of strides per participant was 8.4 ± 3.4, 4.7 ± 2.4, and 7.0 ± 3.4 (mean and ± SD) for the slow, self, and fast conditions. In total, 60 trials and 126 strides were recorded for the slow condition, 58 trials and 105 strides for self, and 51 trials and 66 strides for the fast condition. The mean speeds for each category were 3.6 ± 0.5 km.h^{-1}, 4.6 ± 0.4 km.h^{-1}, and 6.1 ± 0.5 km.h^{-1}, respectively.

The agreement results regarding the spatiotemporal and joint angle parameters were divided and presented as discrete and continuous angular variables. For each, the agreements were shown stratified by speed. Additionally, the last section examines the relationship between MoCap walking speed and the between-system error for each spatiotemporal and kinematic variable across speeds.

3.1. *Agreement for Discrete Variables*

3.1.1. Speed Condition Agreement

The stratified analysis by speed showed that spatiotemporal variables had excellent agreement between systems across all conditions (ICC ≥ 0.95; r ≥ 0.967) (Table 1), with mean biases close to zero (Figure 3) and low MDC values (0.004–0.09), indicating high precision and stability of measurements regardless of speed. In contrast, the reliability of the ROM of angular variables was less consistent, showing low to moderate ICCs (0.482–0.776), mild to strong correlations between the systems (0.54–0.89), and higher MDC values (2.99–6.71), indicating greater overall variability and lower reproducibility for all joints, especially more prominent at the ankle during higher walking speeds.

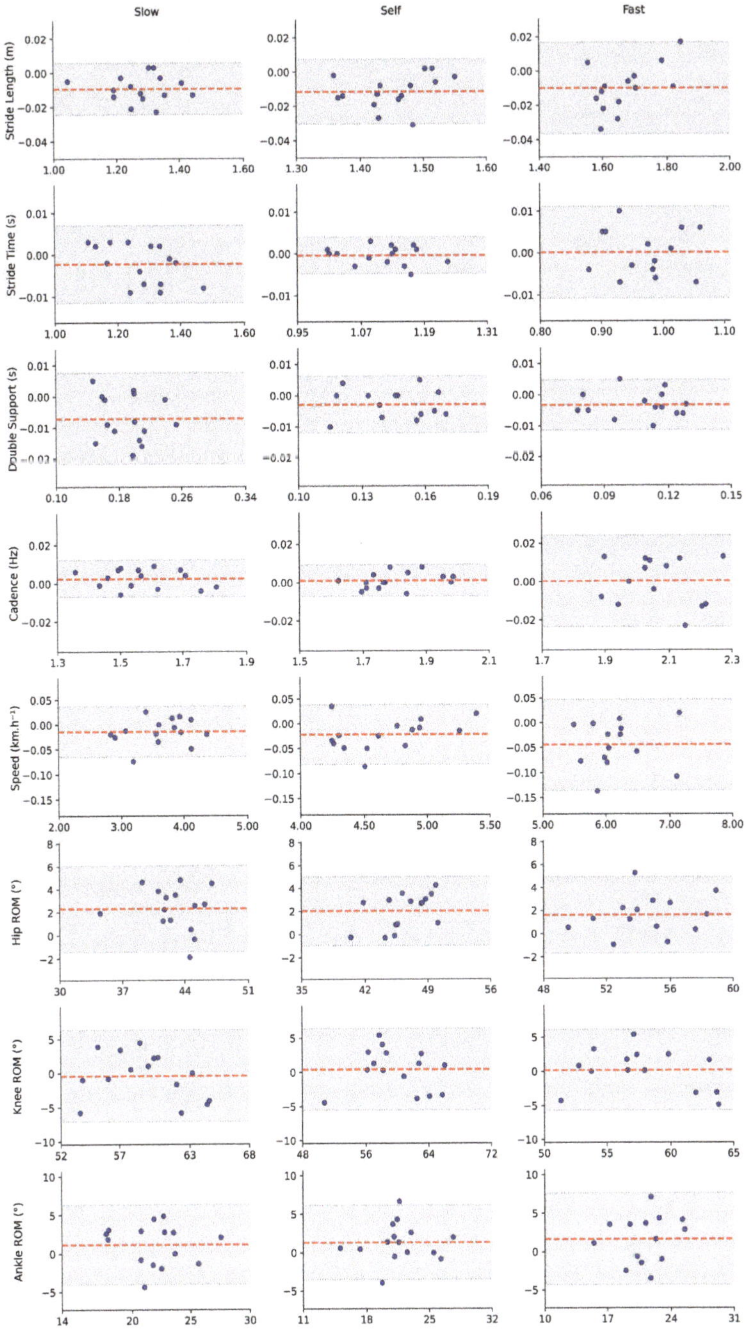

Figure 3. Bland–Altman plots illustrating the agreement between MoCap and OpenCap across various speeds. Each subplot displays the difference between the systems (y-axis) versus the mean of.

both systems (x-axis) for a specific variable, separated by speed: Slow (**left**), Self (**Center**), and Fast (**Right**). The red dashed line indicates the mean bias between methods. The gray shaded area shows the 95% limits of agreement (LoA), while the dotted lines mark the upper and lower LoA boundaries

Table 1. Mean and SD; Bias and its 95% Limits of Agreement (LoA); and agreement coefficients of gait parameters by speed: Intra-Class Correlation (ICC), Pearson's correlation (r), and the minimal detectable change at the 95% confidence level (MDC).

Variable	Speed	MoCap Mean ± SD	OpenCap Mean ± SD	Bias (95% LoA)	ICC (2,1)	r	MDC
Stride Length (m)	Slow	1.286 ± 0.103	1.276 ± 0.102	−0.009 (−0.024, 0.006)	0.993	0.997	0.015
	Self	1.450 ± 0.062	1.439 ± 0.065	−0.012 (−0.030, 0.008)	0.969	0.988	0.019
	Fast	1.664 ± 0.082	1.652 ± 0.086	−0.010 (−0.037, 0.017)	0.984	0.992	0.027
Stride Time (s)	Slow	1.285 ± 0.113	1.283 ± 0.111	−0.002 (−0.012, 0.007)	0.999	0.999	0.009
	Self	1.116 ± 0.069	1.116 ± 0.068	0.000 (−0.005, 0.004)	0.999	0.999	0.004
	Fast	0.977 ± 0.056	0.976 ± 0.058	0.000 (−0.011, 0.011)	0.995	0.995	0.011
Double Support (s)	Slow	0.197 ± 0.036	0.190 ± 0.034	−0.007 (−0.022, 0.008)	0.950	0.973	0.015
	Self	0.149 ± 0.020	0.146 ± 0.018	−0.003 (−0.012, 0.006)	0.957	0.967	0.009
	Fast	0.111 ± 0.019	0.107 ± 0.020	−0.003 (−0.011, 0.005)	0.959	0.973	0.008
Cadence (Hz)	Slow	1.565 ± 0.137	1.568 ± 0.136	0.003 (−0.007, 0.012)	0.999	0.999	0.010
	Self	1.796 ± 0.112	1.797 ± 0.113	0.001 (−0.007, 0.009)	0.999	0.999	0.008
	Fast	2.052 ± 0.118	2.055 ± 0.120	0.000 (−0.024, 0.024)	0.995	0.995	0.024
Walking Speed (km.h^{-1})	Slow	3.614 ± 0.501	3.599 ± 0.505	−0.014 (−0.066, 0.037)	0.998	0.998	0.051
	Self	4.640 ± 0.373	4.616 ± 0.382	−0.022 (−0.082, 0.038)	0.995	0.997	0.060
	Fast	6.106 ± 0.478	6.059 ± 0.481	−0.044 (−0.135, 0.047)	0.992	0.995	0.091
Hip ROM (°)	Slow	41.875 ± 3.290	44.158 ± 3.183	2.318 (−1.427, 6.063)	0.665	0.829	3.745
	Self	45.456 ± 2.684	47.544 ± 3.155	2.031 (−0.960, 5.021)	0.709	0.898	2.990
	Fast	53.845 ± 3.093	55.505 ± 3.431	1.629 (−1.669, 4.926)	0.706	0.823	3.298
Knee ROM (°)	Slow	59.461 ± 4.594	59.079 ± 3.713	−0.389 (−7.010, 6.32)	0.647	0.650	6.711
	Self	60.408 ± 4.804	60.155 ± 4.846	0.412 (−5.549, 6.372)	0.776	0.770	5.960
	Fast	57.890 ± 4.742	57.939 ± 4.533	0.191 (−5.738, 6.120)	0.775	0.774	5.929
Ankle ROM (°)	Slow	21.712 ± 3.203	22.821 ± 3.116	1.164 (−4.038, 6.366)	0.591	0.622	5.202
	Self	21.004 ± 3.715	22.589 ± 3.815	1.313 (−3.550, 6.175)	0.700	0.739	4.862
	Fast	20.590 ± 3.006	22.408 ± 3.508	1.651 (−4.341, 7.643)	0.482	0.538	5.992

3.1.2. Speed vs. System Interaction and Effects

The repeated measures ANOVA did not show any interaction between the system (MoCap, OpenCap) and speed (slow, self, fast) for all variables except for walking speed (km.h^{-1}) (G-G corrected $p = 0.00030$; $\eta p^2 = 0.50$).

Across systems, speed displayed strong main effects for all spatiotemporal variables—cadence, stride time, stride length, double support, walking speed—and for hip ROM (all $p < 0.001$; $\eta p^2 \approx 0.88$–0.95 for spatiotemporal and $\eta p^2 = 0.92$ for hip ROM). Only knee ROM showed a smaller but significant effect of speed (G-G corrected $p = 0.027$; $\eta p^2 = 0.264$), whereas ankle ROM did not change with speed for either system ($p = 0.39$; $\eta p^2 = 0.07$).

Amongst speeds, the system's effects had strong significance in double support ($\eta p^2 = 0.48$), stride length ($\eta p^2 = 0.57$), walking speed ($\eta p^2 = 0.40$), and Hip ROM ($\eta p^2 = 0.70$), with all $p < 0.05$. The other variables, such as cadence, stride time, and knee ROM, were not significant ($p > 0.05$), with minor effects ($\eta p^2 < 0.01$). The only exception was the ankle ROM, which was not significant due to the system effect, but showed a higher effect size ($\eta p^2 = 0.22$).

3.2. *Agreement for Continuous Joint Angle Variables*

Speed Condition Agreement

The results showed global RMSE values below 2° for all assessed joint angles, except for specific moments highlighted in the shaded regions. The ankle presented the highest mean RMSEs (1.77° in Fast, 1.52° in SS, and 1.59° in Slow), possibly reflecting greater sensitivity of this joint to slight differences in event detection and distal segment positioning. The hip and knee exhibited smaller discrepancies between systems, with RMSEs ranging from ~1.00° to 1.52° (Figure 4).

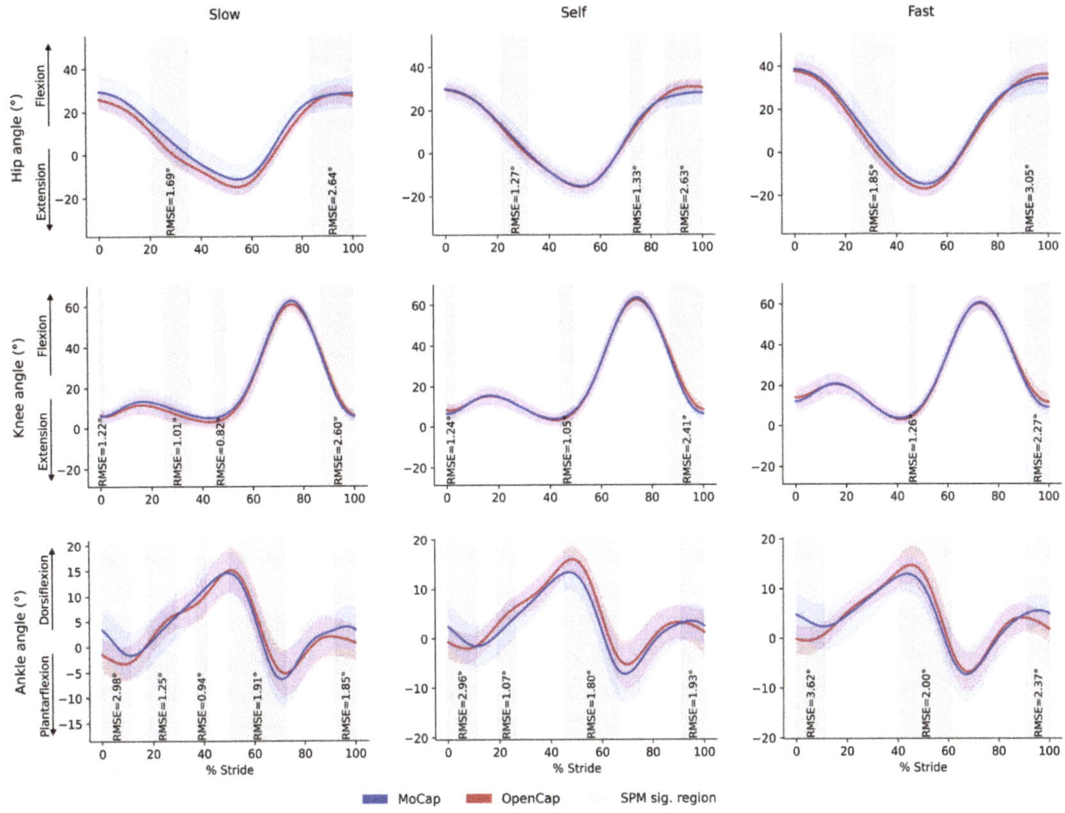

Figure 4. Joint angles across the gait cycle at three speeds for MoCap and OpenCap systems. Mean ± SD of hip, knee, and ankle joint angles over the normalized gait cycle (% stride) for MoCap (blue) and OpenCap (red) at slow, self, and fast speeds. Gray-shaded regions indicate phases with statistically significant differences between systems (SPM sig. region) with corresponding RMSE values shown for each highlighted region.

The calculation of the CoM displacement demonstrated high agreement between systems, with root mean square errors (RMSE) of less than 6 mm in all directions and speeds. The vertical axis (CoM Y) presented the highest absolute values, although the maximum observed difference was only 0.006 m. The anteroposterior (CoM X) and mediolateral (CoM Z) displacements showed slightly smaller errors (0.002–0.003 m) (Figure 5).

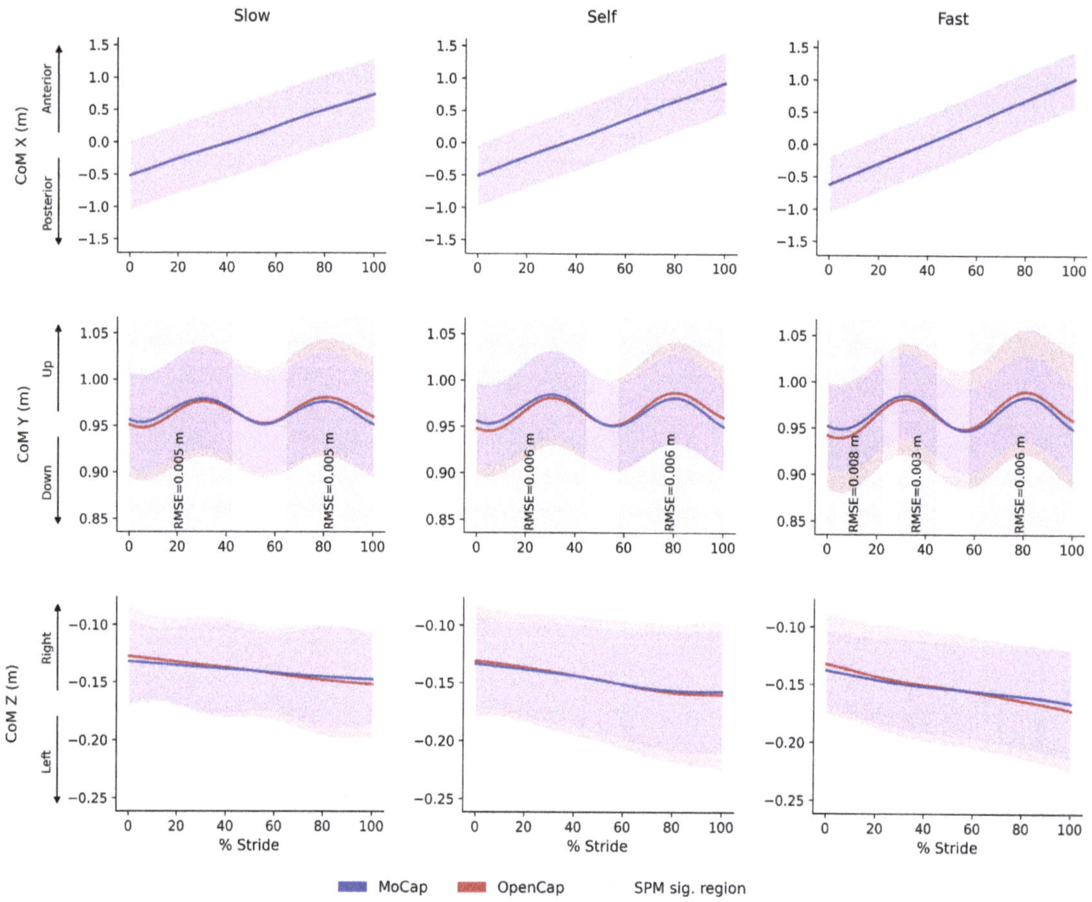

Figure 5. CoM trajectories across the gait cycle at three walking speeds for MoCap and OpenCap systems. Mean ± SD of CoM displacement in the mediolateral (X), vertical (Y), and anteroposterior (Z) directions over the normalized gait cycle (% stride) for MoCap (blue) and OpenCap (red) at slow, self, and fast speeds. Gray-shaded regions indicate phases with statistically significant differences between systems (SPM sig. region) with corresponding RMSE values shown for each highlighted region.

3.3. Relationship and Differences Between Walking Speeds and Between-System Error

The association between MoCap walking speed (km.h^{-1}) and the between-system error showed very low coefficients of determination ($R^2 \leq 0.059$) for all variables, indicating no significant linear relationship. Most parameters had *p*-values above the significance threshold ($p > 0.05$), except for double support (s), which showed a statistically significant association ($p = 0.001$) but with a weak effect ($R^2 = 0.059$). Overall, the between-system error remained consistent across walking speeds, with no evidence of speed-dependent (proportional) bias and only minor, non-significant trends (Figure 6).

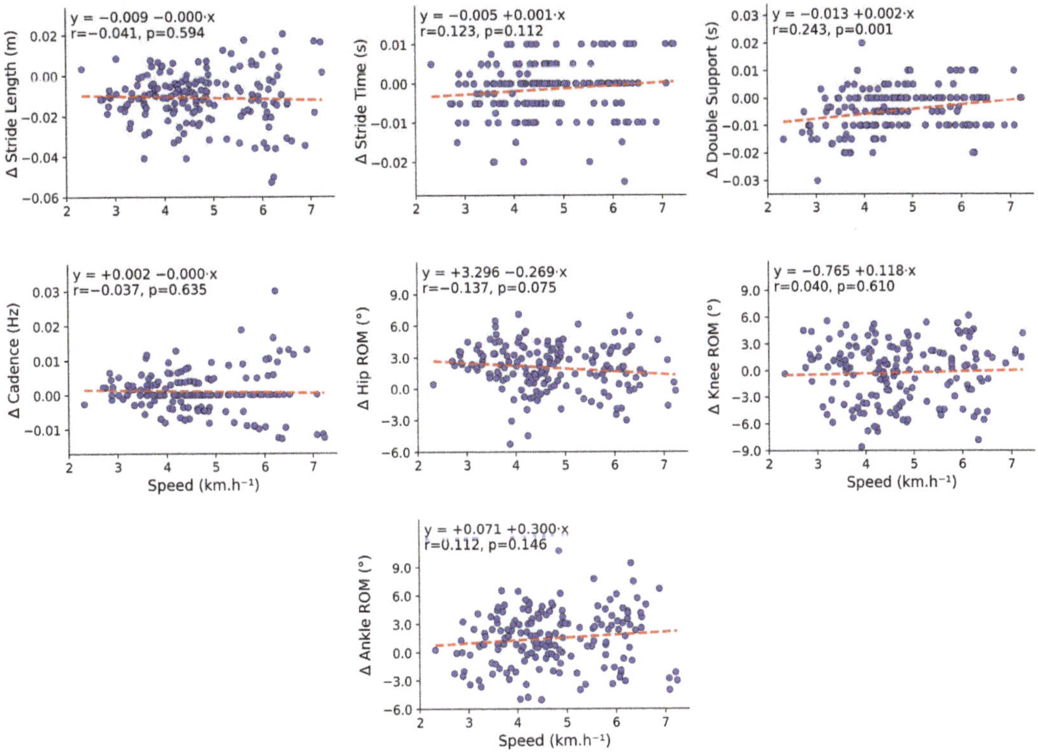

Figure 6. Relationship between MoCap walking speed (km.h^{-1}) and between-system error in spatiotemporal and kinematic variables. Scatterplots of the between-system error (y-axis) for each variable, plotted against MoCap walking speed (km.h^{-1}; x-axis). The red dashed line is the trend line output of the least-squares fit (y = b + a.x); subplot headers report Pearson's r and p.

4. Discussion

The primary analysis of this study demonstrates how biomechanical variables captured by a markerless system (OpenCap) during walking at different speeds align with those from a gold-standard marker-based system (MoCap). To our knowledge, this is the first research to examine these variables across various walking speeds.

4.1. Agreement for Discrete Variables: Spatiotemporal Parameters

Building on previous research, the OpenCap system closely aligns with the MoCap system in terms of spatiotemporal gait variables during walking, particularly at different speeds. Mean biases are close to zero, with high intraclass correlation coefficients and low minimal detectable changes, which supports the reliability of these parameters in the markerless system approach. However, analysis of discrete joint ranges of motion exhibited more variability, especially in hip and ankle movements, where reproducibility ranged from moderate to low. In contrast, continuous kinematic waveforms and CoM displacement demonstrated high consistency between systems over the different speeds proposed, with smaller mean errors.

When analyzing the spatiotemporal data, recent validation studies of OpenCap during overground walking have reported findings consistent with our results, particularly for spatiotemporal variables [7,11,29]. In our study, we observed an almost perfect agreement between OpenCap and MoCap for stride length and stride time, cadence, double support time, and walking speed, with mean biases close to zero, high intraclass correlation coefficients (ICCs), and consistently low minimal detectable changes (MDCs) (for details, see Table 1). This high reliability can be attributed to the robustness of pose estimation algorithms in identifying distal landmarks (e.g., the heel and toes), which serve as direct inputs for calculating events such as touchdown and takeoff [25]. Unlike angular kinematics, which depend on complex estimation of 3D joint centers and segment orientations, spatiotemporal parameters are less vulnerable to errors from camera angles or partial occlusions [7]. These results are consistent with the literature; for example, Martiš et al. [11] found very high correlations ($r \approx 0.94$–1.0) at an average walking speed, while Horsak et al. [10] and Uhlrich et al. [7] reported excellent validity during 'self-selected' natural walking similar to our self-selected speed (~4.5 $km.h^{-1}$). Our findings confirm high reliability, not only at a self-selected, but also at slower and faster speeds. Additionally, our results align with those of Uhlrich et al. [7], who highlighted the strong accuracy of OpenCap for these parameters, not only during walking but across various protocols, including squatting, rising from a chair, and drop jumps, further supporting the system's reliability for these types of variables.

4.2. Agreement for Discrete Variables: Range of Motion Parameters

In contrast, for discrete ROM analysis, both our results and the existing literature show greater limitations. In this study, all the joints presented low to moderate agreement (ICCs ~ 0.48–0.78), with relatively high minimal detectable changes (MDCs) (e.g., 3–7° for all speeds). Precisely, only the knee demonstrated a moderate to strong edge agreement over all walking speeds (ICC ~ 0.65–0.78, MDC ~ 5.9–6.7°). Such a difficulty in reporting higher reliability for joint ROMs was noted by Turner et al. [28], who found good validity for hip and knee motion in the sagittal plane but lower reliability for the ankle during uni- and bilateral movements, as well as jumping. Comparable findings were reported by Horsak et al. [10], who, in a repeatability study of OpenCap, identified the hip and ankle as the joints with the highest variability and noted high MDC values for both, further emphasizing them as challenging joints for this system. Other tasks, such as landing, showed that the hip and ankle remain the joints most prone to errors [30]. Even though continuous joint angle waveforms show high similarity between systems (RMSE < 2° in our case), localized differences in specific phases of the gait cycle, as revealed by our SPM analysis, can shift minimum or maximum values. Since the calculation of discrete ROM relies solely on these two extreme data points, it is inherently more vulnerable to localized errors. In contrast, metrics like RMSE are based on averaging, which spreads the error across the entire gait cycle and can mask these brief, peak-related discrepancies. This difference in calculation methods may explain why discrete ROM measures exhibit lower reproducibility, even when the underlying continuous waveforms appear highly consistent (see Figure 4).

Also, despite constant algorithm system updates, it is worth noting that the pose estimation model continues to struggle with detecting markers from discrete angle joints, which are limited by sparse and noisy keypoints [31]. Aiming to improve marker detection for enhancing accuracy and generalizability for walking and other motor tasks, Falisse et al. [31] recently integrated a Long Short-Term Memory (LSTM) model into OpenCap, which predicts the 3D position of 43 denser anatomical markers based on the 3D position of 20 sparser keypoints. In their study, the new marker enhancer decreased the overall RMSE (error metric) of kinematic angle joints compared to a marker-based system, from 5.3° (older OpenCap system) to 4.1° (LSTM model). In our case, despite the already integrated LSTM model in OpenCap, the higher MDC reported in the ROM from the lower limb joints at all measured speeds still shows the difficulty for their developers to enhance the system in this situation.

Furthermore, the limited volume calibration used for OpenCap could worsen the higher metric errors observed in the discrete ROM variables, as only a small number of trials were conducted. Although designed to mimic natural walking over the ground, this approach may result in less data being analyzed compared to treadmill trials, even though, in this case, the data quality depends on the position of the safety bars [12]. Additionally, from this methodological standpoint, our study meets the highest standard possible by using OpenCap during walking. The use of two cameras at front-side strategic angles can cover the largest possible area without significant errors [7]. Currently, the best results from this markerless system are achieved either in this way or when the model is updated.

Unlike spatiotemporal variables, for which normative values can be established to detect minimal clinical differences (see Section 4.5), variables such as discrete joint ROMs have not yet been standardized due to the unpredictable behavior of pathological gait [32,33]. For example, when comparing the MDC for hip flexion-extension ROM obtained with OpenCap and MoCap systems (2.99°) to the Minimal Clinically Important Difference (MCID) recently reported for chronic stroke patients (5.81° for the affected and 2.86° for the unaffected limb; Guzik et al. [34], our results show that the system's measurement variability stays below the level of clinically meaningful change. This indicates that the markerless system can detect improvements in hip sagittal motion that are relevant for rehabilitation. The MDC, which accounts for approximately 51% of the MCID for the affected limb, further confirms the system's sensitivity to key changes in hip movements. Along with the knee results, where the MDC (5.96°) was lower than the MCID values reported by Guzik et al. [35] (6.8–8.5°), these findings verify that OpenCap's measurement accuracy for major lower-limb joints is within clinically acceptable ranges. Therefore, even small rehabilitation-related changes in sagittal plane kinematics can be reliably identified by the markerless system for stroke patients.

4.3. Agreement for Continuous Variables: Center of Mass Displacement

In the analyses of continuous joint angle waveforms, the RMSE values were consistently low across all walking speeds (<2° for the hip, knee, and ankle), indicating high similarity between joint profiles and remaining below the acceptable thresholds for gait variables [27]. This result reinforces previous findings with OpenCap, which also reported reduced discrepancies between marker-based and markerless systems, particularly for sagittal plane joints [7,10]. Moreover, our continuous joint angle values across all walking speeds were considerably low, with global RMSEs ranging from ~1.00° to 1.77°. This indicates a higher accuracy than that reported in prior gait studies with OpenCap, where RMSE values generally ranged between ~4° and 7° [11,29]. Similarly, the analysis of CoM displacement showed high agreement between systems, with an RMSE of less than 6 mm in all directions and speeds. The vertical axis (CoM Y) presented the largest absolute values, although the maximum difference was only 0.006 m. The anteroposterior (CoM X) and mediolateral (CoM Z) displacements exhibited even more minor errors (0.002–0.003 m). These findings confirm that, in addition to joint angles, OpenCap also provides reliable estimates of CoM trajectories, even at different overground walking speeds. This result, consistent with previous findings, has been reported in validation studies of markerless systems compared to marker-based methods, demonstrating high accuracy for CoM trajectories during self-selected walking [36].

Furthermore, the initial OpenCap study also emphasized the accuracy of this method in capturing three-dimensional CoM displacement, providing reliable measurements [7].

This robustness, observed in our study even at different speeds, can be attributed to the calculation method: OpenCap provides the input kinematic data (i.e., the 3D position of each body segment), which is then utilized by the OpenSim software for biomechanical analysis. Within OpenSim, the CoM is a model-based calculation derived from a full-body musculoskeletal model scaled to each participant's anthropometry. This method computes the total-body CoM as a mass-weighted average of all individual segments. This integrative approach makes the CoM calculation less sensitive to minor errors [37].

4.4. *Agreement for Continuous Variables: Range of Motion Parameters*

The use of SPM was essential to interpret the results from the continuous joint angle waveforms, as we identified localized differences at specific points of the gait cycle (e.g., near toe-off), but without a relevant impact on the overall mean error (~1.00° to 1.77°) (see Figure 4). Previous studies with OpenCap have also reported discrepancies at critical events, such as initial contact and take-off [11,30]. Taken together, these findings emphasize that even when overall RMSE values are low, local discrepancies can still account for errors in specific measures, such as ROM.

4.5. *Relationship and Differences Between Walking Speeds and Between-System Error*

Additionally, when examining the relationship between walking speeds and the between-system error, represented by the error deltas (Δ), these relationships were all low ($R^2 \leq 0.059$) for all variables. In other words, the between-system error for spatiotemporal parameters (e.g., stride length, cadence) and all discrete joint ROMs (hip, knee, and ankle) remained consistent across the tested walking paces, with no trend toward greater errors at higher speeds. These findings, suggesting the absence of proportional bias for most variables, align with a growing body of evidence demonstrating high agreement for spatiotemporal parameters in markerless systems, both at self-selected speeds [29] and across different walking speeds [16,38,39]. The only variable with a distinct behavior was double support time, which exhibited a statistically significant but very weak correlation with speed ($p = 0.001$, $R^2 = 0.059$). Evidence in the literature corroborates this greater sensitivity of double support, as it represents a brief interval in which both feet are in contact with the ground, making it more prone to discrepancies between analytical methods, with accuracy varying according to walking speed (~78.7% to 84.5%) [40].

The repeated-measures ANOVA (system × speed) reinforced this pattern. For both systems, the speed exerted robust main effects on all spatiotemporal variables—cadence, stride time, stride length, double support, and walking speed—as well as on hip ROM (all $p < 0.001$; and large ηp^2 between 0.88 and 0.95 for spatiotemporal variables and 0.92 for the hip). This behavior is expected and widely described in the gait literature [24,41,42]. Knee ROM also varied significantly with speed, albeit with a more negligible effect ($p = 0.027$), but still supported by larger effect sizes ($\eta p^2 = 0.264$). Here, the interaction between speed and system was not significant ($p = 0.12$), but the strong effect size ($\eta p^2 = 0.16$) raises concerns and practical relevance regarding the speed magnitudes that influence differences between OpenCap and Mocap.

In contrast, ankle ROM remained unchanged with increased speed ($p = 0.39$). This lack of significant impact on the ankle should be interpreted with caution, given that the effect size was relatively weak ($\eta p^2 = 0.07$). Otherwise, given the lower reliability and higher measurement variability we previously identified for discrete ankle ROM (ICCs as low as 0.482), it would be plausible that this measurement noise might have masked a true, albeit smaller, physiological effect of speed on this joint. Even when reporting the impact of speed for both systems (the average between OpenCap and Mocap), this result still highlights the difficulty of the OpenCap system in detecting differences in walking speeds at distal joints, particularly at the ankle ROM.

It is also worth noting that no significant interactions were found between systems (MoCap, OpenCap) and speed (slow, self, fast) for any variable, except for walking speed (km.h^{-1}). Post hoc analysis showed that OpenCap estimated slightly lower values than MoCap at all speeds (differences that increased with speed, from −0.014 and −0.046 km.h^{-1}), but of minimal magnitude, a pattern similar to that reported by other authors [11,40]. Methodologically, while MoCap calculates speed using physical markers on the feet and pelvis, OpenCap depends on musculoskeletal models and computer vision-based reconstruction. This methodological difference could explain the results, which show a slight but consistent underestimation of the forward displacement of the mid-hip, likely contributing to the significant bias and larger effect size ($\eta p^2 = 0.50$) in the lower velocity measurement when the actual speed increases. This indicates that although there is a minimal systematic bias, both systems equivalently capture the relative changes in walking speed.

In addition, from a practical point of view, the Minimal Clinically Important Differences (MCID) may reinforce such a behavior [32,33]. Indeed, Bohannon et al. [33] reported a range of 0.36–0.61 km.h^{-1} for detecting minimal significant differences at comfortable speeds in the clinical environment. Replicating our results and considering the self-selected speed as the comfortable one, the underestimation by OpenCap of the Self speed (i.e., the 5 km.h^{-1} recorded would actually be about 5.03 km.h^{-1}, a roughly 0.03 km.h^{-1} error) would account for 8.3% of the minimal detectable difference reported by the authors (0.36 km.h^{-1}). This means that even subtle speed differences, which were notably reported between OpenCap and Mocap systems in the present study, would not have a significant clinical impact. The same interpretation might be extended to slow and fast speeds, which had errors ranging from 4.7% to 13.9%, respectively, related to those presented by Bohannon et al. [33] for indicating actual clinical differences.

Despite the overall strong agreement, some possible sources of error need attention. Double support time, for instance, although there was no interaction between speed and system ($p = 0.09$), a strong effect size ($\eta p^2 = 0.19$) was reported, which could indicate differences between the systems as speed increases. In fact, this result would not be surprising, as it relies on accurately detecting contact events; therefore, slight shifts in the virtual markers could introduce bias [11,29]. In addition, methodological differences between systems may influence walking speed, as factors such as pelvis estimation and camera angle directly affect this measurement [11,29]. Therefore, the interaction observed for walking speed appears to reflect systematic biases related to modeling and capture, rather than a limitation in the system's ability to detect speed changes.

4.6. Limitations

A key limitation is the limited capture volume of the OpenCap system, which restricts data collection to a walking distance of about 4 m. As a result, only a small number of strides could be recorded per trial. It would not represent a flaw in our experimental design but an inherent limitation of the system itself. While repeating trials helps reduce this issue, it may still affect the representativeness of gait dynamics over more prolonged walking bouts.

Furthermore, the present study may not be discussed in an integral manner with other types of pathological gaits. Since regular walking already involves a standardized process that is expected by physicians and engineers responsible for developing algorithms to capture the most reliable biomechanical parameters from human locomotion, this process still requires more time to yield similar outcomes in pathological conditions. In this circumstance, our results may not be entirely representative of clinical populations, where gait patterns are more variable.

5. Conclusions

This study demonstrated that the OpenCap system produces strong agreement with most gait parameters analyzed during walking at various speeds when compared to MoCap. OpenCap had excellent agreement with MoCap for spatiotemporal gait variables across different walking speeds, with minimal mean biases and outstanding reproducibility. At the same time, from the joint angle standpoint, discrete joint ROM measures revealed greater variability, particularly at the hip and ankle, across all speeds. In contrast, continuous joint angle waveforms for the hip, knee, and ankle, as well as CoM displacement, displayed high consistency between systems across all tested speeds. Taken together, these findings highlight a nuanced profile for OpenCap. While it functions as a robust tool for spatiotemporal parameters and continuous kinematics, the identified limitations necessitate caution, especially in clinical settings with varying speeds. However, it is important to contextualize the magnitude of these errors. For the less reliable discrete ROM measures, the observed mean biases were within ranges often considered acceptable for clinical interpretation in gait analysis. Additionally, this systematic bias was smaller than the minimal detectable change (MDC) for these variables, indicating the system is sufficiently sensitive to track clinically significant progress time.

While the present validation was performed with a group of healthy participants, caution should be exercised when applying these findings to clinical populations. Pathological gait patterns often include asymmetrical movements, compensatory postures, and limited joint excursions, which could affect the accuracy of markerless motion capture. Future research should evaluate OpenCap's performance in individuals with neurological or orthopedic impairments, such as those with post-stroke, Parkinson's, or post-surgical gait, to determine if the good precision observed in healthy walking conditions also applies to pathological situations.

Author Contributions: Conceptualization, J.L.S. and P.C. (Paolo Cavallari); methodology, E.F.d.B., J.L.S. and S.C.; software, E.F.d.B. and S.C.; validation, J.L.S., E.F.d.B. and S.C.; formal analysis, E.F.d.B., J.L.S. and S.C.; investigation, E.F.d.B., J.L.S. and S.C.; resources, V.C., P.C. (Paolo Capodaglio) and P.C. (Paolo Cavallari); data curation, E.F.d.B. and S.C.; writing—original draft preparation, E.F.d.B. and J.L.S.; writing—review and editing, J.L.S., S.C., V.C., P.C. (Paolo Capodaglio), M.P.T., L.A.P.-T. and P.C. (Paolo Cavallari); supervision, L.A.P.-T. and P.C. (Paolo Cavallari); project administration, J.L.S., P.C. (Paolo Cavallari); funding acquisition, E.F.d.B. All authors have read and agreed to the published version of the manuscript.

Funding: This study was financed in part by the Coordenação de Aperfeiçoamento de Pessoal de Nível Superior—Brasil (CAPES)—Finance Code 001.

Institutional Review Board Statement: The study was conducted in accordance with the Declaration of Helsinki and approved by the "Comitato Etico di Ateneo dell'Università degli Studi di Milano" (council 23/23).

Informed Consent Statement: Informed consent was obtained from all subjects involved in the study. Written informed consent has been obtained from the patients to publish this paper.

Data Availability Statement: The authors will provide the raw data supporting this article's conclusions without unnecessary restriction.

Acknowledgments: The authors would like to thank the Fondazione Mariani for all the support in maintaining and assisting with the Laboratorio di Analisi del Movimento del Bambino (LAMB).

Conflicts of Interest: The authors declare no conflicts of interest.

Abbreviations

The following abbreviations are used in this manuscript:

CoM	Center of Mass
G-G	Greenhouse–Geisser
ICC	Intraclass Correlation Coefficients
LoA	Limits of Agreement
MDC	Minimal Detectable Change
MoCap	Marker-based Motion Capture
.mot	Joint Angle Data
ROM	Range of Motion
RMSE	Root Mean Square Error
SPM	Statistical Parametric Mapping
TD	Touchdown
TO	Take-off
.trc	Three-dimensional Marker Position

References

1. Hausdorff, J.M. Gait Dynamics, Fractals and Falls: Finding Meaning in the Stride-to-Stride Fluctuations of Human Walking. *Hum. Mov. Sci.* **2007**, *26*, 555–589. [CrossRef]
2. Gomeñuka, N.A.; Oliveira, H.B.; Silva, E.S.; Costa, R.R.; Kanitz, A.C.; Liedtke, G.V.; Schuch, F.B.; Peyré-Tartaruga, L.A. Effects of Nordic Walking Training on Quality of Life, Balance and Functional Mobility in Elderly: A Randomized Clinical Trial. *PLoS ONE* **2019**, *14*, e0211472. [CrossRef]
3. Baker, R. Gait Analysis Methods in Rehabilitation. *J. Neuroeng. Rehabil.* **2006**, *3*, 4. [CrossRef]
4. Monteiro, E.P.; Franzoni, L.T.; Cubillos, D.M.; de Oliveira Fagundes, A.; Carvalho, A.R.; Oliveira, H.B.; Pantoja, P.D.; Schuch, F.B.; Rieder, C.R.; Martinez, F.G.; et al. Effects of Nordic Walking Training on Functional Parameters in Parkinson's Disease: A Randomized Controlled Clinical Trial. *Scand. J. Med. Sci. Sports* **2017**, *27*, 351–358. [CrossRef]
5. Prasanth, H.; Caban, M.; Keller, U.; Courtine, G.; Ijspeert, A.; Vallery, H.; Von Zitzewitz, J. Wearable Sensor-Based Real-Time Gait Detection: A Systematic Review. *Sensors* **2021**, *21*, 2727. [CrossRef]
6. Upadhyay, A.; Shukla, A.; Sharma, M.; Abraham, A. Simple yet Robust Markerless Motion Capture System Using Deep Learning. *Eng. Appl. Artif. Intell.* **2025**, *160*, 111905. [CrossRef]
7. Uhlrich, S.D.; Falisse, A.; Kidziński, Ł.; Muccini, J.; Ko, M.; Chaudhari, A.S.; Hicks, J.L.; Delp, S.L. OpenCap: Human Movement Dynamics from Smartphone Videos. *PLoS Comput. Biol.* **2023**, *19*, e1011462. [CrossRef] [PubMed]
8. Wang, J.; Xu, W.; Wu, Z.; Zhang, H.; Wang, B.; Zhou, Z.; Wang, C.; Li, K.; Nie, Y. Evaluation of a Smartphone-Based Markerless System to Measure Lower-Limb Kinematics in Patients with Knee Osteoarthritis. *J. Biomech.* **2025**, *181*, 112529. [CrossRef]
9. Min, Y.-S.; Jung, T.-D.; Lee, Y.-S.; Kwon, Y.; Kim, H.J.; Kim, H.C.; Lee, J.C.; Park, E. Biomechanical Gait Analysis Using a Smartphone-Based Motion Capture System (Opencap) in Patients with Neurological Disorders. *Bioengineering* **2024**, *11*, 911. [CrossRef] [PubMed]
10. Horsak, B.; Kainz, H.; Dumphart, B. Repeatability and Minimal Detectable Change Including Clothing Effects for Smartphone-Based 3D Markerless Motion Capture. *J. Biomech.* **2024**, *175*, 112281. [CrossRef] [PubMed]
11. Martiš, P.; Košutzká, Z.; Kranzl, A. A Step Forward Understanding Directional Limitations in Markerless Smartphone-Based GAIT Analysis: A Pilot Study. *Sensors* **2024**, *24*, 3091. [CrossRef] [PubMed]
12. Svetek, A.; Morgan, K.; Burland, J.; Glaviano, N.R. Validation of OpenCap on Lower Extremity Kinematics during Functional Tasks. *J. Biomech.* **2025**, *183*, 112602. [CrossRef]
13. de Borba, E.F.; da Silva, E.S.; de Liz Alves, L.; Da Silva Neto, A.R.; Inda, A.R.; Ibrahim, B.M.; Ribas, L.R.; Correale, L.; Peyré-Tartaruga, L.A.; Tartaruga, M.P. Fatigue-Related Changes in Running Technique and Mechanical Variables After a Maximal Incremental Test in Recreational Runners. *J. Appl. Biomech.* **2024**, *40*, 424–431. [CrossRef]
14. Jaén-Carrillo, D.; Ruiz-Alias, S.A.; Chicano-Gutiérrez, J.M.; Ruiz-Malagón, E.J.; Roche-Seruendo, L.E.; García-Pinillos, F. Test-Retest Reliability of the MotionMetrix Software for the Analysis of Walking and Running Gait Parameters. *Sensors* **2022**, *22*, 3201. [CrossRef]
15. Moran, M.F.; Rogler, I.C.; Wager, J.C. Inter-Session Repeatability of Marker-Less Motion Capture of Treadmill Running Gait. *Appl. Sci.* **2023**, *13*, 1702. [CrossRef]
16. Walker, J.; Thomas, A.; Lunn, D.E.; Nicholson, G.; Tucker, C.B. Concurrent Validity of Theia3D Markerless Motion Capture for Detecting Sagittal Kinematic Differences between Gait Speeds. *J. Sports Sci.* **2025**, *43*, 1560–1571. [CrossRef]

17. Middleton, A.; Fritz, S.L.; Lusardi, M. Walking Speed: The Functional Vital Sign. *J. Aging Phys. Act.* **2015**, *23*, 314–322. [CrossRef] [PubMed]
18. Bona, R.L.; Gomeñuka, N.A.; Storniolo, J.L.L.; Bonezi, A.; Biancardi, C.M. Self-Selected Walking Speed in Individuals with Transfemoral Amputation: Recovery, Economy and Rehabilitation Index. *Eur. J. Physiother.* **2020**, *22*, 133–140. [CrossRef]
19. Peyré-Tartaruga, L.; Passos-Monteiro, E. A New Integrative Approach to Evaluate Pathological Gait: Locomotor Rehabilitation Index. *Clin. Transl. Degener. Dis.* **2016**, 86–90. [CrossRef]
20. Peng, Y.; Wang, W.; Wang, L.; Zhou, H.; Chen, Z.; Zhang, Q.; Li, G. Smartphone Videos-Driven Musculoskeletal Multibody Dynamics Modelling Workflow to Estimate the Lower Limb Joint Contact Forces and Ground Reaction Forces. *Med. Biol. Eng. Comput.* **2024**, *62*, 3841–3853. [CrossRef]
21. Davis III, R.B.; Ounpuu, S.; Tyburski, D.; Gage, J.R. A Gait Analysis Data Collection and Reduction Technique. *Hum. Mov. Sci.* **1991**, *10*, 575–587. [CrossRef]
22. Lai, A.K.M.; Arnold, A.S.; Wakeling, J.M. Why Are Antagonist Muscles Co-Activated in My Simulation? A Musculoskeletal Model for Analysing Human Locomotor Tasks. *Ann. Biomed. Eng.* **2017**, *45*, 2762–2774. [CrossRef]
23. Rajagopal, A.; Dembia, C.L.; DeMers, M.S.; Delp, D.D.; Hicks, J.L.; Delp, S.L. Full-Body Musculoskeletal Model for Muscle-Driven Simulation of Human Gait. *IEEE Trans. Biomed. Eng.* **2016**, *63*, 2068–2079. [CrossRef]
24. Winter, D.A. *Biomechanics and Motor Control of Human Movement*; John Wiley & Sons: Hoboken, NJ, USA, 2009; ISBN 0470398183.
25. Zeni, J.A., Jr.; Richards, J.G.; Higginson, J. Two Simple Methods for Determining Gait Events during Treadmill and Overground Walking Using Kinematic Data. *Gait Posture* **2008**, *27*, 710–714. [CrossRef]
26. Mishra, P.; Pandey, C.M.; Singh, U.; Gupta, A.; Sahu, C.; Keshri, A. Descriptive Statistics and Normality Tests for Statistical Data. *Ann. Card. Anaesth.* **2019**, *22*, 67–72. [CrossRef] [PubMed]
27. McGinley, J.L.; Baker, R.; Wolfe, R.; Morris, M.E. The Reliability of Three-Dimensional Kinematic Gait Measurements: A Systematic Review. *Gait Posture* **2009**, *29*, 360–369. [CrossRef]
28. Turner, J.A.; Chaaban, C.R.; Padua, D.A. Validation of OpenCap: A Low-Cost Markerless Motion Capture System for Lower-Extremity Kinematics during Return-to-Sport Tasks. *J. Biomech.* **2024**, *171*, 112200. [CrossRef] [PubMed]
29. Horsak, B.; Eichmann, A.; Lauer, K.; Prock, K.; Krondorfer, P.; Siragy, T.; Dumphart, B. Concurrent Validity of Smartphone-Based Markerless Motion Capturing to Quantify Lower-Limb Joint Kinematics in Healthy and Pathological Gait. *J. Biomech.* **2023**, *159*, 111801. [CrossRef] [PubMed]
30. Lima, Y.L.; Collings, T.; Hall, M.; Bourne, M.N.; Diamond, L.E. Validity and Reliability of Trunk and Lower-Limb Kinematics during Squatting, Hopping, Jumping and Side-Stepping Using OpenCap Markerless Motion Capture Application. *J. Sports Sci.* **2024**, *42*, 1847–1858. [CrossRef]
31. Falisse, A.; Uhlrich, S.D.; Chaudhari, A.S.; Hicks, J.L.; Delp, S.L. Marker Data Enhancement for Markerless Motion Capture. *IEEE Trans. Biomed. Eng.* **2025**, *72*, 2013–2022. [CrossRef]
32. Daynes, E.; Barker, R.E.; Jones, A.V.; Walsh, J.A.; Nolan, C.M.; Man, W.D.C.; Singh, S.J.; Greening, N.J.; Houchen-Wolloff, L.; Evans, R.A. Determining the Minimum Important Differences for Field Walking Tests in Adults with Long–Term Conditions: A Systematic Review and Meta-Analysis. *Eur. Respir. Rev.* **2025**, *34*, 240198. [CrossRef]
33. Bohannon, R.W.; Glenney, S.S. Minimal Clinically Important Difference for Change in Comfortable Gait Speed of Adults with Pathology: A Systematic Review. *J. Eval. Clin. Pract.* **2014**, *20*, 295–300. [CrossRef]
34. Guzik, A.; Drużbicki, M.; Perenc, L.; Wolan-Nieroda, A.; Turolla, A.; Kiper, P. Establishing the Minimal Clinically Important Differences for Sagittal Hip Range of Motion in Chronic Stroke Patients. *Front. Neurol.* **2021**, *12*, 700190. [CrossRef]
35. Guzik, A.; Drużbicki, M.; Wolan-Nieroda, A.; Turolla, A.; Kiper, P. Estimating Minimal Clinically Important Differences for Knee Range of Motion after Stroke. *J. Clin. Med.* **2020**, *9*, 3305. [CrossRef] [PubMed]
36. Oonk, G.A.; Kempe, M.; Lemmink, K.A.P.M.; Buurke, T.J.W. Examining the Concurrent Validity of Markerless Motion Capture in Dual-Athlete Team Sports Movements. *J. Sports Sci.* **2025**, *45*, 1–12. [CrossRef]
37. Delp, S.L.; Anderson, F.C.; Arnold, A.S.; Loan, P.; Habib, A.; John, C.T.; Guendelman, E.; Thelen, D.G. OpenSim: Open-Source Software to Create and Analyze Dynamic Simulations of Movement. *IEEE Trans. Biomed. Eng.* **2007**, *54*, 1940–1950. [CrossRef] [PubMed]
38. Mentiplay, B.F.; Perraton, L.G.; Bower, K.J.; Pua, Y.H.; McGaw, R.; Heywood, S.; Clark, R.A. Gait Assessment Using the Microsoft Xbox One Kinect: Concurrent Validity and Inter-Day Reliability of Spatiotemporal and Kinematic Variables. *J. Biomech.* **2015**, *48*, 2166–2170. [CrossRef] [PubMed]
39. Scataglini, S.; Abts, E.; Van Bocxlaer, C.; Van den Bussche, M.; Meletani, S.; Truijen, S. Accuracy, Validity, and Reliability of Markerless Camera-Based 3D Motion Capture Systems versus Marker-Based 3D Motion Capture Systems in Gait Analysis: A Systematic Review and Meta-Analysis. *Sensors* **2024**, *24*, 3686. [CrossRef]
40. Cerfoglio, S.; Ferraris, C.; Vismara, L.; Amprimo, G.; Priano, L.; Bigoni, M.; Galli, M.; Mauro, A.; Cimolin, V. Estimation of Gait Parameters in Healthy and Hemiplegic Individuals Using Azure Kinect: A Comparative Study with the Optoelectronic System. *Front. Bioeng. Biotechnol.* **2024**, *12*, 1449680. [CrossRef]

41. Fukuchi, C.A.; Fukuchi, R.K.; Duarte, M. Effects of Walking Speed on Gait Biomechanics in Healthy Participants: A Systematic Review and Meta-Analysis. *Syst. Rev.* **2019**, *8*, 153. [CrossRef]
42. Bohannon, R.W. Comfortable and Maximum Walking Speed of Adults Aged 20–79 Years: Reference Values and Determinants. *Age Ageing* **1997**, *26*, 15–19. [CrossRef] [PubMed]

sensors

MDPI

Article

Inferring Mental States via Linear and Non-Linear Body Movement Dynamics: A Pilot Study

Tad T. Brunyé [1,2,*], Kana Okano [2], James McIntyre [2,3], Madelyn K. Sandone [2], Lisa N. Townsend [4], Marissa Marko Lee [2], Marisa Smith [2] and Gregory I. Hughes [1,2]

1 U.S. Army DEVCOM Soldier Center, Natick, MA 01760, USA
2 Center for Applied Brain and Cognitive Sciences, Tufts University, Medford, MA 02155, USA
3 Department of Electrical and Computer Engineering, Tufts University, Medford, MA 02155, USA
4 U.S. Army DEVCOM Soldier Center Simulation and Training Technology Center (STTC), Orlando, FL 32826, USA
* Correspondence: thaddeus.t.brunye.civ@army.mil

Highlights

What are the main findings?

- This pilot study shows that body movement trajectories predict acute stress with moderate-to-high accuracy; workload and uncertainty were not reliably classified.
- The most informative movement-related features were primarily linear spectral and statistical measures, rather than non-linear chaos/complexity metrics.

What is the implication of the main finding?

- Whole-body movement sensing can serve as a low-burden indicator of acute stress for real-time sensing in the context of adaptive human–machine systems.
- Effective monitoring of workload and uncertainty may require larger training samples or multimodal fusion such as pairing with eye, voice, or peripheral physiology.

Abstract: Stress, workload, and uncertainty characterize occupational tasks across sports, healthcare, military, and transportation domains. Emerging theory and empirical research suggest that coordinated whole-body movements may reflect these transient mental states. Wearable sensors and optical motion capture offer opportunities to quantify such movement dynamics and classify mental states that influence occupational performance and human–machine interaction. We tested this possibility in a small pilot study ($N = 10$) designed to test feasibility and identify preliminary movement features linked to mental states. Participants performed a perceptual decision-making task involving facial emotion recognition (i.e., deciding whether depicted faces were happy versus angry) with variable levels of stress (via a risk of electric shock), workload (via time pressure), and uncertainty (via visual degradation of task stimuli). The time series of movement trajectories was analyzed both holistically (full trajectory) and by phase: lowered (early), raising (middle), aiming (late), and face-to-face (sequential). For each epoch, up to 3844 linear and non-linear features were extracted across temporal, spectral, probability, divergence, and fractal domains. Features were entered into a repeated 10-fold cross-validation procedure using 80/20 train/test splits. Feature selection was conducted with the T-Rex Selector, and selected features were used to train a scikit-learn pipeline with a Robust Scaler and a Logistic Regression classifier. Models achieved mean ROC AUC scores as high as 0.76 for stress classification, with the highest sensitivity during the full movement trajectory and middle (raise) phases. Classification of workload and uncertainty states was less successful. These findings demonstrate the potential of movement-based sensing to infer stress states in applied settings and inform future human–machine interface development.

https://doi.org/10.3390/s25226990

Keywords: inertial measurement units; optical motion capture; cognitive state estimation; workload; uncertainty; machine learning; movement dynamics

1. Introduction

Across occupational domains, ranging from sports to healthcare, military, and transportation, individuals operate in dynamic environments that frequently induce states of stress, variable workloads, and moments of uncertainty [1–3]. Stress often arises from threats or risks and can trigger heightened arousal, narrowed attentional focus, and impaired learning and memory [4–6]. Workload reflects the cognitive demands imposed by a task relative to an individual's available resources, and excessive workload can impair performance (increasing errors and response latencies) by overwhelming attentional and executive systems [7–9]. Uncertainty occurs when information is ambiguous, incomplete, or conflicting, and it is associated with slower decision-making, reduced confidence, and strategic hesitation [10–12]. Due to these transient cognitive and affective states negatively influencing cognitive function and task execution [9,13–17], the accurate, real-time detection of these mental states can support adaptive systems that enhance safety, training, and performance under pressure. Such systems may include artificial intelligence (AI)-enhanced training simulators, stress- and workload-aware decision aids, or cognitive monitoring modules in occupational settings.

Traditional methods for cognitive state estimation, including sensors such as electroencephalography (EEG), functional near-infrared spectroscopy (fNIRS), and pupillometry, can offer valuable insights but often require instrumentation that can be cumbersome and sensitive to motion artifacts, limiting their applicability in naturalistic or mobile environments [18–20]. Increasingly, attention has turned to human movement sensing as a promising alternative for assessing cognitive states. Movement-based sensing offers a scalable and minimally intrusive alternative to conventional psychophysiological measures, enabling cognitive-state estimation in naturalistic, mobile settings. Rooted in embodied cognition, this approach assumes that mental states are not merely internal processes but are expressed through and shaped by the body. Behavioral cues, such as erratic gestures during confusion, postural stiffening under stress, or coordination shifts under cognitive load, reflect this link [21–28].

Sensor technologies, particularly optical motion capture (OMC) and inertial measurement units (IMUs), enable the high-resolution tracking of body or object movement. OMC systems use synchronized camera arrays to track markers in 3D space with sub-millimeter precision, ideal for simulated or constrained environments. IMUs offer mobile, lower-cost alternatives for field use, using accelerometers, gyroscopes, and magnetometers to track linear and angular motion. These sensing modalities enable the extraction of both linear features (such as velocity, acceleration, and positional displacement), and non-linear features that quantify signal complexity, predictability, and structure across time. Non-linear metrics such as entropy, fractal dimension, and Lyapunov exponents can capture chaotic or unstable movement patterns that may signal underlying changes in cognitive state. Together, linear and non-linear features offer a complementary view: linear metrics capture overt movement dynamics, while non-linear metrics may reveal subtle irregularities or fluctuations linked to mental processes. For example, recent research has demonstrated that non-linear features of walking, running, eye movements, brain activity, and heart rate have been useful for characterizing mental and physical states such as stress, workload, uncertainty, task competence, and postural stability [29–38]. Together, linear and non-linear features may provide unique value for mental state classification. Prioritizing these features is critical, affording input into machine learning pipelines that classify mental states with high temporal resolution and without the need for intrusive physiological instrumentation.

In occupational contexts, movement sensing can be used to quantify training progress, assess coordination, and analyze task performance [39,40]. However, few studies have examined whether dynamic whole-body movements, captured during task performance, can serve as a real-time proxy for evolving cognitive states such as stress, uncertainty, or workload [38]. Related work includes demonstrating postural immobility [41], posterior sway [42,43], or increased overall postural sway [44] when encountering aversive stimuli, and anterior sway when encountering positive or appealing stimuli [43,45]. Whereas this prior work focuses primarily on whole-body postural sway related to emotional experiences, herein we focus on the movement of occupational tools in response to three additional cognitive and affective states: stress, workload, and uncertainty. Identifying such movement-based indicators could enable early detection of cognitive strain, support adaptive training systems, and inform the development of human–machine interfaces for performance augmentation. These insights may also guide future integration of IMU-based sensing in wearable systems for occupational use.

The present pilot study addresses this gap by leveraging OMC to track movement trajectories while participants perform a decision-making task. Given the exploratory nature and small sample size (N = 10), the study was intended to establish feasibility and identify promising analytic approaches for future, larger-scale investigations. Participants experienced controlled manipulations of stress (via risk of electric shock), workload (via time pressure), and uncertainty (via stimulus clarity). Movement trajectories were segmented into task-relevant temporal phases, and several high-dimensional linear and non-linear features were extracted across temporal, spectral, probability, divergence, and fractal domains. Trajectory features were extracted using established Python libraries, and predictive models were evaluated using repeated cross-validation.

We had three main hypotheses. First, that stress would be most reliably classified from movement dynamics, relative to workload and uncertainty. Second, that predictive sensitivity would peak during the controller-raising phase, reflecting anticipatory arousal. And third, that both linear and non-linear features would contribute meaningfully to classification.

2. Materials and Methods

We conducted a human subjects experiment to test whether features quantified from movement dynamics afford classification of varied mental states. The study was approved by the institutional review boards at Tufts University and the U.S. Army Combat Capabilities, Army Research Laboratory (APPROVALS #24-089 and STUDY00005440).

2.1. *Participants, Design & Procedure*

A total of 18 (15 male, 3 female; Mean age 22.5) active duty military participants volunteered after providing written informed consent. Ten participants had complete datasets for analysis (8 male, 2 female; Mean age 23.3); data from eight participants were excluded due to incomplete motion capture records or missing behavioral data, resulting in 10 complete datasets suitable for analysis. Each participant completed two sessions on separate days, providing 20 sessions for analysis; during each session, they completed a perceptual decision-making task. Stress was manipulated in a within-participants manner: one session involved an acute stress induction, while the other did not, with the order counterbalanced across participants. During each session, participants experienced four conditions corresponding to the 2 $\times$ 2 within-participants design, with low versus high workload, and low versus high uncertainty conditions.

In the stress session, participants wore a StressX Pro Belt (SETCAN Corporation, Winnipeg, MB, Canada) that randomly administered 4–8 electric torso shocks. Shocks were delivered using a current-limited stimulator (compliance up to 4.5 kV), with pulses of ≤150 ms, peak current limited to 1 mA, and mean delivered energy of 55 mJ per pulse. In the no-stress session, the belt instead delivered innocuous tactile vibrations. This level of torso shock is commonly used in research settings, is considered uncomfortable but not painful, and carries minimal risk to participant health and safety; however, it is sufficient to increase physiological stress responses [4,46,47]. During each session, participants performed four testing blocks of a task involving the discrimination of happy versus angry facial expressions (i.e., a perceptual decision-making task involving facial emotion recognition); a total of 200 white male faces were generated with the FaceGen Modeller software (v. 3.5; Singular Inversions, Inc., Toronto, ON, Canada). Note that we used only white male faces to limit potential influences of sex, race, and ethnicity on emotional decision-making; intensity of facial expressions was pilot tested to ensure reliable perceptual discrimination between the two classes (happy, angry), even under conditions of clarity masking. Example faces are provided in Figure 1. The four blocks corresponded to the 2 × 2 matrix of workload (low, high) and uncertainty (low, high) conditions. Condition order was randomized for each session.

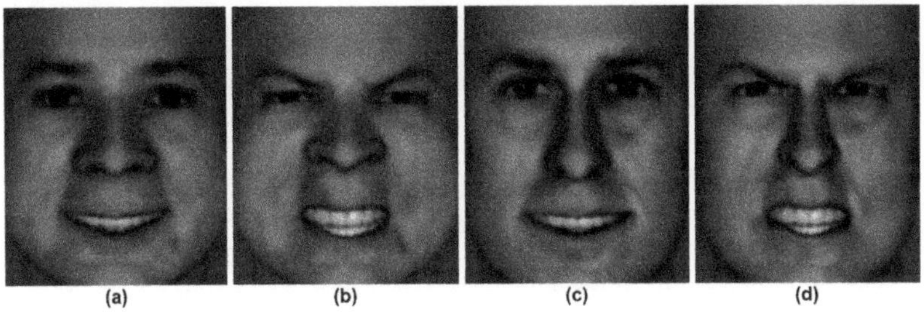

Figure 1. Two example faces with happy (panels (**a**,**c**)) versus angry (panels (**b**,**d**)) facial expressions.

Each block of the perceptual decision-making task included five minutes of trials, with each trial including a sequence of five faces. In a single trial, each of the five faces would appear sequentially from either left-to-right or right-to-left, on a large Cave Automatic Virtual Environment (CAVE) screen measuring 14′ wide by 8′ tall and running at 8K resolution (with the Unity engine [48]). Based on which of the four blocks the participant was experiencing, the faces appeared at different timing intervals corresponding to low (6 s) or high (3.6 s) workload, and at different visual clarities corresponding to low (50% clarity) or high (35% clarity) uncertainty. Timing intervals, clarities, and facial emotion intensities were determined via pilot study to ensure they similarly modulated accuracy across low versus high conditions. During trials, participants were instructed to classify each face as happy or angry and respond by aiming a controller (KWA PTS Centurion CM4 C4-10) at the face and either pressing a button (in response to a happy face) or pulling the trigger (in response to an angry face). Within a trial, faces needed to be responded to in order of appearance.

During each trial, participants would begin with the controller lowered, raise it in response to the first face appearing, and then move it laterally to aim at and respond to each face. The accuracy of each response was recorded alongside movements tracked with 6DOF (roll, pitch, yaw, and x, y, z position) at 20–25 Hz via OMC (TRACKPACK/E, Advanced Realtime Tracking, GmbH, Weilheim, Germany). Retroreflective markers were affixed along the longitudinal axis of the controller to capture translational and rotational motion, with two additional off-axis markers mounted at the end of the controller at distinct lateral offsets to disambiguate orientation. Trigger pulls were recorded by detecting a discrete pulse emitted from an IR laser integrated into the controller (Flash Kit distributed by Laser Ammo USA, Inc., Great Neck, NY, USA).

As manipulation checks, we measured three specific outcomes. First, we assessed the effectiveness of our stress induction by administering the state-trait anxiety inventory (STAI-S, [49]) before, during, and after task performance. Second, we evaluated task accuracy under the varied workload and uncertainty conditions (i.e., low, high) to determine if task performance was effectively degraded under high workload and uncertainty. The timeline of the overall procedure is depicted in Figure 2.

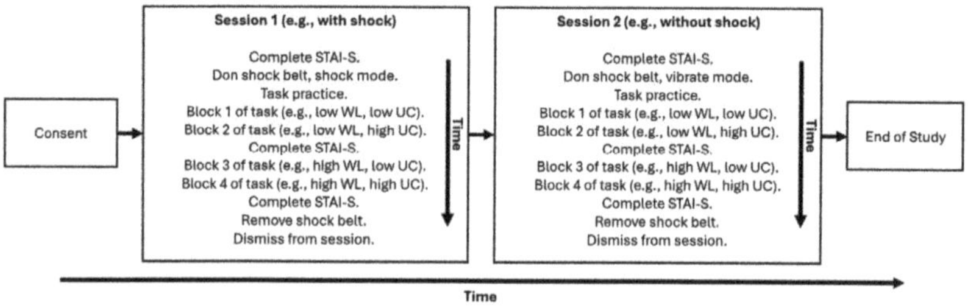

Figure 2. Summarized timeline of the overall experimental procedure, beginning with consenting and ending with dismissal. WL = workload, UC = uncertainty. Note that whether participants received shock or not was balanced across sessions, and block/condition pair order was randomized.

Additional research instruments were used but not analyzed or reported herein. These included eye-tracking glasses manufactured by SensoriMotoric Instruments (SMI; model SMI ETG2, Boston, MA, USA), a Zephyr Bioharness (Medtronic Healthcare, Boulder, CO, USA), the positive and negative affect schedule (PANAS, [50]), a custom fatigue scale, a virtual reality simulator sickness questionnaire (VRSQ, [51]), and salivary biosamples.

2.2. Data Processing

Data were collected from a total of 1649 trials. Each began with a lowered controller and proceeded with decisions being made for the sequence of five faces. Each trial's time series of movement data was divided into multiple temporal epochs: an early lowered epoch, a middle raising epoch, a late aiming epoch, and face-to-face decision-making epochs (i.e., from face 1 to face 2, from face 2 to face 3, and so forth). This resulted in a total of 7773 epochs for analysis. From these, we removed 467 epochs (i.e., 6%) with data loss due to tracking error, and 63 trials (i.e., <1%) after manual visual inspection of trajectories for artifacts of body repositioning, scenario pauses, or other rare events. This resulted in a total of 7243 epochs for analysis.

To parse raise phases from the time series, we took a 6-s period before the first decision (i.e., button press or trigger pull). To parse the raise phase into early, middle, and late epochs, a dynamically set velocity threshold was applied per trial using a k-Means clustering algorithm (from scikit-learn) on the velocity magnitude with two clusters for movement and stillness. We then split each raise trial trajectory from the beginning of the first movement to the end of the final movement as the 'raising' period. This allowed us to capture the full raise segment, including any hesitations that may be present. Example raise trial movement trajectories are depicted in Figure 3.

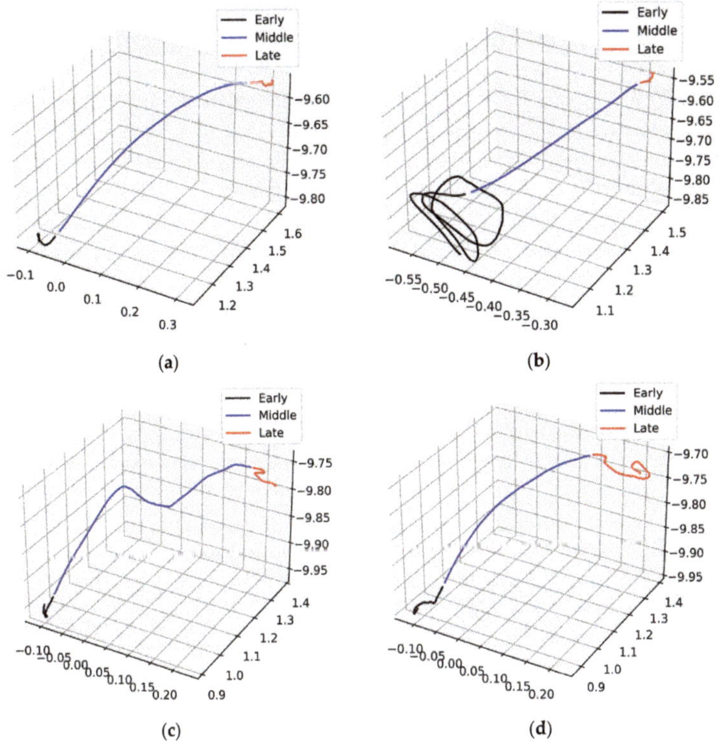

Figure 3. (**a**–**d**) Example time-series *raise* trial movement data, demonstrating the inherent variability of movement trajectories during *raise* trials, and parsed into early, middle, and late epochs.

To parse *face-to-face* epochs from the time series (i.e., Face 1 to Face 2, and so forth), we used the 3-s periods before each decision was made for faces 2–5 (note that the trajectory preceding Face 1 is included in the late aiming epoch). These inter-face epochs were collapsed into a single *face-to-face* epoch for analysis; if decisions were not made (e.g., trial timeout), these epochs were not used. Example face-to-face epoch movement trajectories are depicted in Figure 4.

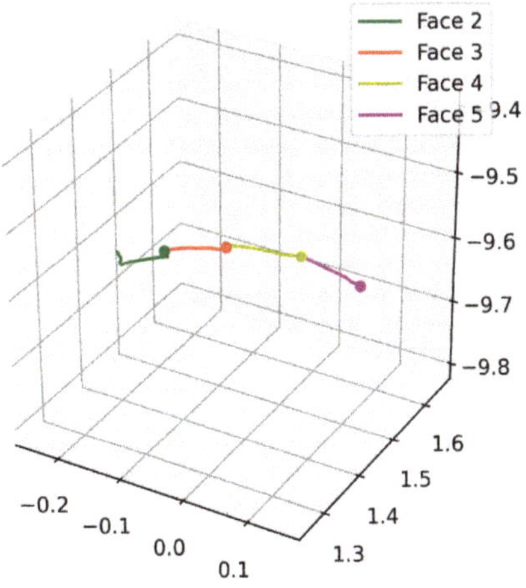

Figure 4. Example time-series *face-to-face* trial movement data for one consecutive set of faces.

These four *raise* and *face-to-face* epochs were carried forward for pre-processing movement trajectories. We did not analyze any trials where the participant did not respond to the stimulus given the lack of appreciable controller movement. Upon visual inspection of our data, all trials showed primarily translational rather than rotational movement (i.e., *x*-, *y*-, *z*-axes; predominately upward or lateral). Thus, analyses are restricted to the former.

To derive features from the 7243 epoch trajectories, we leveraged three Python (v3.12) packages: the Time Series Feature Extraction Library (TSFEL v0.2.0 [52]), the Time Series FeatuRe Extraction on basis of Scalable Hypothesis tests library (TSFRESH v0.21.1 [53]) and the Nonlinear Analysis Core's NONANLibrary (v2.2.0.0 [54]). Together, these packages calculate features across the probability, temporal, divergence, spectral, and fractal domains. Parameters followed default implementations from each library's documentation [52–54]. For example, TSFEL features were extracted with a 256-sample window and 50% overlap, and TSFRESH used standard hypothesis-testing parameters for relevance filtering. NONAN features were computed using established chaos and fractal estimators (e.g., Lyapunov exponent, approximate entropy). The corresponding GitHub pages of each package contain full feature lists. Features were calculated using velocity (V) and each of the X, Y, and Z translational axes, resulting in a maximum of 3844 features per temporal segment (i.e., early raise, middle raise, late raise, and face-to-face). For clarity, the Y axis reflects up/down (superior-inferior) movement, the X axis reflects left/right (medial-lateral) movement, and the Z axis reflects forward/backward (anterior–posterior) movement, all relative to the participant's perspective.

Data analysis tested whether levels of stress (via threat of electric shock), workload (via time pressure), and/or uncertainty (via visual degradation) could be reliably classified from movement epoch features.

2.3. Data Analysis

Data analysis used a repeated (10 times) 10-fold cross-validation (i.e., 100 iterations), using 80% of the data for training and 20% for testing in each fold. We then used the Terminating Random Experiments Selector (T-Rex Selector) [55] for feature selection on the training set; this selector uses dummy variables to [38,56] control the false discovery rate (FDR), which was set at 0.05.

The features selected from the training set were used to construct a scikit-learn (version 1.4.0) pipeline consisting of a Robust Scaler followed by a Logistic Regression model. Using these selected features, predictions were generated with the trained pipeline. The logistic regression classifier used an L2 penalty with the 'lbfgs' solver, maximum 1000 iterations, and class-balanced weighting to account for any minor label imbalance. Parameters were selected based on conventional defaults in sci-kit-learn and validate in prior cognitive state classification studies using similar data scales [38,56]. To prevent data leakage across folds, all epochs from a given participant were assigned to a single partition within each iteration such that no participant contributed data to both training and testing sets, ensuring independence between training and test samples.

We selected logistic regression as our primary classifier due to its interpretability, stability in small-sample contexts, and reduced risk of overfitting relative to more complex algorithms. Given the modest size of our dataset, we did not compare multiple models, as doing so could yield inflated performance estimates from limited data. Future work with larger datasets will enable systematic benchmarking of alternative classifiers (e.g., SVM, random forest, or ensemble methods) to evaluate potential performance gains.

3. Results

Data from the three manipulation checks demonstrated generally successful stress and uncertainty manipulations. As a pilot study with a limited sample size, results should be interpreted cautiously and viewed as preliminary indicators of potential signal strength. The high stress condition increased STAI scores (M = 38.4, SD = 10.6) during the task, relative to the low stress condition (M = 33.2, SD = 7.72), with marginal significance, $F(1, 9) = 3.13$, $p = 0.10$. The uncertainty manipulation was effective, with high uncertainty conditions associated with significantly lower accuracy (M = 0.71, SD = 0.14) relative to low uncertainty conditions (M = 0.84, SD = 0.11), $F(1, 9) = 63.19$, $p < 0.001$. Finally, the workload manipulation led to numerically lower accuracy in the high (M = 0.76, SD = 0.14) versus low (M = 0.78, SD = 0.14) workload conditions, but this difference did not reach significance, $F(1, 9) = 2.24$, $p < 0.17$. A post hoc power analysis was conducted for the three manipulation check ANOVAs, is detailed in Table 1. Given the small sample size of this pilot study, the stress and workload manipulations were likely underpowered to detect medium effects, whereas the uncertainty manipulation achieved high power.

Table 1. Results of post hoc power analyses conducted for the manipulation check ANOVAs ($\alpha = 0.05$, $N = 10$), including partial eta-squared values and statistical power.

	F(1, 9)	η_p^2	f	Power
Stress	3.13	0.26	0.59	0.46
Uncertainty	63.19	0.88	2.71	0.99
Workload	2.24	0.20	0.05	0.35

ROC AUC scores are provided in Table 2. For Stress, predictive models built on the full 6-s window of movement trajectory data achieved an average ROC AUC score of 0.76, indicating that trajectory information captured up to six seconds prior to the decision is effective for predicting stress levels. This predictive capability appears to be primarily driven by the lowered (early epoch) and raise (middle epoch) movements, which individually reached ROC AUC scores of 0.66 and 0.70, respectively.

Table 2. Mean ROC AUC scores for stress, uncertainty, and workload classification across movement epochs. AUC (area under the ROC curve) values reflect model discriminability, where 0.5 is chance and 1.0 is perfect classification. N/A indicates that the feature selector identified no discriminative features, which occurs when no voting level meets the requirement that the estimated false discovery proportion (FDP) remains below the target false discovery rate (FDR), suggesting either weak signals or true null conditions. * = this result is due only to task demands, which necessitates faster face-to-face responding in the high workload condition.

	Full Raise	Early Raise	Middle Raise	Late Raise	Face-to-Face
Stress	0.76	0.66	0.70	0.58	0.69
Uncertainty	0.57	0.55	N/A	0.53	0.56
Workload	0.54	0.50	N/A	0.53	0.94 *

F1 scores from the 100 cross-validation iterations are depicted in Figure 5. The spread of scores indicates consistent model reliability, with limited outliers and a median that aligns with the overall mean. This stability suggests that the predictive model is generalizable across different subsamples of the data, rather than overfitting to any specific partition. Across iterations, classification metrics for stress averaged approximately 0.70–0.75 accuracy, 0.72 precision, and 0.70 recall, consistent with the observed ROC AUC of 0.76 and indicating overall balanced sensitivity and specificity across folds.

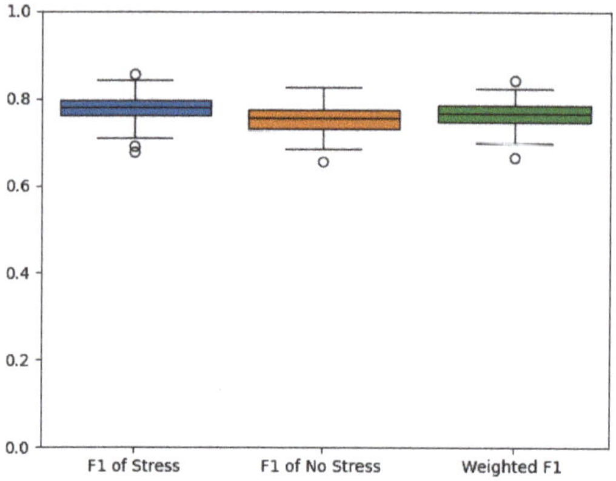

Figure 5. F1 scores from the 100 (10 repeated 10-fold) cross-validation iterations. Dots indicate outliers.

To illustrate model performance consistency, Figure 6 presents a representative confusion matrix from a cross-validation iteration, normalized over the true labels. This iteration achieved a notably strong ROC AUC score of 0.84, reflecting a particularly high discriminative capability. Of course, not all confusion matrices were this strong, as evidenced by the overall mean ROC AUC score of 0.76.

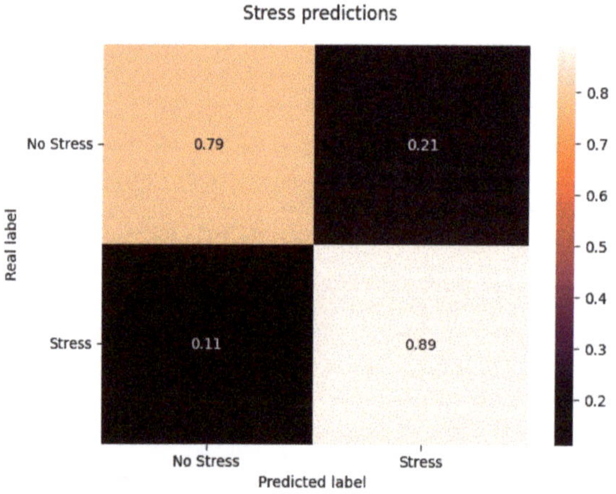

Figure 6. Confusion matrix from a sample cross-validation iteration, normalized over the true labels. The predictions from this iteration achieve an ROC AUC score of 0.84.

The most frequently selected features, from all iterations, are listed in Table 3; all the tabulated features were selected in 100% of iterations. Note that the most frequently selected features are derived from linear spectral analysis or basic statistical operations on the time series. While some involve non-linear mathematical transforms (e.g., mel scaling, absolute values), none are non-linear dynamical features in the sense of chaos or complexity metrics such as entropy or Lyapunov exponents.

A key feature emerging across all iterations is the Spectrogram mean coefficient at 7.26 Hz, extracted from the velocity magnitude signal using the TSFEL package. This feature consistently exhibited a positive coefficient in the Logistic Regression model, indicating that elevated values at this frequency are predictive of increased stress. Note that other consistently selected features (Table 3) showed variably positive or negative coefficients, making them less straightforward to explain.

Table 3. The most frequently selected features (selected in 100% of iterations), alongside a brief description of feature characteristics.

Feature	Analysis Package	Description
Spectrogram Mean Coefficient (7.26 Hz)	TSFEL	The mean spectral amplitude (at 7.26 Hz) for the velocity magnitude signal.
Spectral Amplitude Decrease	TSFEL	The average rate at which spectral amplitude declines from lower to higher frequencies.
Mel-Frequency Cepstral Coefficient	TSFEL	The 10th mel-frequency cepstral coefficient reflecting spectral envelope shape.
84th FFT Frequency (14 Hz) Magnitude	TSFRESH	Magnitude of the 84th discrete Fourier transform (FFT) coefficient (14 Hz) from the velocity magnitude signal.
Minimum of X-axis Value	TSFEL	Minimum observed value along the X-axis signal.
53rd FFT Frequency (8.83 Hz) Magnitude	TSFRESH	Magnitude of the 53rd discrete FFT coefficient (8.83 Hz) from the velocity magnitude signal.

Figure 7 presents a boxplot comparing the distributions of this key feature across stress and no-stress conditions. The figure includes 95% confidence intervals and highlights statistical significance at the $p < 0.001$ level. The clear separation between the two groups reinforces the feature's utility as a discriminative marker of stress. Physiologically, this may correspond to subtle muscular tremors associated with posture maintenance, which are known to intensify under stress conditions. While speculative, this interpretation is supported by existing literature and aligns with prior work demonstrating the impacts of acute stress on motor control and tremors [57–60].

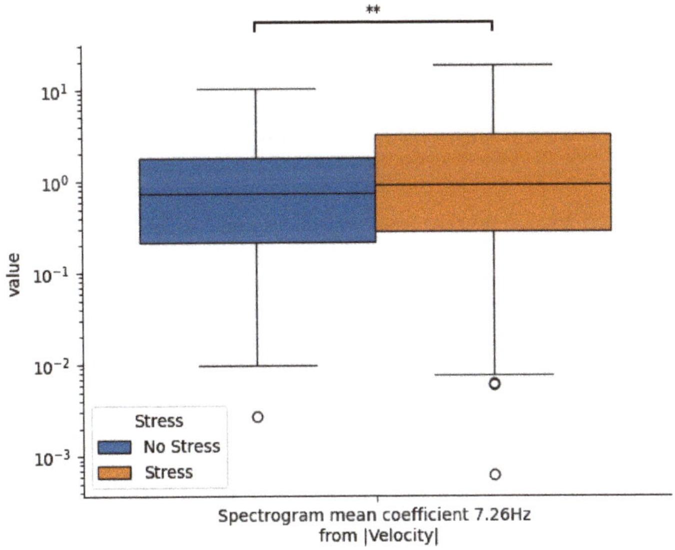

Figure 7. Box plot distinguishing stress and no-stress conditions for a notable feature. Including 95% confidence intervals and an indication of pairwise statistical significance (** $p < 0.001$). Dots indicate outliers.

In contrast, models predicting Uncertainty and Workload did not yield significant performance. As shown in Table 2, ROC AUC scores for these conditions rarely exceeded 0.57, and in some cases, feature selection failed entirely, suggesting either a lack of distinguishable signal within the movement data or limitations in capturing these psychological states through trajectory-based features alone.

4. Discussion

Results of this initial pilot study demonstrate that high-resolution movement dynamics, captured via OMC, can serve as reliable indicators of acute stress during a simulated perceptual decision-making task involving facial emotion recognition. Given the modest pilot sample size ($N = 10$) and power analysis outcomes, these findings should be interpreted as preliminary and hypothesis-generating. Larger samples will be required to confirm the reliability of the observed stress-related movement patterns. Using a rich set of linear and non-linear features extracted from temporally segmented trajectories, we were able to classify stress states with moderate to high accuracy (ROC AUC = 0.76), particularly during the early and middle epochs. In contrast, classification models for uncertainty and workload failed to reach meaningful predictive performance; this was not particularly surprising given that these two variables were not robustly manipulated. That limitation aside, this pattern could suggest that movement-based indicators are more tightly coupled with stress-related arousal than with task-related ambiguity or cognitive demand in this context.

The finding that movement trajectories, particularly during the early and middle stages of the controller raise, were predictive of stress aligns with the embodied cognition framework, which posits that mental states are reflected in motor behavior [26,61,62]. The consistent emergence of a velocity-domain feature (Spectrogram mean coefficient at 7.26 Hz) as a reliable stress marker may point to subtle oscillatory dynamics or microtremors induced by heightened neuromuscular tension under stress. Such stress-related movement variability likely reflects increased sympathetic activation affecting fine motor stability, consistent with prior evidence linking arousal to motor jitter and co-contraction patterns [13,21,57,60]. The spectrogram mean coefficient reflects average signal power within a narrow frequency band, and elevated power near 7 Hz may indicate transient oscillatory instabilities or micromovements during posture transitions [58,60]. These frequency components may be linked to increased co-contraction of muscle groups or involuntary motor unit firing under stress, consistent with prior research showing that stress alters neuromuscular control strategies [63]. In the context of the raising phase, such perturbations could represent subtle tremor-like dynamics superimposed on otherwise smooth movement, offering a physiologically plausible marker of acute stress. These findings build upon prior work linking gross motor variability to stress and extend this literature by demonstrating sensitivity within a tightly controlled, goal-directed, upper-body movement context [21,22]. Notably, the stress signal was strongest during the raising phase, likely reflecting anticipatory arousal and preparatory control, rather than stimulus-driven decision-making [13,64]; it is also the longest continuous movement epoch, providing a rich time series that extended across vertical space. Early movement phases during perceptual decision-making tasks may be a window into pre-conscious motoric stress responses.

Contrary to our hypotheses, movement trajectories failed to yield reliable classifiers for workload and uncertainty. This likely reflects that the time-pressure manipulation, while effective in pilot testing, did not elicit a significant behavioral change in accuracy. Future studies should employ more immersive or sustained workload demands; for example, multitasking, dual-task tracking, or resource-sharing paradigms, which may evoke stronger workload effects, with downstream consequences for movement dynamics. This may reflect either limitations in how these mental states manifest behaviorally or inadequacies in the current sensing or feature extraction approach. While stress is known to elicit global changes in muscular tension, posture, and movement vigor, workload and uncertainty may influence more internal cognitive operations (such as attentional allocation, executive control, or decision latency) that are not readily detectable through pre-decisional gross motor features alone. Alternatively, the lack of predictive power could reflect the constrained movement space inherent in the controller-based task, which may have limited expression of compensatory strategies or behavioral adaptations to cognitive strain. It is also possible that workload and uncertainty modulate movement dynamics only under more prolonged, intense, or ecologically complex task settings, or that individual differences in working memory capacity or strategy use attenuated consistent expression of movement-based markers. Indeed, whereas our manipulation checks demonstrated the success of our stress and uncertainty manipulations, our workload manipulation numerically altered task accuracy but this difference was non-significant. More intense workload manipulations may lead to different results.

This study contributes to a growing body of work suggesting that whole-body or object-based movement trajectories can be used to infer internal cognitive-affective states [38,56,65–67]. Unlike traditional psychophysiological methods, movement tracking (particularly with IMUs) offers a scalable and minimally intrusive means of state assessment, particularly valuable in real-world occupational settings where other state sensing modalities may prove impractical. Our results highlight the utility of combining temporal segmentation with a broad feature extraction approach to capture both overt movement dynamics and hidden non-linear patterns. Importantly, our use of repeated cross-validation and a conservative feature selection approach (T-Rex Selector) reduces the risk of overfitting and provides confidence in the generalizability of findings across individuals and over time.

The specificity of movement-based features to stress, rather than workload or uncertainty, highlights the need to consider the phenomenology of each mental state and its likely behavioral correlates. Stress, as a physiological and psychological response to threat, appears more likely to manifest in muscle activation and subtle movement jitter than are states like uncertainty, which may involve more covert deliberative processes [10,17,38,60]. Future studies may benefit from multimodal approaches that pair movement data with eye tracking, voice analysis, or peripheral physiological signals to capture a broader array of cognitive-affective states [19,20,38].

Several limitations warrant caution in interpreting these findings. First, as a pilot study, the modest sample size and homogeneity of the participant pool may limit generalizability. The study was designed only to test analytic feasibility and identify candidate movement features for follow-on validation. Future work should increase participant numbers using high-throughput IMU-based data collection or multi-site collaborations to improve sample diversity (e.g., to balance male/female ratio, increase age range) and increase statistical power. Replication in larger, more diverse cohorts will be important for confirming robustness of our findings and population-level generalizability. Second, while the task was well-controlled, it may not reflect the full complexity of real-world contexts where stress, workload, and uncertainty co-occur dynamically and vary over longer timescales wherein neuromuscular fatigue may cooccur. Third, our labels for stress, workload, and uncertainty were derived from experimental manipulations rather than subjective or continuous self-reports, potentially limiting granularity and relevance to phenomenological expressions of these states. Integrating concurrent subjective or physiological measures would allow calibration between experimentally imposed and self-experienced stress, workload, and uncertainty. Fourth, although the predictive model performed well for stress, it remains correlational in nature, and the underlying mechanisms linking specific movement patterns to internal states require further elucidation, potentially via neurophysiological validation. Finally, our use of logistic regression prioritized model interpretability and stability over marginal accuracy gains from more complex algorithms. Future work with larger, more balanced datasets could explore ensemble and kernel-based methods to assess potential performance improvements.

Although the facial emotion recognition task provided precise experimental control, it represents a simplified abstraction of occupational performance. Translating these findings to dynamic, real-world settings will require adapting movement-sensing systems to unconstrained environments and integrating with context-aware data streams. Future work should explore how movement-related features interact with other sensor modalities, examine generalizability across tasks and populations, and evaluate the feasibility of real-time state detection in training settings and field-deployable systems using IMUs or camera-based systems. There is also promise in applying deep learning approaches capable of learning latent features from raw time series, although care must be taken to ensure interpretability and avoid overfitting. Indeed, the current analytic approach provides relatively high transparency and interpretability, identifying concrete linear and non-linear features that can be explored in future work.

5. Conclusions

In conclusion, this pilot study provides preliminary evidence that some cognitive states may be inferable from fine-grained features of movement during a stressful perceptual decision-making task. These findings support the potential of movement-based sensing as a low-burden method for real-time cognitive state monitoring and inspire future sensor integration into adaptive training or performance augmentation systems. The failure to classify workload and uncertainty points to the complexity of behavioral correlates of cognition and suggests the need for multimodal and task-specific sensing approaches. Overall, this work contributes to the development of next-generation human–machine systems that are sensitive to the fluctuating cognitive state of the user.

Author Contributions: Conceptualization, T.T.B. and G.I.H.; methodology, T.T.B., L.N.T., G.I.H. and K.O.; formal analysis, J.M.; data curation, T.T.B., K.O., M.K.S., M.M.L., M.S. and G.I.H.; writing—original draft preparation, T.T.B., M.K.S. and J.M.; writing—review and editing, K.O., L.N.T., M.M.L., M.S. and G.I.H.; visualization, J.M.; supervision, T.T.B.; funding acquisition, T.T.B. and G.I.H. All authors have read and agreed to the published version of the manuscript.

Funding: This research was funded by the U.S. Army DEVCOM Soldier Center, grant number W911-QY-19-R-0003 (awarded to Tufts University). The views expressed in this article are solely those of the authors and do not reflect the official policies or positions of the Department of Army, the Department of Defense, or any other department or agency of the U.S. government.

Institutional Review Board Statement: This study was conducted in accordance with the Declaration of Helsinki and approved by the Institutional Review Board of the U.S. Army Combat Capabilities Command Army Research Laboratory (protocol code #24-089, approved 10 October 2024) and Tufts University (protocol code STUDY00005440, approved 13 December 2024).

Informed Consent Statement: Informed consent was obtained from all subjects involved in this study.

Data Availability Statement: Given the highly specialized and potentially sensitive nature of participants (i.e., military personnel) and the relatively small sample size that can lead to unintentional identity ascertainment, deidentified data are only available by request to the corresponding author.

Conflicts of Interest: The authors declare no conflicts of interest. Staff from the funding agency (T.T.B., G.I.H., and L.N.T.) played a role in the design of the study; in the collection, analyses, and interpretation of data; in the writing of the manuscript; and in the decision to publish the results.

Abbreviations

The following abbreviations are used in this manuscript:

AI	Artificial Intelligence
CAVE	Cave Automatic Virtual Environment
EEG	Electroencephalography
DEVCOM	Combat Capabilities Development Command
fNIRS	Functional Near-Infrared Spectroscopy
FDP	False Discovery Proportion
FDR	False Discovery Rate
FFT	Fast Fourier Transform
IMU	Inertial Measurement Unit
IR	Infrared
NONAN	Nonlinear Analysis Core
OMC	Optical Motion Capture
PANAS	Positive and Negative Affect Schedule
ROC	Receiver Operating Characteristic
AUC	Area Under the Curve
SMI	SensoMotoric Instruments
STAI	State-Trait Anxiety Inventory
TSFEL	Time Series Feature Extraction Library
TSFRESH	Time Series Feature Extraction on basis of Scalable Hypothesis tests
VRSQ	Virtual Reality Sickness Questionnaire
6DOFs	Six Degrees of Freedom

References

1. MacDonald, W. The Impact of Job Demands and Workload on Stress and Fatigue | EBSCOhost. Available online: https://openurl.ebsco.com/contentitem/doi:10.1080%2F00050060310001707107?sid=ebsco:plink:crawler&id=ebsco:doi:10.1080%2F00050060310001707107 (accessed on 11 August 2025).
2. Liu, D.; Peterson, T.; Vincenzi, D.; Doherty, S. Effect of Time Pressure and Target Uncertainty on Human Operator Performance and Workload for Autonomous Unmanned Aerial System. *Int. J. Ind. Ergon.* **2016**, *51*, 52–58. [CrossRef]
3. Phillips-Wren, G.; Adya, M. Decision Making under Stress: The Role of Information Overload, Time Pressure, Complexity, and Uncertainty. *J. Decis. Syst.* **2020**, *29*, 213–225. [CrossRef]
4. Brunyé, T.T.; Goring, S.A.; Navarro, E.; Hart-Pomerantz, H.; Grekin, S.; McKinlay, A.M.; Plessow, F. Identifying the Most Effective Acute Stress Induction Methods for Producing SAM- and HPA-Related Physiological Responses: A Meta-Analysis. *Anxiety Stress Coping* **2025**, *38*, 263–285. [CrossRef]
5. Russell, G.; Lightman, S. The Human Stress Response. *Nat. Rev. Endocrinol.* **2019**, *15*, 525–534. [CrossRef]
6. Oken, B.S.; Chamine, I.; Wakeland, W. A Systems Approach to Stress, Stressors and Resilience in Humans. *Behav. Brain Res.* **2015**, *282*, 144–154. [CrossRef] [PubMed]
7. Plass, J.L.; Moreno, R.; Brünken, R. *Cognitive Load Theory*; Cambridge University Press: Cambridge, UK, 2010; ISBN 978-0-521-86023-9.
8. Sweller, J. Chapter Two—Cognitive Load Theory. In *Psychology of Learning and Motivation*; Mestre, J.P., Ross, B.H., Eds.; Academic Press: Cambridge, MA, USA, 2011; Volume 55, pp. 37–76.
9. Engström, J.; Markkula, G.; Victor, T.; Merat, N. Effects of Cognitive Load on Driving Performance: The Cognitive Control Hypothesis. *Hum. Factors* **2017**, *59*, 734–764. [CrossRef]
10. Brunyé, T.T.; Gardony, A.L. Eye Tracking Measures of Uncertainty during Perceptual Decision Making. *Int. J. Psychophysiol.* **2017**, *120*, 60–68. [CrossRef]
11. Aston, S.; Nardini, M.; Beierholm, U. Different Types of Uncertainty in Multisensory Perceptual Decision Making. *Philos. Trans. R. Soc. B Biol. Sci.* **2023**, *378*, 20220349. [CrossRef] [PubMed]
12. Peterson, D.K.; Pitz, G.F. Confidence, Uncertainty, and the Use of Information. *J. Exp. Psychol. Learn. Mem. Cogn.* **1988**, *14*, 85–92. [CrossRef]
13. Vine, S.J.; Moore, L.J.; Wilson, M.R. An Integrative Framework of Stress, Attention, and Visuomotor Performance. *Front. Psychol.* **2016**, *7*, 1671. [CrossRef] [PubMed]

14. Brunyé, T.T.; Goring, S.A.; Cantelon, J.A.; Eddy, M.D.; Elkin-Frankston, S.; Elmore, W.R.; Giles, G.E.; Hancock, C.L.; Masud, S.B.; McIntyre, J.; et al. Trait-Level Predictors of Human Performance Outcomes in Personnel Engaged in Stressful Laboratory and Field Tasks. *Front. Psychol.* **2024**, *15*, 1449200. [CrossRef]
15. Bruggen, A. An Empirical Investigation of the Relationship between Workload and Performance. *Manag. Decis.* **2015**, *53*, 2377–2389. [CrossRef]
16. Smith, J.D.; Jackson, B.N.; Church, B.A. The Cognitive Architecture of Uncertainty. *Anim. Behav. Cogn.* **2019**, *6*, 236–246. [CrossRef]
17. Morgado, P.; Sousa, N.; Cerqueira, J.J. The Impact of Stress in Decision Making in the Context of Uncertainty. *J. Neurosci. Res.* **2015**, *93*, 839–847. [CrossRef]
18. Seok, D.; Lee, S.; Kim, M.; Cho, J.; Kim, C. Motion Artifact Removal Techniques for Wearable EEG and PPG Sensor Systems. *Front. Electron.* **2021**, *2*, 685513. [CrossRef]
19. Peck, E.M.; Afergan, D.; Yuksel, B.F.; Lalooses, F.; Jacob, R.J.K. Using fNIRS to Measure Mental Workload in the Real World. In *Advances in Physiological Computing*; Fairclough, S.H., Gilleade, K., Eds.; Springer: London, UK, 2014; pp. 117–139; ISBN 978-1-4471-6392-3.
20. Sirois, S.; Brisson, J. Pupillometry. *WIREs Cogn. Sci.* **2014**, *5*, 679–692. [CrossRef] [PubMed]
21. Doumas, M.; Morsanyi, K.; Young, W.R. Cognitively and Socially Induced Stress Affects Postural Control. *Exp. Brain Res.* **2018**, *236*, 305–314. [CrossRef] [PubMed]
22. Richer, R.; Koch, V.; Abel, L.; Hauck, F.; Kurz, M.; Ringgold, V.; Müller, V.; Küderle, A.; Schindler-Gmelch, L.; Eskofier, B.M.; et al. Machine Learning-Based Detection of Acute Psychosocial Stress from Body Posture and Movements. *Sci. Rep.* **2024**, *14*, 8251. [CrossRef]
23. Ghanavati, T.; Salavati, M.; Karimi, N.; Negahban, H.; Ebrahimi Takamjani, I.; Mehravar, M.; Hessam, M. Intra-Limb Coordination While Walking Is Affected by Cognitive Load and Walking Speed. *J. Biomech.* **2014**, *47*, 2300–2305. [CrossRef]
24. Mitra, S.; Knight, A.; Munn, A. Divergent Effects of Cognitive Load on Quiet Stance and Task-Linked Postural Coordination. *J. Exp. Psychol. Hum. Percept. Perform.* **2013**, *39*, 323–328. [CrossRef]
25. Givens, D.B.; White, J. *The Routledge Dictionary of Nonverbal Communication*; Routledge: London, UK, 2021; ISBN 978-0-429-29366-5.
26. Hutchins, E.; Palen, L. Constructing Meaning from Space, Gesture, and Speech. In *Discourse, Tools and Reasoning: Essays on Situated Cognition*; Resnick, L.B., Säljö, R., Pontecorvo, C., Burge, B., Eds.; NATO ASI Series; Springer: Berlin/Heidelberg, Germany, 1997; pp. 23–40; ISBN 978-3-662-03362-3.
27. Melinger, A.; Levelt, W.J.M. Gesture and the Communicative Intention of the Speaker. *Gesture* **2004**, *4*, 119–141. [CrossRef]
28. Brunyé, T.T.; Haga, Z.D.; Houck, L.A.; Taylor, H.A. You Look Lost: Understanding Uncertainty and Representational Flexibility in Navigation. In *Representations in Mind and World: Essays Inspired by Barbara Tversky*; Zacks, J.M., Taylor, H.A., Eds.; Routledge: New York, NY, USA, 2017; pp. 42–56; ISBN 978-1-315-16978-1.
29. Lorås, H.; Sandseter, E.B.H.; Sando, O.J.; Storli, L. Distinct Clusters of Movement Entropy in Children's Exploration of a Virtual Reality Balance Beam. *Front. Psychol.* **2023**, *14*, 1227469. [CrossRef]
30. Goodridge, C.M.; Gonçalves, R.C.; Arabian, A.; Horrobin, A.; Solernou, A.; Lee, Y.T.; Lee, Y.M.; Madigan, R.; Merat, N. Gaze Entropy Metrics for Mental Workload Estimation Are Heterogenous during Hands-off Level 2 Automation. *Accid. Anal. Prev.* **2024**, *202*, 107560. [CrossRef]
31. Keshmiri, S. Entropy and the Brain: An Overview. *Entropy* **2020**, *22*, 917. [CrossRef]
32. Valenza, G.; Allegrini, P.; Lanatà, A.; Scilingo, E.P. Dominant Lyapunov Exponent and Approximate Entropy in Heart Rate Variability during Emotional Visual Elicitation. *Front. Neuroeng.* **2012**, *5*, 3. [CrossRef] [PubMed]
33. Parbat, D.; Chakraborty, M. A Novel Methodology to Study the Cognitive Load Induced EEG Complexity Changes: Chaos, Fractal and Entropy Based Approach. *Biomed. Signal Process. Control.* **2021**, *64*, 102277. [CrossRef]
34. Ekizos, A.; Santuz, A.; Schroll, A.; Arampatzis, A. The Maximum Lyapunov Exponent During Walking and Running: Reliability Assessment of Different Marker-Sets. *Front. Physiol.* **2018**, *9*, 1101. [CrossRef] [PubMed]
35. Winter, L.; Taylor, P.; Bellenger, C.; Grimshaw, P.; Crowther, R.G. The Application of the Lyapunov Exponent to Analyse Human Performance: A Systematic Review. *J. Sports Sci.* **2023**, *41*, 1994–2013. [CrossRef]
36. Richman, J.S.; Moorman, J.R. Physiological Time-Series Analysis Using Approximate Entropy and Sample Entropy. *Am. J. Physiol. Heart Circ. Physiol.* **2000**, *278*, H2039–H2049. [CrossRef] [PubMed]
37. Lau, Z.J.; Pham, T.; Chen, S.H.A.; Makowski, D. Brain Entropy, Fractal Dimensions and Predictability: A Review of Complexity Measures for EEG in Healthy and Neuropsychiatric Populations. *Eur. J. Neurosci.* **2022**, *56*, 5047–5069. [CrossRef]
38. Brunyé, T.T.; McIntyre, J.; Hughes, G.I.; Miller, E.L. Movement Sensing Opportunities for Monitoring Dynamic Cognitive States. *Sensors* **2024**, *24*, 7530. [CrossRef]
39. Biggs, A.T. Developing Scenarios That Evoke Shoot/Don't-Shoot Errors. *Appl. Ergon.* **2021**, *94*, 103397. [CrossRef]
40. Chung, G.K.W.K.; De La Cruz, G.C.; de Vries, L.F.; Kim, J.-O.; Bewley, W.L.; de Souza e Silva, A.; Sylvester, R.M.; Baker, E.L. *Determinants of Rifle Marksmanship Performance: Predicting Shooting Performance with Advanced Distributed Learning Assessments*; University of California Los Angeles: Los Angeles, CA, USA, 2004.

41. Azevedo, T.M.; Volchan, E.; Imbiriba, L.A.; Rodrigues, E.C.; Oliveira, J.M.; Oliveira, L.F.; Lutterbach, L.G.; Vargas, C.D. A Freezing-like Posture to Pictures of Mutilation. *Psychophysiology* **2005**, *42*, 255–260. [CrossRef]
42. Woodward, S.H.; Shurick, A.A.; Alvarez, J.; Kuo, J.; Nonyieva, Y.; Blechert, J.; McRae, K.; Gross, J.J. Seated Movement Indexes Emotion and Its Regulation in Posttraumatic Stress Disorder. *Psychophysiology* **2015**, *52*, 679–686. [CrossRef] [PubMed]
43. Brunyé, T.T.; Hayes, J.F.; Mahoney, C.R.; Gardony, A.L.; Taylor, H.A.; Kanarek, R.B. Get in My Belly: Food Preferences Trigger Approach and Avoidant Postural Asymmetries. *PLoS ONE* **2013**, *8*, e72432. [CrossRef]
44. Kosonogov, V.; Martínez-Selva, J.M.; Torrente, G.; Carrillo-Verdejo, E.; Arenas, A.; Sánchez-Navarro, J.P. Head Motion Elicited by Viewing Affective Pictures as Measured by a New LED-Based Technique. *Multisensory Res.* **2019**, *32*, 575–588. [CrossRef]
45. Behnke, M.; Bianchi-Berthouze, N.; Kaczmarek, L.D. Head Movement Differs for Positive and Negative Emotions in Video Recordings of Sitting Individuals. *Sci. Rep.* **2021**, *11*, 7405. [CrossRef] [PubMed]
46. Brunyé, T.T.; Giles, G.E. Methods for Eliciting and Measuring Behavioral and Physiological Consequences of Stress and Uncertainty in Virtual Reality. *Front. Virtual Real.* **2023**, *4*, 951435. [CrossRef]
47. Okano, K.; Lee, M.M.; Hart-Pomerantz, H.; Smith, M.; Sandone, M.K.; Harvey, T.; Brunyé, T.T. Effects of Repeated Cranial Electrotherapy Stimulation on Physiological and Behavioral Responses to Acute Stress: A Double-Blind Randomized Clinical Trial. *Front. Hum. Neurosci.* **2025**, *19*, 1641801. [CrossRef] [PubMed]
48. Unity Technologies, Inc. Unity3d Engine 2022. Available online: https://unity.com/releases/editor/whats-new/2022.3.62f3#notes (accessed on 11 August 2025).
49. Spielberger, C.D.; Gorsuch, R.L.; Lushene, P.R.; Vagg, P.R.; Jacobs, G.A. *Manual for the State-Trait Anxiety Inventory*; Consulting Psychologists Press: Palo Alto, CA, USA, 1983.
50. Watson, D.; Clark, L.A.; Tellegen, A. Development and Validation of Brief Measures of Positive and Negative Affect: The PANAS Scales. *J. Personal. Soc. Psychol.* **1988**, *54*, 1063–1070. [CrossRef]
51. Kim, H.K.; Park, J.; Choi, Y.; Choe, M. Virtual Reality Sickness Questionnaire (VRSQ): Motion Sickness Measurement Index in a Virtual Reality Environment. *Appl. Ergon.* **2018**, *69*, 66–73. [CrossRef]
52. Barandas, M.; Folgado, D.; Fernandes, L.; Santos, S.; Abreu, M.; Bota, P.; Liu, H.; Schultz, T.; Gamboa, H. TSFEL: Time Series Feature Extraction Library. *SoftwareX* **2020**, *11*, 100456. [CrossRef]
53. Christ, M.; Braun, N.; Neuffer, J.; Kempa-Liehr, A.W. Time Series FeatuRe Extraction on Basis of Scalable Hypothesis Tests (Tsfresh—A Python Package). *Neurocomputing* **2018**, *307*, 72–77. [CrossRef]
54. UNO Biomechanics Nonlinear-Analysis-Core/NONANLibrary 2020. Available online: https://www.mathworks.com/matlabcentral/fileexchange/71907-uno-biomechanics-nonlinear-analysis-toolbox (accessed on 11 August 2025).
55. Machkour, J.; Muma, M.; Palomar, D.P. The Terminating-Random Experiments Selector: Fast High-Dimensional Variable Selection with False Discovery Rate Control. *Signal Process.* **2022**, *231*, 109894. [CrossRef]
56. Koenig-Robert, R.; Quek, G.L.; Grootswagers, T.; Varlet, M. Movement Trajectories as a Window into the Dynamics of Emerging Neural Representations. *Sci. Rep.* **2024**, *14*, 11499. [CrossRef] [PubMed]
57. Saleh, S.M.; Mahdi, A.; Kamel, A.Z.; Jawad, H.F.; Saad, A. Prevalence and Factors Associated with Enhanced Physiologic Tremor among Health Personnel: A Cross-Sectional Study. *Int. J. Occup. Saf. Ergon.* **2025**, 1–8. [CrossRef] [PubMed]
58. Hwang, I.-S.; Chen, Y.-C.; Wu, P.-S. Differential Load Impact upon Arm Tremor Dynamics and Coordinative Strategy between Postural Holding and Position Tracking. *Eur. J. Appl. Physiol.* **2009**, *105*, 945–957. [CrossRef]
59. Charles, P.D.; Esper, G.J.; Davis, T.L.; Maciunas, R.J.; Robertson, D. Classification of Tremor and Update on Treatment. *Am. Fam. Physician* **1999**, *59*, 1565–1572. [PubMed]
60. Budini, F.; Mocnik, R.; Tilp, M.; Crognale, D. Mental Calculation Increases Physiological Postural Tremor, but Does Not Influence Physiological Goal-Directed Kinetic Tremor. *Eur. J. Appl. Physiol.* **2022**, *122*, 2661–2671. [CrossRef]
61. Wilson, M. Six Views of Embodied Cognition. *Psychon. Bull. Rev.* **2002**, *9*, 625–636. [CrossRef]
62. Dove, G. On the Need for Embodied and Dis-Embodied Cognition. *Front. Psychol.* **2010**, *1*, 242. [CrossRef]
63. Lakie, M. The Influence of Muscle Tremor on Shooting Performance. *Exp. Physiol.* **2010**, *95*, 441–450. [CrossRef]
64. Nieuwenhuys, A.; Oudejans, R.R.D. Anxiety and Perceptual-Motor Performance: Toward an Integrated Model of Concepts, Mechanisms, and Processes. *Psychol. Res.* **2012**, *76*, 747–759. [CrossRef]
65. Freeman, J.B.; Ambady, N. MouseTracker: Software for Studying Real-Time Mental Processing Using a Computer Mouse-Tracking Method. *Behav. Res. Methods* **2010**, *42*, 226–241. [CrossRef] [PubMed]
66. Freeman, J.; Dale, R.; Farmer, T. Hand in Motion Reveals Mind in Motion. *Front. Psychol.* **2011**, *2*, 59. [CrossRef] [PubMed]
67. Balaban, C.D.; Cohn, J.; Redfern, M.S.; Prinkey, J.; Stripling, R.; Hoffer, M. Postural Control as a Probe for Cognitive State: Exploiting Human Information Processing to Enhance Performance. *Int. J. Hum.–Comput. Interact.* **2004**, *17*, 275–286. [CrossRef]

MDPI AG
Grosspeteranlage 5
4052 Basel
Switzerland
Tel.: +41 61 683 77 34

Sensors Editorial Office
E-mail: sensors@mdpi.com
www.mdpi.com/journal/sensors

www.ingramcontent.com/pod-product-compliance
Lightning Source LLC
LaVergne TN
LVHW070448061126
851858LV00011B/188